ableau

Strategies
en Master

Ryan Sleeper

Beijing · Boston · Farnham · Sebastopol · Tokyo

Practical Tableau

by Ryan Sleeper

Published by O'Reilly Media, Inc., 1005 Gravenstein Highway North, Sebastopol, CA 95472.

O'Reilly books may be purchased for educational, business, or sales promotional use. Online editions are also available for most titles (*http://oreilly.com/safari*). For more information, contact our corporate/institutional sales department: 800-998-9938 or *corporate@oreilly.com*.

Editor: Virginia Wilson	**Indexer:** Ellen Troutman-Zaig
Production Editor: Melanie Yarbrough	**Interior Designer:** David Futato
Copyeditor: Jasmine Kwityn	**Cover Designer:** Karen Montgomery
Proofreader: Kim Cofer	**Illustrator:** Rebecca Demarest

April 2018:   First Edition

Revision History for the First Edition

2018-04-03:   First Release

See *http://oreilly.com/catalog/errata.csp?isbn=9781491977316* for release details.

978-1-491-97731-6

[LSI]

This book is dedicated to my grandmothers, Nancy Boyd and Ruth Sleeper

Table of Contents

Part II. Chart Types

Part III.   Tips and Tricks

Part IV.   Framework

Part V.   Storytelling

Foreword

It's more important than ever before to be fluent in the language of data. Our world is full of an ever-increasing amount of data in the form of tables, spreadsheets, and databases about our businesses, our interactions, our cities, our environment, our personal health. The topics and applications are endless.

When it comes to quickly and effectively processing data to find and share impactful stories, there's no software quite like Tableau. It allows you to drag and drop your data onto a digital canvas that brings it to life. In addition, Tableau gives you the ability to share what you create with your audience so they can come to understand as well.

And there's no resource quite like this book as you embark on the journey from beginner to expert and develop your skills working with data using Tableau. Ryan Sleeper is a true master of the art and science of data visualization, and he has created an amazing resource of practical tutorials that start with the basics, move to more advanced topics, and include often missed but critically important design tips along the way.

Ryan has earned the coveted title of Tableau Zen Master not only by becoming an expert in the software, but also by graciously and effectively helping others to build their skills as well. His award-winning Tableau Public visualizations have enlightened and delighted people all over the world on topics such as baseball player valuation, the cost of living, traffic patterns, and stock valuations, to name just a few.

So in picking up this book, you're setting off on a journey to learn from the best. The combination of Tableau's powerful software and Ryan's clear and concise way of explaining how to use it mean each step along the way will be a pleasure.

I wish you all the best. The world in which we live—our communities and our planet itself—are depending on each one of us becoming not just fluent in the language of data, but eloquent.

— Ben Jones
Director of Outreach Programs
Tableau Software
@DataRemixed

Preface

Eight years ago, my then-boss asked our team of three analysts to try using a "new" tool called *Tableau*. All three of us did the first thing that came naturally and attempted to replicate our existing Excel reports in Tableau. I found that transitioning from Excel-based reporting was not always seamless, but have since realized that it was because I did not have a go-to resource to help me connect the dots between my existing reporting knowledge and what I was learning in Tableau. I'm grateful I stuck with Tableau because over time I realized how flexible and powerful the software is.

As of 2018, Tableau has been named a leader in the Gartner Magic Quadrant for Business Intelligence and Analytics Platforms for six consecutive years. Tableau works because it helps you unlock the benefits of visualizing data:

- Reduced time to insight
- Increased accuracy of insights
- Improved engagement

Tableau has made it possible for me to find thousands of insights in data that have led to tangible actions and real returns for the dozens of globally known brands I have consulted for. In addition to the value added during my day job, I have had the honor of being named a Tableau Zen Master twice, won Tableau's Iron Viz Championship in 2013, and authored the Tableau Public Visualization of the Year in 2015.

The data visualization tips, tutorials, and strategies contained in this book are the 100 ideas that made this all possible.

This Book's Purpose

When I started using Tableau, there weren't many resources available for learning the tool. There were (and still are) a lot of individual posts and videos on the web, but I found it challenging to tie everything together in a way that helped me get the most out of Tableau. I have an MBA and a master's in sport business management, as well as undergraduate degrees in marketing and psychology. Before I began my career, I had not taken a single class about data or analytics. This made it even more challenging to get started with Tableau, and despite all of my previous accomplishments, I would say that my learning curve looked like this:

The long, flat line before I started to figure things out represents about two years of self-teaching and growing pains. In many ways, this experience makes me uniquely qualified to help you reduce your own learning curve. *I wrote this book because it's the one I wish I had when I started using Tableau.* My hope is that this selection of topics, combined with my firsthand knowledge of potential pitfalls, and the practical style of communication, will make your learning curve look like this:

This Book's Audience

This book is best for a "201-level" Tableau user. Most Tableau users have some foundational "101-level" knowledge, but do not have the need for extremely technical "601-level" skills. After all, Tableau's mission is to help you see and understand your data as easily as possible. This book is targeted specifically at helping you build on the foundational knowledge and take your applications of Tableau to the next level. That being said, I have two big caveats:

- Part I covers the core concepts that I find most important when using Tableau. The chapters in that part make it possible for a brand-new Tableau user to learn how to use Tableau with this book alone. For more experienced users, it also offers a review of basic concepts to ensure they have the prerequisites required to build on their knowledge in later chapters.
- Beyond technical "how-tos," this book also offers a strategic framework for data visualization and discusses storytelling techniques. Furthermore, many of the tips and tricks in *Practical Tableau* were invented by me personally, and may be considered advanced. It is my belief that there is something for every Tableau user in this book, regardless of experience level.

This Book's Structure

Practical Tableau is organized into five parts:

Part I

The chapters in this part help you get started from scratch using Tableau. By the end of Part I, you will have the ability to use Tableau immediately and the foundational prerequisites to apply the "201-level" material.

Part II

Part II consists of step-by-step tutorials that walk you through how to build a variety of charts in Tableau. More importantly, each tutorial also explains uses for each chart type in a business context, which helps you choose the right tool for the job in your analyses. Many of the chart types explained here are not available "out-of-the-box" through Tableau's "Show Me" functionality, so you are sure to add some advanced approaches to your Tableau toolbelt. For the charts that are easy to create with Show Me, there are often innovative twists added to take the standard charts to the next level.

Part III

The various topics covered in this part will help ensure you're known as the Tableau guru at your office. This part covers everything from innovative uses of parameters, working with dates, color theory, making your Tableau workbooks run efficiently, designing for mobile devices, and much more.

Part IV

These chapters discuss the INSIGHT framework for data visualization. The INSIGHT framework is a proprietary process that has been used in the construction of hundreds of Tableau dashboards. Following a strategic framework helps you align the requirements of diverse end users to maximize the effectiveness of your data visualization.

Part V
> The book concludes by outlining tangible tactics for storytelling with data. Regardless of how good you become at the technical aspects of Tableau, without some attention to the intangible aspects of data visualization, you will not be as successful as you can be. This part discusses data visualization theory and the psychological components of communicating with data. You will learn specific and actionable tips that you can begin implementing in your work immediately.

O'Reilly Safari

Safari (formerly Safari Books Online) is a membership-based training and reference platform for enterprise, government, educators, and individuals.

Members have access to thousands of books, training videos, Learning Paths, interactive tutorials, and curated playlists from over 250 publishers, including O'Reilly Media, Harvard Business Review, Prentice Hall Professional, Addison-Wesley Professional, Microsoft Press, Sams, Que, Peachpit Press, Adobe, Focal Press, Cisco Press, John Wiley & Sons, Syngress, Morgan Kaufmann, IBM Redbooks, Packt, Adobe Press, FT Press, Apress, Manning, New Riders, McGraw-Hill, Jones & Bartlett, and Course Technology, among others.

For more information, please visit *http://oreilly.com/safari*.

How to Contact Us

Please address comments and questions concerning this book to the publisher:

> O'Reilly Media, Inc.
> 1005 Gravenstein Highway North
> Sebastopol, CA 95472
> 800-998-9938 (in the United States or Canada)
> 707-829-0515 (international or local)
> 707-829-0104 (fax)

We have a web page for this book, where we list errata, examples, and any additional information. You can access this page at *http://bit.ly/practical-tableau*.

To comment or ask technical questions about this book, send email to *bookquestions@oreilly.com*.

For more information about our books, courses, conferences, and news, see our website at *http://www.oreilly.com*.

Find us on Facebook: *http://facebook.com/oreilly*

Follow us on Twitter: *http://twitter.com/oreillymedia*

Watch us on YouTube: *http://www.youtube.com/oreillymedia*

Acknowledgments

No one achieves anything remarkable in a community without the support of that community, and I am certainly no exception to that rule. What I have found most unique about my experience with Tableau is its relentlessly kind and selfless community. I would not have been able to write this book without the knowledge shared and the inspiration provided by Tableau's user community. While some of these users are mentioned throughout the chapters of *Practical Tableau*, there are far too many individuals to name that have helped me along the way. If you have answered somebody's question on Tableau's user forums, posted a visualization to Tableau Public, attended a user group meeting, or wrote a blog post about Tableau: thank you.

Thank you, Ben Jones, Director of Outreach Programs at Tableau. Ben inspired me very early in my career and gave me the confidence to push the Tableau envelope. Quite simply, I would not have had the opportunity to write this without Ben Jones and Tableau Public.

Thank you to my family for helping me develop a worldview that motivated me to do something like this and for your support along the way; even if at times I had trouble explaining exactly what I do.

Special thanks to my wife, Amy, for allowing me to share some of our private life through data visualization and letting me disappear to the coffee shop almost every Saturday and Sunday for quite a while to document the ideas you're about to read.

PART I

Fundamentals

CHAPTER 1

How to Learn Tableau: My Top Five Tips

Tableau's mission is to help people see and understand their data, and I can tell you that after you've mastered a few of the fundamentals, it is an extremely easy way to do just that. For basic analyses, such as looking at a measure such as sales, and slicing and dicing that measure by a dimension such as region, I'm not sure anything could be easier than Tableau. However, there can be a substantial learning curve required to get exactly what you want out of the software. In fact, for me personally it has been a career-long education spanning eight years using Tableau. While I've been through some growing pains and experienced some frustration learning the tool, I mostly view my lack of perfection as good news. The challenge keeps my job interesting and I continue to get excited discovering innovative solutions to complex problems that have led to several successful visualizations.

This chapter shares my top tips for how to learn Tableau, whether you have a budget of $0 or $5,000.

Tip #5: Follow the Community

Cost: $0

The first of my top five tips is to follow the Tableau community. I have learned several software programs during my career in digital analytics and data visualization, and bar none, Tableau has the most selfless community of the bunch. The great thing about following the community is that you can tailor the list of users you focus on to align with your own uses of Tableau. Perhaps you want to follow users sharing advanced technical know-how, members of the community who are applying Tableau in your own industry, or users more focused on design and user experience.

I've put together a Twitter list, Data Viz Heroes (*https://twitter.com/ryanvizzes/lists/data-viz-heroes/*), that might be a good starting point for you. These are just a few of my favorite users to learn Tableau from. Remember, this is not a comprehensive list of every outstanding Tableau user, but a short list of users whose style aligns with how I want to use the software.

Some of these users have created aggregated learning resources from several users in the community. One of my favorites is the Data + Science Tableau Reference Guide (*http://www.dataplusscience.com/TableauReferenceGuide/*), maintained by Jeffrey Shaffer (@HighVizAbility (*https://twitter.com/HighVizAbility*)). If you can't quite find what you're looking for, there is an active community of Tableau users answering specific questions on the community forums.

Lastly, get involved with a local Tableau User Group. This is a free resource where you can meet local Tableau users and learn from what others are doing. Many of my Data Viz Heroes often speak at these meetings. These user groups are all over the world— use this handy Tableau User Group map (*https://community.tableau.com/community/groups*) to find the one closest to you and reach out to the leader to get involved.

Tip #4: Take a Training Class

Cost: $13–$6,000 per day

No matter how many blog posts you've read, sometimes you just need to talk to somebody who can help you connect the dots between what you are learning. Attending a Tableau training or data visualization workshop can help you take your skills a significant step forward in a short amount of time. Tableau training comes in many shapes and sizes, and as with the tip about following the community, you should choose your Tableau training based on what you are hoping to get out of the software at this point in your development.

If you would like a recorded training, I recommend the resources available at O'Reilly's Safari Books Online (*https://www.safaribooksonline.com/*), Udemy, Pluralsight, or Playfair Data TV (*https://www.playfairdata.tv/*). Several of these recorded trainings are taught by qualified instructors, including my Data Viz Heroes.

If you are in need of in-person training, you can attend a one-day training at Tableau's annual customer conference, a group training conducted by Tableau, an on-site training conducted by Tableau, or an on-site training conducted by a third-party trainer. I attended a group training conducted by Tableau during my second year using the software, and a condensed "analyst" training at a Tableau conference in my third year using it. I can personally attest to the value that attending an in-person training provides.

I'd be a bad consultant if I didn't mention my Tableau training offering (*http://bit.ly/2uEPaYO*) and encourage you to get in touch if you are interested in my personal training services.

Tip #3: Read Up

Cost: $35–$45

There are simply some good books on Tableau available to learn from. This is a great starting point for learning Tableau, and one we sometimes take for granted. When I started using Tableau ("Back in my day…."), there was only one book that I can remember, and it was a very short one. There are now dozens of such resources available. I'm obviously biased toward the book you are currently reading, but among several other great options, here are two that I vouch for:

- *Tableau Your Data!* by Dan Murray (Wiley)

  This book is possibly the best all-around—ahem, non–*Practical Tableau*—resource for getting started with Tableau. It provides some of the basic fundamentals, but also discusses more advanced features and Tableau Server.
- *Communicating Data with Tableau* by Ben Jones (O'Reilly)

  In my opinion, Ben's book is the best second step, as it is more strategic and provides some ways to think about your approach to data visualization after you have the fundamentals down. It also offers several hands-on walkthroughs for different applications of Tableau.

Tip #2: Practice

Cost: $0

There is no substitute for on-the-job training with your own data and unique business problems. The more challenges you come across and push through to an eventual solution, the more unique tools you get to add to your toolbelt to solve increasingly complex problems that emerge. This may sound obvious, so I will offer an extra tip to help you get the most out of your practice: start a weekly internal meetup.

I call mine Tableau Tuesday. During Tableau Tuesday, a group of 5–10 internal Tableau users get together to train, share case studies of our own work, and/or work collaboratively through challenging situations. These Tableau Tuesday events lead to valuable discussion and ensure that the entire team is continuously learning.

Tip #1: Tableau Public

Cost: $0

I credit Tableau Public as the primary reason for my personal success with Tableau, and thus, it is my number one tip for how to learn Tableau. Tableau Public (*https://*

public.tableau.com/s/) is a free tool that has almost all of the same functionality as Tableau Desktop (Personal). You can currently connect to and explore Excel, text files, and Google Sheets with up to 15 million rows.

The only catch with Tableau Public is that your files have to be saved to the web, and external audiences can potentially find your work. For this reason, it is not a suitable option for private business data. I actually view this as a positive. This forces you to find topics and data outside of your normal work environment. As I described in my Tableau customer story (*https://www.tableau.com/de-de/learn/stories/digital-analytics-consultancy-agency-turns-data-stories*), Tableau Public is my sandbox to try new approaches to data visualization that in a business setting may not be as appreciated. The cool thing is, these "attempts to fly" are often eventually figured out, and frequently make it into my daily corporate work.

You can also download many of the workbooks you find on Tableau Public. This provides an amazing bevy of dashboards that you can use as a learning resource by downloading, looking under the hood, and reverse engineering. There is an option for the publisher to disallow this feature, but there are still thousands of downloadable dashboards—including every single one of mine (*http://www.ryansleeper.com/data-visualizations/*). I previously had just one dashboard that was not downloadable, *The Cost of Attending the Baseball Championship Series*, and that was because it included stadium data of Kauffman Stadium in Kansas City and Citi Field in New York worth thousands of dollars to create. Well, I'm proud to report that even the 2015 Tableau Public Visualization of the Year is now available to download for free!

I unlocked this dashboard for two reasons, which I'll relate here because they illustrate the spirit of Tableau Public. Steve Wexler of Data Revelations wrote a post called "In Praise of Tableau Public." (*http://bit.ly/2p56WiV*) In the post, Steve describes all of the things that I love about Tableau Public. Then I came to a line that said, "Unless you indeed have proprietary data please, please, please don't stop your workbooks from being downloaded." That's three pleases. It reminded me of how important Tableau Public is as a resource for people to learn from and have discussions around approaches to data visualization.

Second, after the announcement that this viz received the honor of Tableau Public Viz of the Year, I was immediately asked personally from a new user for the original copy so they could see how it was created. It simply didn't feel right to keep the dashboard locked. My hope is that Tableau users of any experience level have the opportunity to learn from Tableau Public dashboards so they can incorporate innovations into their own work and continue pushing the envelope in their own ways.

That's it my for my top five tips for how to learn Tableau. Trust me when I say that *everybody* is learning! The key is to be persistent. Tableau is user-friendly enough and has so many resources available that anybody who is committed can become an expert.

CHAPTER 2

Which Tableau Product Is Best for Me?

I always say that there are five to ten topics that I wish somebody had told me the first day I used Tableau. The next several chapters address those topics, and will help you start using Tableau immediately! The first thing you need to know is what products you should download to get started. Tableau is growing at a rapid pace and there are still regular updates to all of its products, as well as the product ecosystem itself, making product selection a potentially confusing topic for a beginner.

It helps to understand that Tableau is a *brand*, and not a specific *product*. When somebody asks you to "download Tableau," they could be talking about Tableau Reader, Tableau Public, Tableau Desktop (Personal), Tableau Desktop (Professional), Tableau Server, Tableau Online, and so on.

This chapter provides an introduction to Tableau's product ecosystem so you can make the choice that best suits your individual requirements.

Which Tableau Product Is Best for Me?

The decision on which Tableau product to download comes down to four key attributes:

Connectivity
　　What data sources do you need to access?

Distribution
　　Who do you want to see your dashboard and how will you share it with them?

Automation
　　Do you need your work to update automatically on a refresh schedule?

Security

Do you require an on-premise level of security or can your work be saved in the cloud?

From here, I will share a brief synopsis of each product, how each answers the four questions just mentioned, and who might get the best use out of each product.

Tableau Desktop: Personal

Tableau Desktop: Personal is the entry point for the paid development versions of the software. It allows you to keep your workbooks private, but connection and distribution options are limited.

Connectivity	Excel, text files, Access, statistical files, shape files, spatial files, and Tableau files
Distribution	Offline or Tableau Public
Automation	Not available
Security	As good as your personal computer/server's security
Best for	Those that only need to connect to flat data files; those that need the most cost-effective version that will keep their data private

Tableau Desktop: Professional

Tableau Desktop: Professional is similar to Tableau Desktop: Personal in that it is a development version of Tableau. Both the Personal and Professional versions have all of the same development capabilities, but the Professional version provides full access to every data type and distribution channel currently available in the software.

Connectivity	All possible connections in Tableau
Distribution	Offline, Tableau Server, or Tableau Public (all possible distribution options in Tableau)
Automation	Not available
Security	As good as your personal computer/server's security
Best for	Those that need to connect to data in databases; those that need the capability to publish to Tableau Server

Tableau Reader

Tableau Reader is a free download that allows you to open "packaged workbooks," which are Tableau workbooks that are saved in a special way by Tableau Desktop users so the data and visualizations are in the same file. Tableau Reader allows you to open and interact with Tableau workbooks, but not develop them. Development capabilities could be considered an obvious fifth key attribute, but as Tableau Reader is the only product listed that does not provide these capabilities, I have not listed it as a key consideration. This product works much like a PDF viewer, where a developer of a document saves it in a certain way so that it can be opened by a PDF reader.

Connectivity	*.twbx* files only (packaged workbooks)
Distribution	Offline
Automation	Not available
Security	As good as your personal computer/server's security
Best for	People that need an affordable way to view and interact with colleagues' Tableau workbooks

Tableau Public

Tableau Public is another free download, but this product actually provides development capabilities. The catch is that the workbooks have to be saved to Tableau's public cloud, making this an unsuitable choice for proprietary business data.

Connectivity	Excel, text files
Distribution	Cloud (Public)
Automation	Not available
Security	Limited; your workbooks are potentially accessible by anyone on the web, but you are able to restrict the ability for someone to download your files
Best for	Journalists; sharing publicly available data (and Tableau know-how) with the world; practicing Tableau for free; trying the software

Tableau Online

Tableau Online is similar to Tableau Server, but it is hosted via a third-party partner of Tableau. This product still has the advantages of cloud distribution and automatic refreshes, but it is hosted off premise, which can result in security challenges for certain organizations. Like Tableau Server, Tableau Online requires additional per-user licensing, even if those users already have access to Tableau Desktop.

Connectivity	Workbooks that have been published to Tableau Online and that you have been granted access to
Distribution	Cloud
Automation	Available via data refresh schedules
Security	As good as Tableau's third-party host
Best for	Those that need to access/distribute workbooks in the cloud; those that want to automate workbook refreshes; those that want to edit workbooks in the cloud (limited capability); those that are OK having their data and workbooks hosted off premise

Tableau Server

Tableau Server provides a central repository for all of your Tableau workbooks that can be accessed by your business users via a web browser. Tableau Server also has the advantage of data refresh capabilities as well as a way for your organization to keep its data and workbooks on premise in the case that your organization requires that level of security. Tableau Server requires additional user licenses, even if you already have a Tableau Desktop license:

Connectivity	Workbooks that have been published to Tableau Server and that you have been granted access to
Distribution	On-premise or cloud
Automation	Available via data refresh schedules
Security	As good as your on-premise or server host's security
Best for	Those that need to access/distribute workbooks in the cloud; those that want to automate workbook refreshes; those that want to edit workbooks in the cloud (limited capability); those that need to keep their data and workbooks on premise

Tableau consistently invests in research and development, so it is a good idea to keep an eye out for updates and new products at Tableau's product page (*http://www.tableau.com/products*). Also, if you are part of a nonprofit organization and just getting started with any of the paid products mentioned here, be sure to ask Tableau for special pricing!

CHAPTER 3

An Introduction to Connecting to Data

Once you have chosen the best Tableau product for you, it is time to start finding insights in your data! Much like Tableau's suite of products, data connections come in many shapes and sizes. As of this writing, Tableau Desktop: Personal has seven different types of data connections, and Tableau Desktop: Professional adds another 63 native ways to connect to data. That doesn't even count the ability to access web data through customized connectors or Open Database Connectivity (ODBC).

As you can imagine from the breadth of connection options, you can connect to almost any type of data in Tableau and if you don't see the connection you are looking for, somebody is likely working on a customized solution that will help. I could write an entire book on the different data connections alone, but they all work similarly and are fairly intuitive. So for the purposes of this chapter, I will show you how to get started with one connection type and a few of the ways you can prepare to work with the data.

An Introduction to Connecting to Data in Tableau

When you open Tableau, you will see a screen that looks like this, where you have the option to choose your data connection:

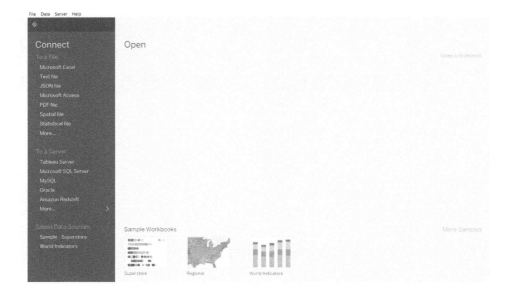

The options under the navigation heading "To a File" can be accessed with Tableau Desktop: Personal. All possible data connections, including to data that resides on a server, can be accessed with Tableau Desktop: Professional.

At the bottom of the left navigation, there are a couple of data sources that come with every download of Tableau. The first, Sample – Superstore, is actually an Excel file, so you can connect to it whether you are using Tableau Desktop: Personal or Tableau Desktop: Professional. I like to train with this data source because it is the most common data source used in online tutorials and during Tableau's own training. To start using it, click it.

The Sample – Superstore data source will be used for every tutorial in this book unless noted otherwise.

After clicking a saved data source, you are immediately thrown into the authoring interface. We discuss getting a lay of the land in Chapter 5, but I actually want to take a step back to show you what happens when you normally connect to a new data source. To get to the data editing interface, click the Data Source tab in the lower-left corner of the authoring interface. You should be taken to a screen that looks like this:

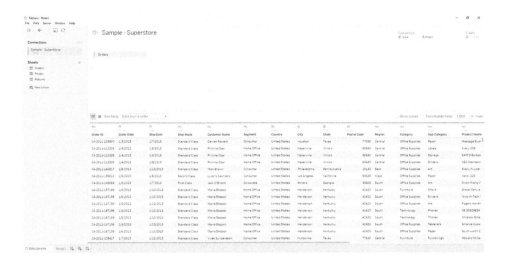

This is the screen you will be presented with when connecting to an Excel or database connection. In Tableau, the Excel workbook is treated as a database and the individual tabs are treated as individual tables within that database. For this reason, you can join tabs to each other if they have at least one field in common. When you join tables, you are appending additional fields to your data source based on shared fields. To do so, simply drag the table (i.e., tab) that you want to join into the data editing interface and tell Tableau what the two tabs have in common. Here's what the Sample – Superstore dataset looks like after I dragged the Returns table into the view and set up a *left* join on Order ID (this means that every field that has a matching Order ID in the table on the right will be appended to the table on the left):

You can even do cross-database joins, even if the data comes from different types of data connections. To do this, you would click Add to the right of Connections, connect to your additional data source, and set up a join just as pictured in the previous image.

If you're working with multiple tables that all have the same column headers, it may make more sense to union, or stack, the tables instead of joining them. Maybe you've got twelve months of web analytics data in one Excel file, but each month's data lives on a separate tab. To union the twelve tabs, you would drag "New Union" from the left navigation onto the data editing interface, then drag the tables that you want to union into the box that appears. When you create a union in Tableau, a column will be added that tells you what sheet the data came from.

After you've retrieved the data you want to work with, there are a few more options for preparing each column. To access them, click the down arrow next to the data type icon for each column:

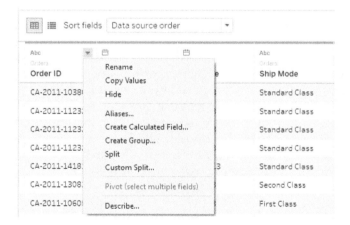

The options are:

Rename
    Allows you to rename the field.

Copy Values
    When nothing is selected, places the value in the first row on your clipboard (preselecting rows before choosing this option will copy your selection).

Hide
    Hides the entire column.

Aliases
    Allows you to assign new names to individual dimension members.

Create Calculated Field

Allows you to create a new field before you start using it within Tableau.

Create Group

Allows you to group different dimension members. This can be handy for quick data clean-up.

Split

Tableau will look at the dimension members in your column and guess the most appropriate way to split them into multiple columns.

Custom Split

The same as Split, but you determine how to separate the dimension members.

Pivot

When you have multiple columns selected, you can transpose them. Note you can only do one data pivot per data source.

Describe

Gives you additional information about the field.

When going through this process for quantitative fields, the string functions are not available, and one additional option is available: Create Bins. This creates equally sized bins, which can be used to make histograms. We will discuss how to make histograms in Chapter 28.

Lastly, you can also change the data type of a column by clicking the data type icon at the top of the column.

It's important to note that any changes you make to the data at this point creates metadata and has no impact on your underlying data source. This means you can make rapid progress in Tableau without the risk of messing up your existing infrastructure.

Another notable task that you may choose to do when connecting to a new data source is to either extract or filter the data source. By default, most data source connections will be live with no filters; these options can be seen in the upper-right corner of the data editor:

Live connections are advisable when you are working with large datasets and/or datasets held on powerful, in-memory databases. Live connections also offer the best security in most large organizations.

Extracts create a snapshot of your data at whatever point they are created. They are typically faster than a live data connection, especially when connecting to a live database. Just remember that extracts have to be refreshed periodically so that you are working with the latest data possible. From within Tableau Desktop, extracts can be refreshed by navigating to Data in the top navigation, hovering over the data source you want to refresh, then hovering over Extract, and clicking Refresh. If you eventually use Tableau Server or Tableau Online, you will see an option to automate the refresh process when you publish from Tableau Desktop.

The final option discussed in this chapter is the ability to filter the entire data source before you start working with it in Tableau. These filters can be created with any combination of fields by clicking the Add button under Filters. This is an easy opportunity to make your workbooks more efficient because you have the ability to filter out the data you don't need for your analysis. For example, if your analysis is about this year's data, don't pull in the last ten years of data! Or maybe you are building the workbook for a stakeholder that is only responsible for one division and they're not allowed to see the performance of other divisions. Adding a filter in this scenario not only makes the data processing more efficient, it will help you manage security to ensure data does not fall into the wrong hands.

With all of these choices, you should be able to set up your data exactly as you wish before you start working with it. However, if you are trying to transition existing Excel reports or working with irregularly shaped data, you may benefit from reading on into Chapter 4, before you get seriously down to work.

Shaping Data for Use with Tableau

The next thing I wish I knew when I first started using Tableau is that there is an optimal way to shape data for use with the software. I'll never forget the day I was introduced to Tableau. The boss walked in and asked three of us in the office to try out this new tool she had heard of for creating data visualizations. The first thing every one of us tried to do is connect to an existing Excel report and re-create it in Tableau. After all, this was supposed to be intuitive—perhaps even *magical*—software, right? We quickly found out that nothing worked as we expected, we couldn't figure out how to make a single chart, and we had to fight the temptation to immediately revert back to our familiar Excel experience.

It's fun to look back, and this now seems like a simple problem to solve, but the scenario I experienced my first time with Tableau is not uncommon. In fact, it's both the most common Tableau adoption scenario that I come across—and the most difficult: first-time users connecting to an existing Excel report without any consideration to the format of the data.

Most existing Excel reports are not set up to work well with Tableau, and if this is the first data source that a first-time user attempts to work with, they are setting themselves up to fail. But don't despair—I can personally attest to what it's like to start using Tableau without any data or visualization software experience. I've always said that there are three or four key things to know when getting started with Tableau, and sometimes you just need somebody to share them with you so you can connect the dots and get started.

Shaping Data for Use with Tableau

This topic is easiest to illustrate, so take a look at the first image, which is meant to be similar to a typical report in Excel:

Sweet Excel Table					
	Q1	Q2	Q3	Q4	Total
Sales	$	$	$	$	$$$$
Profit	$	$	$	$	$$$$
Orders	#	#	#	#	####

There is a title along the top, a column header for each quarter, and a row for each KPI (Sales, Profit, and Orders). In addition, there is a total for each row on the right-hand side of the table.

The format of this report poses several problems for Tableau which, upon connecting, will try to interpret the data source, classify the fields, and set up your workspace:

- There is a title in the first row. The first two rows are critical for Tableau to interpret the data source, so we've immediately gotten off on the wrong foot.

- The column headers are quarters, which will cause Tableau to create a field for each quarter, when in fact the quarters should all be consolidated into one field for date/quarter.

- The KPIs are running down the first column so, by default, Tableau will not interpret these KPIs as unique fields.

- There is a total in the right column. As Tableau totals fields for you, not only is this unnecessary, it will likely lead to double-counting.

The ideal format for Tableau looks like this:

Quarter	Sales	Profit	Orders
Q1	$	$	#
Q2	$	$	#
Q3	$	$	#
Q4	$	$	#

Each column now represents a unique field, so the layout is vertical instead of horizontal. The title and totals have also been removed.

With the data in this shape, Tableau will be able to look at the first row to determine the fields and the second row to classify the data (i.e., type; discrete versus continuous; dimension versus measure). We will discuss the ways Tableau classifies data in the next few chapters.

As one additional tip, if your dataset includes a date field that is not in a traditional date format (as we've shown here with quarters), I recommend adding a column that looks like an actual date. In this case, I've added a column for quarter as date, and chosen the first date in each quarter as the entries:

Date	Quarter	Sales	Profit	Orders
1/1/2018	Q1	$	$	#
4/1/2018	Q2	$	$	#
7/1/2018	Q3	$	$	#
10/1/2018	Q4	$	$	#

Note that I've put the dates in my local (i.e., US) format, but this tip is also true for Tableau users outside of the United States using varying date formats. Your local version of Tableau should recognize the date format that you're used to.

Dates are a special data type in Tableau and by having dates in a date format that the software recognizes, the full functionality of date fields is unlocked.

Finally, if data reshaping is required for you to work with a dataset in Tableau, you can reshape it prior to connecting—which is my personal preference—or use Tableau's data interpreter and data pivot tools when you connect. Regardless of the method you choose, putting some thought into the shape of your data will help you get off to a strong start with your analyses in Tableau.

CHAPTER 5

Getting a Lay of the Land

This chapter provides an overview of the Tableau interface, terminology, and a couple of preliminary things I like to do whenever I start working with a new dataset. While this is certainly not an exhaustive list, it will help you get started authoring in Tableau immediately and will provide a foundation for what's to come.

Tableau Terminology

To walk through some of the most important Tableau terminology, we will use the following key followed by names and definitions:

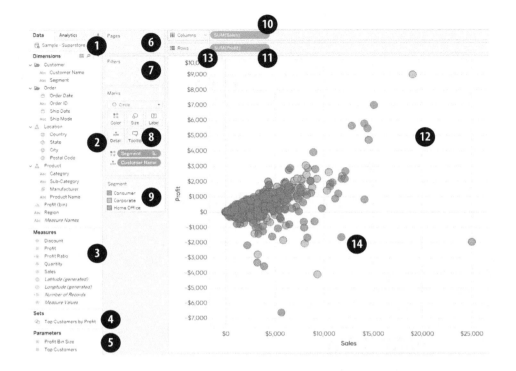

1. *Data Sources*: Displays all of the data connections in the workbook. Note that only one data connection (Sample – Superstore) is being displayed in this example, but you can connect to more than one data source at a time.

2. *Dimensions area of the Data pane*: A list of all of the fields in the data source classified as dimensions (discussed in the next chapter).

3. *Measures area of the Data pane*: A list of all the fields in the data source classified as measures (discussed in the next chapter).

4. *Sets area of the Data pane*: If the data source you are using contains at least one set, or if you have created one or more sets, they will show up here.

5. *Parameters area of the Data pane*: If the workbook you are using contains at least one parameter, or if you have created one or more parameters, they will show up here.

6. *Pages Shelf*: The Pages Shelf allows you to "flip" through a "page" for each dimension member and/or add animation to a view. For example, you can put a dimension for Month of Order Date onto the Pages Shelf and have the view rotate through one month of data at a time.

7. *Filters Shelf*: Any dimension or measure that you filter a view by will be displayed here.

8. *Marks Card (Marks Shelf)*: Each square in this area is called a Marks Card, which are called that because they influence the marks on the view. Each Marks Card resides on the Marks Shelf. Note that depending on the chart type you are creating, additional cards will show up, such as for Shape or Path.

9. *Legend*: There are several different legends that will appear here to show how the marks are encoded, including Color (pictured), Size, and Shape.

10. *Columns Shelf*: Fields placed here will create columns on the view.

11. *Rows Shelf*: Fields placed here will create rows on the view.

12. *Worksheet/View*: Each tab in a Tableau workbook is called a worksheet and the area that displays a data visualization is a view.

13. *"Pill"*: The slang term for fields being used on a worksheet. This term is used due to the oblong shape dimensions and measures inherit once they are placed on a shelf or Marks Card.

14. *Mark*: Each data point on the view.

15. *Show Me* (not pictured): When you click Show Me in the upper-right corner of the authoring interface, you will see thumbnails for 24 different chart types. If you are using a combination of dimensions and measures required to create each respective chart, the thumbnail will be in color; otherwise it will be grayed out. Clicking a full-color thumbnail will draw that visualization with the combination of fields you are using. Show Me provides a nice shortcut to creating several useful chart types, but this book will primarily focus on creating charts manually. I hope that by not relying on Show Me, you'll gain a better understanding of how each visualization in Tableau is created.

I will close this chapter by sharing two things that I like to do when I open a new dataset in Tableau: view the underlying data and view the number of records.

View the Underlying Data

If I am working with a new dataset that has been provided to me, I like to get a general feel for the types of data each field provides. You can easily view this in a tabular form in Tableau in a few different ways:

- Right-click the data connection in the data window and choose View Data.
- Click Data in the top navigation, hover over the data connection, and choose View Data.
- Click the first tab in the bottom of the worksheet view.

Whichever method is used, this provides a snapshot of the data so that you can get a general feel for the types of data that are available, if some fields contain nulls, what fields may be most useful to "slice and dice" your measures, and so on.

If you want to look at one field at a time, a handy trick is to right-click that field on the Dimensions/Measures area of the Data pane and choose Describe. A window will pop up to provide you with helpful information about the respective field.

View the Number of Records

If you look at the bottom of the list of measures on the Measures area of the Data pane, you will see a field called Number of Records. This is a special field that Tableau automatically generates for you, which is indicated by the italic formatting. Number of Records is actually a calculated field that simply equals 1. What this does is adds a column with an entry of 1 to each row of your data, so Tableau can count the number of records in the dataset. To view how many records are in your dataset, on a blank worksheet, drag the Number of Records field to the Text Marks Card:

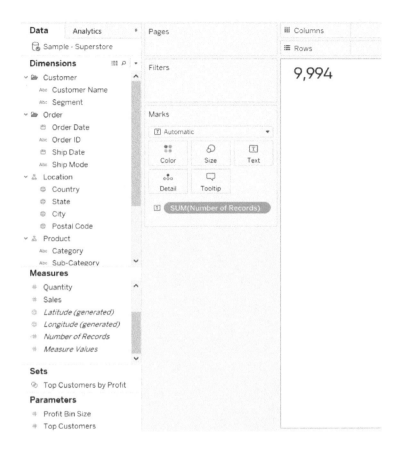

I like to do this when I am getting started with a new dataset for two reasons:

- This provides a quick quality assurance check. For example, if the number of records is lower than you expected, you may need to ensure you haven't filtered the dataset or that the data provider gave you the correct output.

- Having a ballpark idea of the number of records in a dataset can provide a clue on whether I need to take extra steps to keep the workbook running efficiently. If I find that I am working with a very large dataset, I may consider additional ways to aggregate the data and/or keep the size of the data in mind when creating calculated fields (as some are more efficient than others). Efficiency tips are covered in Chapter 58.

After I've got a feel for the size of the data and the type of data I have available, I start creating views and doing some discovery analytics, which we will discuss in future chapters.

CHAPTER 6

Dimension Versus Measure

When you connect to data, Tableau will classify each field as a dimension or a measure. Tableau will then group the fields by their dimension or measure classification on the lefthand side of the workspace. Having a good understanding of the differences between dimensions and measures makes it much easier to work with the data in Tableau.

What Is a Measure?

According to Tableau's Knowledge Base, a measure is a field that is a dependent variable; that is, its value is a function of one or more dimensions. Tableau treats any field containing numeric (quantitative) information as a measure.

Consider the following bar chart, created in Tableau with the Sales measure from the Sample – Superstore dataset:

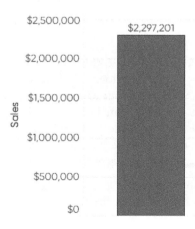

Sales is quantitative, so by default, Tableau will guess that the field is a measure. It can be considered a dependent variable, because a measure by itself does not provide much value. The value of $2,297,201 is meaningless by itself. It is dependent on context that comes in the form of being broken down by dimensions.

What Is a Dimension?

According to Tableau's Knowledge Base, a dimension is a field that can be considered an independent variable. By default, Tableau treats any field containing qualitative, categorical information as a dimension.

Here is the same Sales measure from before, broken down by the dimension of Region:

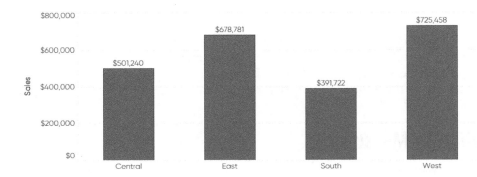

Now that our sales total has been broken down by region, we are able to start gaining insights from the data. One insight that emerges is that the South region has relatively low sales compared to the other regions. This is a descriptive insight that materialized only when we combined measures and dimensions together.

Generally, the measure is the number; the dimension is what you "slice and dice" the number by.

That being said, there can be exceptions to this rule, so it helps to understand how Tableau treats these types of fields. Consider a business that has unique numerical order IDs for each sale (i.e., order 1 is assigned the number 1, order 2 is assigned the number 2, etc.). Looking at the definition just provided, Tableau will classify this Order ID field as a measure the first time you connect to a dataset containing the field. However, Order ID is a dimension because we would "slice and dice" a measure, such as Sales, by Order ID to see how much revenue we brought in per order.

Another rule of thumb I follow is that if it doesn't make sense to sum up a number, it is likely a dimension. That's the case with the hypothetical Order ID field just mentioned. There would never be any value in adding up all of our Order ID numbers to get the total, and sure enough, this field should be a dimension instead of a measure.

One more case that comes to mind where Tableau can misclassify fields is when you have a field that should be a measure, that has the word NULL in the first entry under the column header in your data. The word NULL would be seen as a string value to Tableau, and thus qualitative, which would cause Tableau to classify the field as a dimension.

The good news is that any field that is misclassified can easily be reclassified by right-clicking the field from within the Dimensions or Measures area of the Data pane and choosing "Convert to dimension" or "Convert to measure" as appropriate. The same thing can be achieved by dragging and dropping the field into the Dimensions or Measures area of the Data pane.

An understanding of how dimensions and measures work in Tableau, combined with the basic data preparation just mentioned (when applicable), will make it easier to create visualizations moving forward.

CHAPTER 7

Discrete Versus Continuous

The second big way Tableau classifies each field you are using is as discrete or continuous. This classification has an impact on what types of visualizations you can create as well as how they will look, so having a good grasp on what this distinction means is core to your understanding of how Tableau looks at your data.

It is easy to know if a field is being used as discrete or continuous based on its color. Blue indicates that a field is discrete, while green indicates that a field is continuous. If your first guess was that these colors represented whether a field was a dimension or measure, you are not alone. The thought that blue represents dimensions and green represents measures is the most common myth in Tableau. It's easy to understand why because, by default, dimensions are categorized as discrete variables, and thus have a small blue icon in front of them in the Dimensions area of the Data pane. Measures are categorized as continuous variables, so they are prefaced with a green icon in the Measures area of the Data pane.

I assure you that the color-coding identifies discrete versus continuous fields and not dimensions versus measures. Measures can actually be used as discrete fields or continuous fields, and the same is true for some dimensions, such as dates.

So what does this mean for your visualizations? I will illustrate using two rules of thumb I have when considering if a field should be used as discrete or continuous: *Discrete fields draw headers; continuous fields draw axes.*

Take a look at the following visualizations that look at sales by month. In the first chart, I am using date as a *discrete* field:

Sales by Month: Discrete

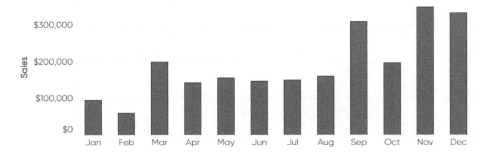

Notice that there is a *discrete* header for each month.

In the second chart, I am using the same exact data, but I have changed the Date dimension from discrete to *continuous*:

Sales by Month: Continuous

As you can see, I now have a *continuous* axis of time. Since the axis is continuous, I cannot change the order of the dates; they follow a chronological order from oldest date on the left to most recent date on the right. On the other hand, when the Date dimension is being used as discrete (as pictured in the first image), I am able to change the order of the dates. For example, I could sort the bars in descending order, with the month with the highest sales first, and the month with the lowest sales last. Which brings me to my second rule when determining whether I should use a field as discrete or continuous:

Discrete fields can be sorted; continuous fields cannot

So how might you use this in the real world? If you know that you want to look at a trend over a continuous period of time, you would want to use a continuous date, which will be colored green on the view. If your analysis requires you to have discrete marks that can be sorted, you would use the field as discrete, which will be colored blue on the view.

This date example is just one of many possibilities, but remembering the two rules outlined in this chapter will help you understand how the use of discrete and continuous fields are impacting the data visualizations you create in Tableau.

CHAPTER 8

Five Ways to Make a Bar Chart/An Introduction to Aggregation

Now that we've gone through some fundamental topics, such as dimension versus measure and discrete versus continuous, and you have an overview of the authoring interface, you're ready to start creating visualizations in Tableau. This chapter shares five different ways to create a bar chart and provides an introduction to the topic of aggregation.

Perhaps the most important lesson from this chapter is a line I hear myself saying almost every day: *there is always more than one way to do the same thing in Tableau.* You will find your own techniques, form your own habits, and hear different opinions—and they likely will all have merit. You truly can take multiple paths to get to the same end result in Tableau. We are about to discuss *five* different ways to create a bar chart, and it's not even a comprehensive list!

Five Ways to Create a Bar Chart in Tableau

Option #1

The easiest way to start a bar chart in Tableau is to simply double-click the measure you want to visualize from the Measures area of the Data pane. Let's double-click the Sales measure. By default, this will place a continuous pill for Sales on the Rows Shelf, which creates a vertical bar.

Option #2

You could have got to this same place by left-clicking and dragging the Sales measure from the Measures area of the Data pane to the Rows Shelf.

Option # 3

"Pre-select" the Sales measure by clicking it, then click "horizontal bars" in the Show Me options. This creates a different orientation than the first two approaches because the Sales measure is placed on the Columns Shelf instead of the Rows Shelf. If you prefer the vertical orientation, you can click the Swap icon (pictured here), use the Ctrl-W shortcut, or drag and drop the Sales measure from the Columns Shelf to the Rows Shelf:

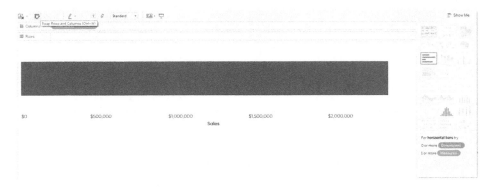

Option #4

You can change the mark type on an existing view to Bar. Let's say you are looking at the Sales measure by Year of Order Date as a line graph. You can convert the line graph to a bar chart by changing the mark type on the Marks Shelf from Automatic (line) to Bar:

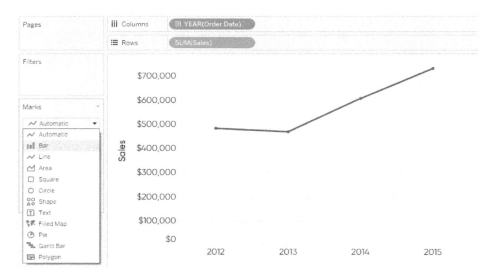

Option #5

Similar to option #2, but if you *right*-click and drag the Sales measure from the Measures area of the Data pane to the Rows Shelf, you will be presented with the option to choose the data aggregation before the bar chart is created:

An Introduction to Aggregation in Tableau

By default, every measure on a view in Tableau is aggregated in some way. It can be easy to not notice this when you're getting started because the default aggregation is SUM, and that works for most situations. Look back at the views created through the five approaches in the previous section; the Sales measure is preceded by the word SUM to show you how the field is being aggregated. There are several other aggregation options in Tableau, and the choice will influence your analysis. Here is a list of some of the options and the results you can expect to see for each choice (using the Sales measure):

SUM

All of the sales added up together

AVG

All of your sales added up, divided by the number of records

MEDIAN

When sorted, the sales amount for the record in the exact middle of your data

CNT

A count of all records with sales

CNTD
> A count of distinct sales amounts

MIN
> The smallest sales value in your data

MAX
> The largest sales value in your data

Knowing that there are always multiple approaches to the same solution in Tableau and having an understanding of aggregation will help tremendously as we start working with different visualizations and creating calculated fields in future chapters.

CHAPTER 9

Line Graphs, Independent Axes, and Date Hierarchies

In the previous chapter, I shared five different ways to make a bar chart in Tableau. This chapter walks you through how to build another key data visualization: the line graph. For all the fancy visualizations I enjoy building with Tableau, at the end of the day, bar charts and line graphs are two of the most effective options available. While we're at it, we'll touch on some related topics, including date hierarchies and independent axes, so you can master this foundational graph.

How to Make a Line Graph in Tableau

A line graph is similar to a bar chart in Tableau in that you are looking at one or more measures with the option to "slice and dice" it by one or more dimensions. The important distinction between the bar chart and line graph is that the line graph should include an element of time. Let's build out a line graph using the Sample – Superstore dataset using Order Date as our element of time.

First, use any of the five methods discussed in Chapter 35 to create a bar chart that adds SUM(Sales) to the Rows Shelf. I'm going to simply double-click the Sales measure to start the view.

At this point, you could also double-click your element of time (Order Date) to start a line graph, but there is a better way. As with measures, dates also have an aggregation and can be used as continuous or discrete fields. The choices you make for these two classifications has an impact on how the visualization will look. Fortunately, it is easy to see all of the options if instead of double-clicking the Order Date dimension, you right-click and drag it to the Columns Shelf. Before Tableau generates the visualization, you will see the following options:

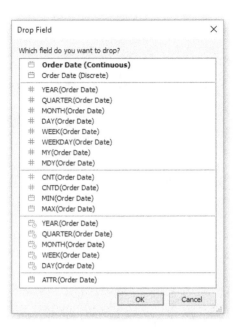

As you can see, each option has a blue or green icon next to it. Remember, the blue color coding in Tableau indicates discrete, while green color coding indicates continuous. The choice of whether you select a discrete or continuous option should be based on what type of visualization you want to create. Let's say that we want to look at a *continuous* trend over time, which means we can ignore the blue options for now.

The next choice we have is how granular we want the continuous trend to be. This is called the DatePart and includes options such as year, quarter, month, week, and day. For this analysis, let's say we want to see a monthly trend over time. With these two requirements in mind, we know that we should pick the choice with a green icon with an aggregation of Month, which is the fourth choice from the bottom. After making this selection, the line graph looks like this:

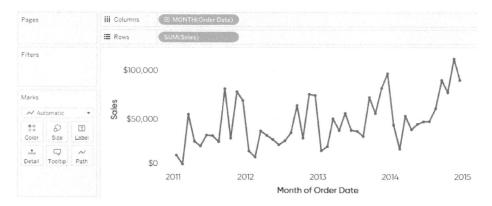

The small circles on each data point are called "markers" can be added by clicking on the Color Marks Card and choosing one of the "Markers:" options under Effects.

Independent Axes in Tableau

The line graph created in the previous section can now be sliced and diced by additional dimensions by simply dragging them to the Columns Shelf or Rows Shelf and dropping them in front of the continuous fields on the view (currently MONTH(Order Date) or SUM(Sales)). To demonstrate how axes work across multiple columns or rows in Tableau, I will drag the Ship Mode dimension to the Rows Shelf:

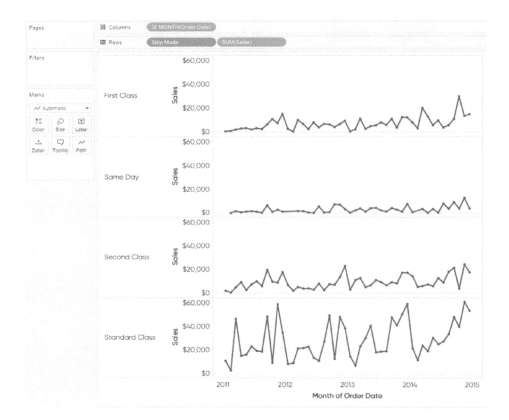

Notice that, by default, each row shares the same axis range from $0 to approximately $60,000, which is the largest range across all four ship modes. This default setting where the axes share the same range is helpful because it provides an apples-to-apples comparison across the four rows. However, it can be difficult to see the trends for each individual row. If you would like the four axes to have their own axis range, right-click any of the axes and choose "Edit axis." You will be presented with a dialog box where you can choose "Independent axis ranges for each row or column":

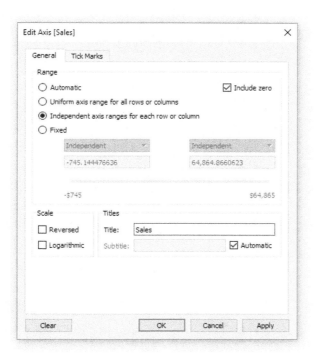

Upon making this selection, you will see your trend graph change so that each row has its own unique range:

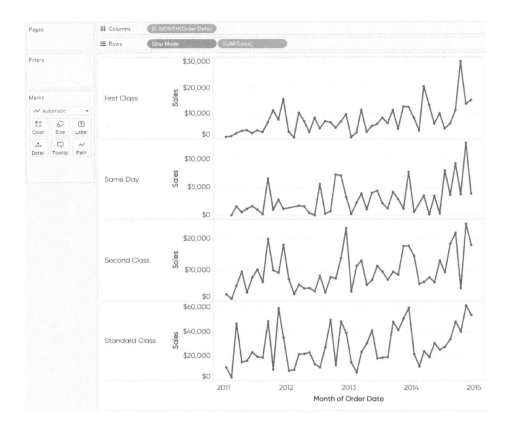

Date Hierarchies in Tableau

For the final section in this chapter, let's take a step back by building the line graph again, this time by first double-clicking the Sales measure and Order Date dimension. At this point, your line graph should look similar to this:

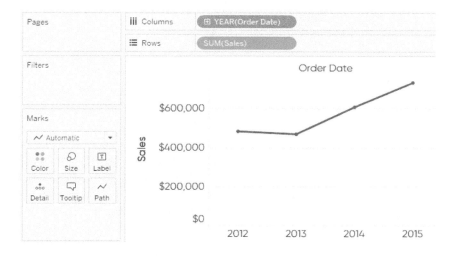

The blue YEAR(Order Date) pill is telling us that date is being aggregated by year and being used as a *discrete* field. When dates are being used as discrete fields, you will see a + sign on the field, which indicates this field has a hierarchy. Dates are one of the few special dimensions in Tableau that automatically receive a hierarchy, and it goes in this order: Year > Quarter > Month > Day.

To utilize the hierarchy, simply click the + sign on the field. The field will expand to the next level of the hierarchy and provide a different view. Here's how this same view looks if I click the + on Year, then click the + on Quarter:

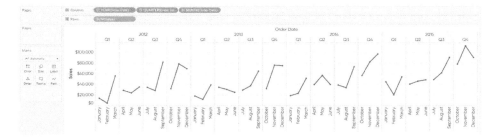

You can also drill back "up" by clicking the – sign that appears on fields where the + has already been clicked. What's nice about these fields is that, because they are discrete, they can be moved around into different orders to quickly create different analyses. The fields are processed in order, so with the last line graph pictured, the Sales measure is first cut by Year, then Quarter, then Month. To demonstrate a couple of possibilities, let's first remove Quarter from the view, leaving us with Year and Month:

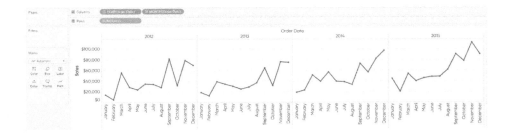

At this point, we have a pretty standard analysis, where our years and months go in chronological order from oldest to most recent. This creates a seasonal analysis where you can compare four calendar years to each other. Look what happens when you simply change the order of Year and Month by dragging the Month pill in front of the Year pill:

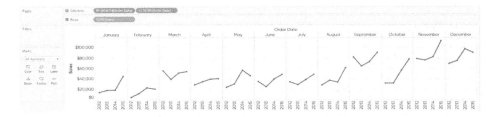

The fields are processed in order, so now the Sales measure is first cut by Month, then Year. This completely changes the analysis into a four-year trend per month.

While line graphs may seem simple on the surface, they are extremely powerful visualizations, and Tableau provides the flexibility to use them for many different analyses.

CHAPTER 10

Marks Cards, Encoding, and Level of Detail

The Marks Cards in Tableau provide some of the most powerful functionality in the program because they allow you to modify a view's design, visualization type, user experience, and granularity of analysis all in one place. This chapter provides an overview of the Marks Cards available in the authoring interface as well as an introduction to the concept of a view's *level of detail*.

In Chapter 5, you saw that the default location of the Marks *Shelf* (or Shelves), which contain the Marks *Cards*, are located on the left side of the view to the right of the Data pane and under the Filters Shelf. The Marks Shelf and Marks Cards include the word "marks" because they change the marks, or data points, on a view.

An Explanation of Level of Detail

To help illustrate how each Marks Card impacts the marks on a view, we will be using this simple scatter plot looking at Profit Ratio and Sales:

As you can see on the Marks Shelf, there are six different Marks Cards: Color, Size, Label, Detail, Tooltip, and Shape. Note that the Shape Marks Card is not available for every view, but appeared because we are creating a scatter plot in this example. To help explain what each of these cards does, I'm going to start a little out of order and discuss the Detail Marks Card first.

I'm starting with the Detail Marks Card because level of detail is a critical aspect of analyzing data in Tableau, but it took me a while when I started using Tableau to realize its importance. It's not a difficult concept, but just one of those that wasn't explained to me early on. Once you wrap your head around the topic of level of detail, your authoring in Tableau will feel much more fluid and it will be easier to use the powerful level of detail expressions functionality in Chapter 16.

The first thing you need to know is that every visualization has a level of detail. It helps me to think about level of detail as the most granular level where the analysis takes place. Consider the preceding scatter plot. At this point, we are not slicing and dicing the Profit Ratio and Sales measures by any dimension. For that reason, you see just a single mark, which represents the intersection of Profit Ratio and Sales for every record combined in the Sample – Superstore dataset. As you add dimensions to the view, the analysis becomes more granular, so the level of detail changes. For example, if we wanted to do this Profit Ratio versus Sales comparison at the customer level, we can drag and drop the Customer Name dimension from the Dimensions area of the Data pane to the Detail Marks Card, which results in the following:

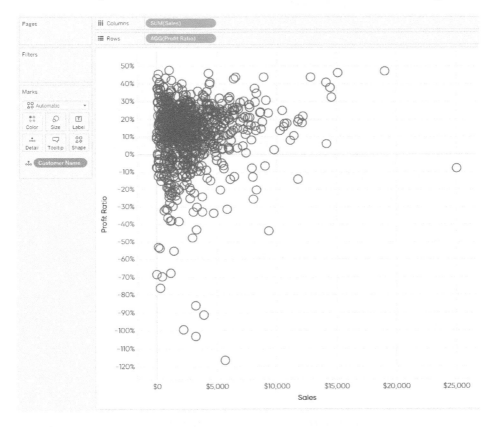

We have changed the most granular level of the analysis from the entire file to customer. Another handy feature of Tableau is you can look in the lower-left corner of the worksheet for a summary of the view. When we changed the level of detail for this scatter plot, the mark count changed from 1 (the entire file) to 793 (the number of customers).

Note that adding dimensions in other places on the view will also change the level of detail, but the Detail Marks Card is available to make the analysis more granular without changing the structure of the view if needed.

An Introduction to Encoding

The Color, Size, and Shape Marks Cards all allow you to "encode" the marks on a view. Encoding marks adds depth to an analysis by mapping marks to colors, sizes, and/or shapes. Here's how the scatter plot view looks if we put Segment on the Color Marks Card, Sales on the Size Marks Card, and Category on the Shape Marks Card:

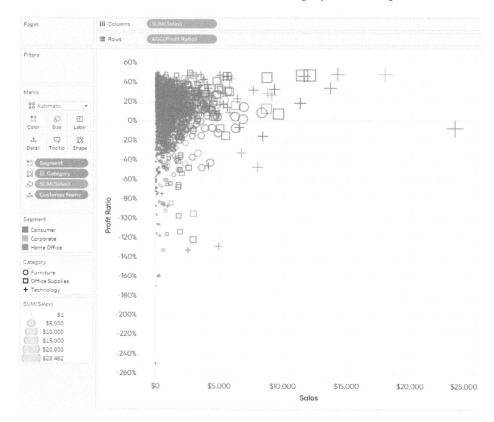

There are now three different legends corresponding with the encoding that was just added. For consistency, this encoding will conveniently carry through on other views as they are created. For example, if I color a new view by the Segment dimension, Consumer will still be identified as blue, Corporate will still be identified as orange, and Home Office will still be identified as red. These colors can be changed by clicking the color legend and mapping new colors.

These three Marks Cards can also be used to change all the marks on the view instead of mapping to a specific dimension. Instead of placing a dimension on the Marks Cards, click each card to experiment with changing the color, size, or shapes for all of the marks at the same time. Simple changes to the Marks Cards can substantially improve the design of a data visualization.

Label and Tooltip Marks Cards

The Label and Tooltip Marks Cards can both be used to add written information to a view. The difference is that whatever information is added as a label will show up on the view itself, while any information added to the tooltips will only show up when an end user hovers over marks on the view.

This is an important distinction that should be considered when you are authoring in Tableau. For example, if your visualization will be printed or copied and pasted as a screenshot, you would want to add the information to Label to ensure the information is shown on the view. On the other hand, if you know your end users will be interacting with Tableau, you may opt to save some on-screen real estate by providing the information through tooltips.

As with the other Marks Cards, labels and tooltips can be customized with specific information by dragging and dropping fields onto the Label and Tooltip Marks Cards, respectively. You can click into each of these two Marks Cards to toggle them on and off, change the formatting, and even type in additional information.

The six Marks Cards introduced in this chapter can dramatically improve the depth, design, and user experience of your visualizations. Utilizing this functionality will not only help your analyses, it will make your final product more effective with end users.

CHAPTER 11

An Introduction to Filters

Tableau provides the ability to filter individual views or even entire data sources on dimensions, measures, or sets (see Chapter 15). This filtering capability can serve a variety of purposes, including minimizing the size of the data for efficiency purposes, cleaning up underlying data, removing irrelevant dimension members, and setting measure or date ranges for what you want to analyze. What's more, most of these filters can be manipulated by you and your end users—a powerful tactic for finding stories in the data. This chapter offers an introduction to filters in Tableau, including extract filters, data source filters, dimension filters, and measure filters.

Dimension Filters in Tableau

For this chapter, we will start with the most granular filters (dimension filters and measure filters) and then work our way out to the more "macro" filters. To help illustrate dimension filters and measure filters, we will use this simple bar chart, which is showing the sales per customer from the Sample – Superstore dataset in descending order (the customer names are sorted in descending order by sum of Sales; one way to achieve this is by clicking the sort descending icon found immediately above the Columns Shelf):

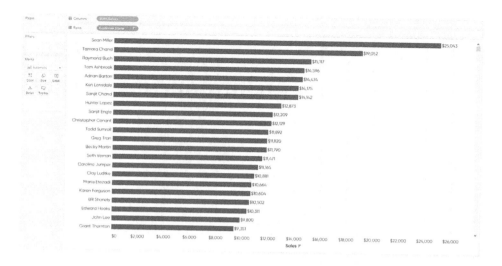

The first, and most basic way to filter out marks on a view, is to select the marks, and then choose to keep or exclude them. Let's say that our boss has an extreme aversion to names that start with the letter "C", so we want to make sure we remove those customers from the report. To do so, you can go through the list of customers, and use multiselect (Ctrl-Click on a PC) to highlight them. After selecting the names that you want to filter, hover over one of the dimension members (in this case, customer names), and click Exclude:

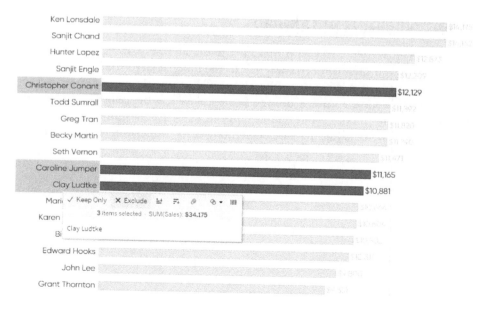

Note that there is also an option to Keep Only, which would do exactly what it sounds like, and *keep only* the selected names on the view.

After choosing Exclude, notice that the Customer Name dimension is added to the Filters Shelf in the upper-left corner of the view:

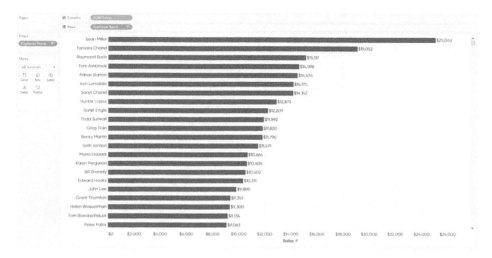

That's because Tableau created a dimension filter for you when you excluded the Customer Name dimension members from the view. You could have got to this same point by dragging the Customer Name dimension from the Dimensions area of the Data pane to the Filters Shelf and manually setting up the dimension filter. Let's take a look under the hood at the options for manually setting up a dimension filter by right-clicking the Customer Name filter and choosing Edit Filter:

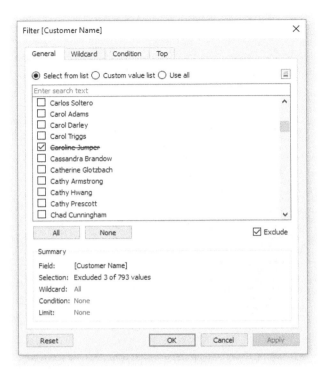

Notice that Tableau created an "Exclude" dimension filter for us when we chose to exclude the three names that start with the letter "C" from the view, as indicated by the box for "Exclude" being checked. There is a summary box at the bottom of the filter that is telling us the criteria for our filter. We currently are excluding 3 of 793 total marks, or customer names, from the view. This manual selection of individual dimension members is the most precise form of filtering, but can also be quite tedious. This is especially true when filtering on the Customer Name dimension, which has 793 individual dimension members.

Fortunately, there are three other tabs at the top of our dimension filter dialog box, which help us refine the filter criteria. Instead of manually selecting all names that start with the letter "C", I'll navigate to the "Wildcard" tab and leverage the "Does not start with" function:

After applying this logic, I am left with 726 of 793 customers—and none whose first names start with "C" so our boss can rest easy! After adding any criteria to one of the four tabs, you can always navigate back to the Summary card on the General tab to see all the rules in the filter. Each rule acts as an AND statement, meaning that the dimension members must meet all criteria to be included or excluded from the view.

There are two additional tabs that can be used to add rules to a dimension filter. The Condition tab allows you to add quantitative thresholds that must be met and the Top tab allows you to focus only on the Top or Bottom dimension members based on a measure of your choosing.

Measure Filters in Tableau

Measure filters are similar to dimension filters, but the filtering options are different between the two. To illustrate, drag the Sales measure from the Measures area of the Data pane to the Filters Shelf. The first difference you'll notice is that before you select the measure filter criteria, you are asked to choose the aggregation of the measure:

I will choose Sum, which is the default for most measures. After making the choice of aggregation, you can choose to filter on a range of values, a minimum threshold, or a maximum threshold:

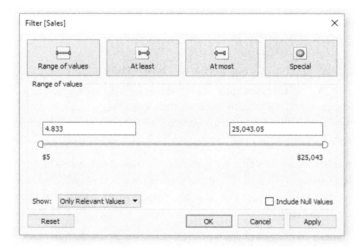

"Range of values" provides the most flexibility and is the best (and only) choice if you want you and your end users to be able to control both the bottom end and top end of the range. For now, I'll change just the bottom end of the range to be $10,000. After changing the low end to $10,000 and clicking OK, my view looks like this:

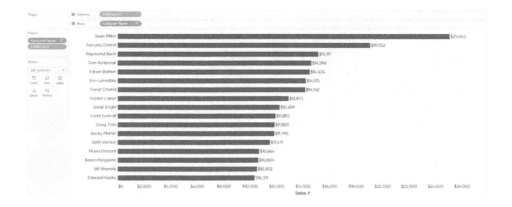

Note that I now have two filters on the Filters Shelf; one dimension filter and one measure filter. All of the filters that you place here will act as a condition in an AND statement. So at this point, in order for a customer name to be shown on the view, it must not start with the letter "C" and sales must be between $10,000 and $25,043.05.

Note that you can add additional dimension or measure filters, even if the fields are not used to generate the view.

More Options with Filters

Sometimes, you want a filter to be permanent and do not have any interest in changing its criteria. Other times, you would like to change the criteria or even let your end users decide what is filtered on the view. Any filter can be shown to you and your end users for easy manipulation by simply clicking a filter from the Filters Shelf and choosing Show Filter. Upon doing so, you will see the filter appear in the upper-right corner of the view. If you're not happy with the default format of the filter, you can click the down arrow in the upper-right corner of the filter being shown on the view and change it. Dimension filters have seven different formats to choose from and measure filters have three different formats.

Lastly, dimension and measure filters are applied to only the worksheet you added it to by default. However, filters can be changed to apply to additional individual worksheets, every worksheet that shares the data source, or as of Tableau 10, even all related data sources. This provides the ability to make filters "global" so that changing their criteria in one place filters the views throughout the workbook. To change the worksheets that a filter is applied to, click the filter on the Filters Shelf, hover over Apply to Worksheets, and make your selection.

Macro Filters

Dimension and measure filters are the most granular form of filtering in Tableau, and will be used most regularly. Occasionally though, you may want to apply a filter at a higher level, such as the data source or extract. This type of "macro" filter provides the benefit of reducing the size of the dataset, one of my top five efficiency tips for working with data in Tableau (listed in Chapter 58).

To add this type of filter, navigate to the data source editor by doing one of the following:

- Right-click the data source from the Data Window and choose Edit Data Source.
- Click Data in the top navigation, hover over the data source of interest, and choose Edit Data Source.
- Click the Data Source tab at the bottom of the authoring interface. Once there, you will see an option to add filters to the live data source or data extract in the top-right corner. After you choose a dimension or measure to use as a filter, the filter dialogs will look very familiar to the filters introduced to this point, only now, the filters will be applied to the entire data source before you create individual views.

CHAPTER 12

An Introduction to Calculated Fields

Possibly the most powerful feature of Tableau is its ability to allow authors to create new data from existing data through calculated fields. Calculated fields can be used to create new dimensions such as segments, or new measures such as ratios. They can also be used with any data type, a multitude of functions and aggregations, as well as logical operators, making the calculated results virtually limitless. This chapter will introduce calculated fields by walking you through how to create two new measures and one new dimension in the Sample – Superstore dataset.

Why Use Calculated Fields?

You may be wondering what's with all the praise regarding calculated fields? After all, I've also suggested that it's best to prepare your data as much as possible before it gets to Tableau, and that data should include all of the required fields for your analysis. Right?

There are many reasons to leverage the calculated fields functionality in Tableau. Here are just a few:

- To segment your data in new ways on the fly
- To prove a concept such as a new dimension or measure before making it a permanent field in the underlying data
- To filter out unwanted results for better analyses
- To take advantage of the power of parameters (introduced in Chapter 14), putting choice in the hands of your end users
- To calculate ratios across many different variables in Tableau, saving valuable database processing and storage resources

To bring the concept of calculated fields to life, let's pretend we are working with the Sample – Superstore dataset, and want to evaluate the average order value (AOV) for the product sub-categories we manage compared to the rest of the company. AOV is defined as total sales revenue divided by the number of orders. While this dataset has Order ID as a dimension, it does not have the number of orders as a measure, which is the denominator for the AOV calculation.

To isolate the number of orders, I will first create a calculated field to count the number of orders. The formula to count the distinct number of orders will be COUNTD of the Order ID dimension. To start a calculated field, you can do one of the following:

- Click the down arrow in the upper-right corner of the Dimensions area of the Data pane and pick Create Calculated Field.
- Right-click a blank space on the left sidebar and choose Create Calculated Field.
- Click Analysis in the top navigation and choose Create Calculated Field.
- Right-click one of the fields you want to use as part of your calculated field, hover over Create, and choose Calculated Field.

For this first calculated field, because I know that I need the Order ID as part of my calculated field, I will start the calculated field by right-clicking the Order ID dimension on the Dimensions area of the Data pane, hovering over Create, and clicking "Calculated field." This opens a new dialog box where I can enter the formula for my calculated field:

On the righthand side of the calculated field dialog box there is a definition of the COUNTD expression. Any time you see a blue color-coding when creating a calculated field, you can click the blue-colored word to get a definition and example of that particular function; this is a great way to learn the syntax. If you do not see the "fly-out" window, click the sideways arrow found on the middle-right of the calculated field dialog box. After clicking the OK button, you will see a new measure for Orders appear on the Measures area of the Data pane—a brand-new measure that we can now use throughout the workbook!

Now that I have my Orders measure, which is the denominator of the AOV calculation I'm after, I can create another calculated field to calculate the total sales revenue divided by the number of orders. To start this calculated field, I will right-click a blank space in the left sidebar and choose Create Calculated Field. I'm presented with a blank calculated field dialog box where I can enter my formula for AOV:

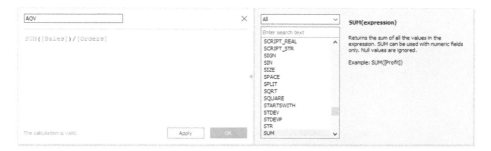

Notice this time that the measure of Sales is aggregated as SUM, but Orders appears to have no aggregation. That's because Orders already has an aggregation of COUNTD in the underlying calculated field that we created in the previous step. Tableau does not allow you to mix aggregated and nonaggregated fields within a calculated field. If you create an invalid calculated field, Tableau will display a red indicator at the bottom of the dialog box that reads "The calculation contains errors." You can click the error message to be provided with a clue for what may be wrong with your calculation.

Also remember that even when Tableau says that a calculation is valid, that's in terms of the syntax, and not in terms of the result you are looking for. To quality check a calculated field and ensure it's properly calculating the result, I like to put the raw "ingredients" on the view and calculate the answer manually. In the case of this tutorial, I would create a quick table showing Orders, Sales, and the newly created AOV measure. I would then divide the sales amount by the number of orders to make sure the correct answer is reflected as AOV:

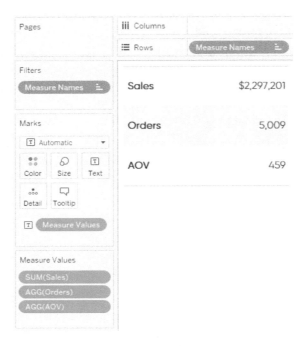

Based on this image, it looks like Tableau has calculated the correct answer: $2,297,201 in total sales divided by 5,009 total orders equals an average order value of $459. By default, calculated fields do not receive number formatting. In the case of AOV, which should be displayed as a currency, you can change this by right-clicking the calculated field on the Measures area of the Data pane, hovering over "Default properties," and clicking "Number format."

More on Aggregating Calculated Fields

Aggregation, introduced in Chapter 8, is an important concept to consider when creating calculated fields. A calculated field for SUM([Profit]) / SUM([Sales]) will give you a very different answer than [Profit] / [Sales], even though both formulas are valid. If you do not provide the aggregation within the calculated field, Tableau will calculate the equation for every record in your analysis, then aggregate the answers for all of the rows together when the calculated field is added to the view. It is critical to quality check calculated fields and ensure you are seeing expected results before integrating the new measures in your work.

To this point, we've created a new measure for Orders and used the Orders measure within a second new calculated field for AOV. Now let's put the new fields to work by answering our business question:

What is the AOV of the product sub-categories I manage compared to everything else?

For the purposes of this illustration, I'll pretend that I manage the Copiers, Machines, and Supplies sub-categories. To answer this question, we will create a third calculated field, this time creating a new Sub-Category Segmentation dimension.

This calculation is slightly different in that we will be incorporating IF/THEN logic to create a segmentation: one segment for the sub-categories I manage (Copiers, Machines, and Supplies) and the other segment for every other sub-category. The formula looks like this:

All this calculation is saying is that if the dimension member of Sub-Category matches copiers, machines, or supplies, I want the data to be classified as "My Sub-Categories." If the dimension member is anything other than those three, I want the data to be classified as "Other." To quality check a dimension calculation such as this one, I like to first place the original dimension on the Rows Shelf, followed by the newly created calculated field to make sure the dimension members are being properly calculated:

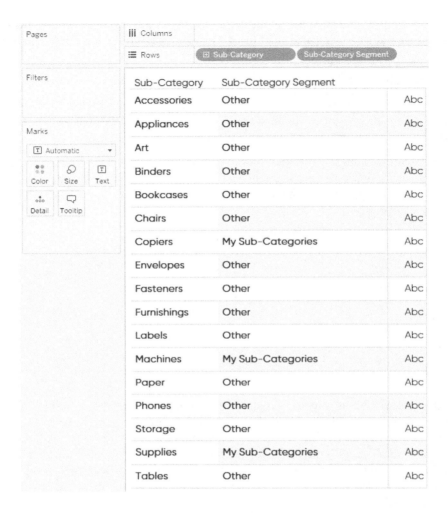

As you can see, my three sub-categories are classified as "My Sub-Categories" in the second column, and everything else is classified as "Other."

I'm now ready to answer my business question by putting the AOV calculated field on the view, then slice and dice the measure by the Sub-Category Segment dimension:

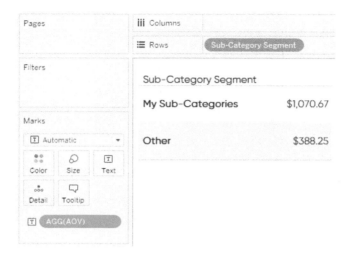

The answer clearly shows the AOV for the product sub-categories that I manage is much higher than the AOV for all of the other sub-categories—maybe it's time I ask for a bonus!

CHAPTER 13

An Introduction to Table Calculations

Tableau comes with several preset calculations that you can compute with the numbers on a view, including running total, difference, percent difference, percent of total, moving average, and more. These predefined calculations are called table calculations because they compute the result based on a virtual table that includes only the numbers on the view. Table calculations provide several benefits, including:

- A fast way to create advanced calculations even without knowing the underlying syntax
- Table calculations can be saved for future use as calculated fields, and because calculated fields can be edited, this is a great way to learn the syntax and the different functions available in Tableau
- Efficient processing—table calculations are computed on a very small subset of the data source, making them an efficient solution for calculating results

To help introduce table calculations and how to use them, we will be using this simple crosstab:

Table calculations are added to measures, so in order to add a table calculation, click a measure that's on the view. The fastest way to add a table calculation is to hover over Quick Table Calculation and choose an option:

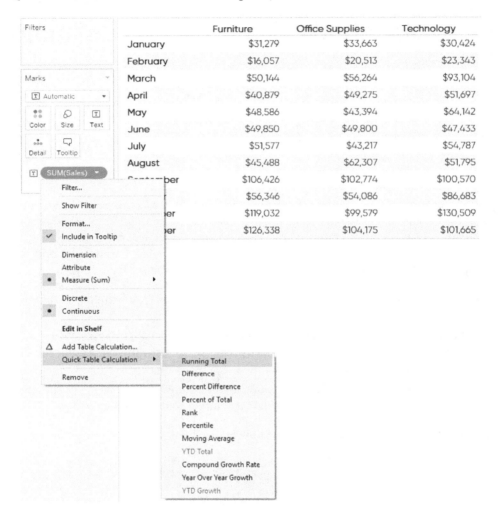

Here's how the view looks after choosing the Running Total table calculation:

Pages	⫶⫶⫶ Columns	⊞ Category		
	≣ Rows	⊞ MONTH(Order Date)		

	Furniture	Office Supplies	Technology
January	$31,279	$64,942	$95,366
February	$16,057	$36,570	$59,913
March	$50,144	$106,408	$199,512
April	$40,879	$90,154	$141,852
May	$48,586	$91,980	$156,122
June	$49,850	$99,650	$147,083
July	$51,577	$94,794	$149,581
August	$45,488	$107,794	$159,589
September	$106,426	$209,200	$309,770
October	$56,346	$110,432	$197,115
November	$119,032	$218,611	$349,120
December	$126,338	$230,512	$332,177

Filters

Marks

⊤ Automatic ▾

Color   Size   Text

Detail   Tooltip

⊤ SUM(Sales) △

Table calculations are defined by how they are (a) partitioned (or grouped), and (b) addressed (or how they are computed). Notice in the example here the running total is being computed from left to right, which is the default *addressing*. This would mean that, by default, the table calculation is being addressed by the Product Category dimension. This leaves the Month dimension as the *partitioning* field. For a running total calculation, this doesn't make a lot of sense. It is easy to change the addressing by changing how the table calculation is being computed. To do this, click the measure with the table calculation again, now identified with a delta symbol, hover over Compute Using, and change how the calculation should be computed (or addressed):

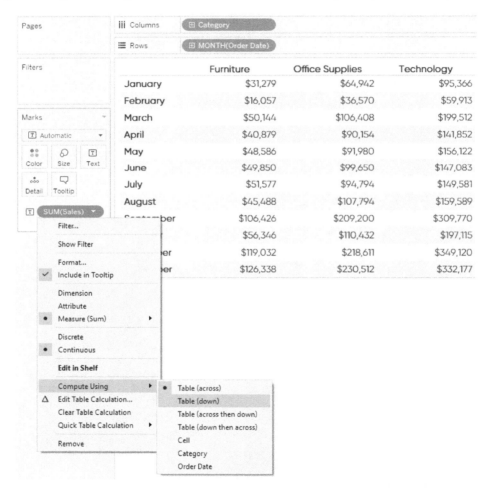

Here's how the crosstab looks after changing the addressing/"Compute Using" to Table (down):

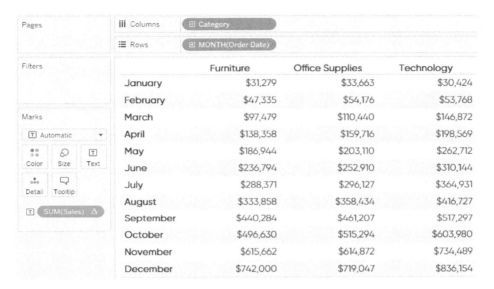

	Furniture	Office Supplies	Technology
January	$31,279	$33,663	$30,424
February	$47,335	$54,176	$53,768
March	$97,479	$110,440	$146,872
April	$138,358	$159,716	$198,569
May	$186,944	$203,110	$262,712
June	$236,794	$252,910	$310,144
July	$288,371	$296,127	$364,931
August	$333,858	$358,434	$416,727
September	$440,284	$461,207	$517,297
October	$496,630	$515,294	$603,980
November	$615,662	$614,872	$734,489
December	$742,000	$719,047	$836,154

Now that the addressing field has been changed to Month and the partitioning field has been changed to Product Category, my result makes a lot more sense for my analysis. I can look at each Product Category column, and look down across months to see how the sales built up throughout the year.

There are many different options available within table calculations that can be accessed by clicking a measure with a table calculation and choosing "Edit table calculation." For just a few possibilities, see one of Tableau's most popular posts, Top 10 Tableau Table Calculations (*http://www.tableau.com/table-calculations*).

I mentioned in the introduction to this chapter that one of the benefits of table calculations is that they provide a way to learn the syntax. To do so, simply double-click a measure with a table calculation to see the underlying formula. This code can be copied into a calculated field so you can take a closer look.

Lastly, even though they are called table calculations, table calculations do not literally have to be used on a table, or crosstab, view. Here is one example I regularly use to add value to a basic monthly line graph:

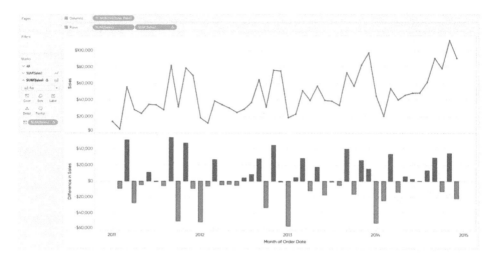

Notice that the first row is a basic monthly trend, while the second Sales pill has a delta symbol, indicating there is a table calculation being applied. This time, I am using the second row to show the month-over-month *difference* in sales—another of the quick table calculation options available in Tableau.

To create this visualization, I started by simply making a line graph showing the sum of Sales by continuous Month of Order Date. I then placed a second occurrence of the Sales measure on the Rows Shelf, which created a second row with the exact same trend. Now that there were two independent pills for the Sales measure, I was able to add a table calculation for month-over-month difference (the second option under "Quick table calculation") to the second pill only.

Each measure also gets its own set of Marks Cards, which means they can be edited independently. After changing the second row so the mark type is bar and the marks are colored by the month-over-month change, the result is the visualization just shown. Now in addition to a typical monthly sales trend, I've provided the month-over-month difference values and visualization, which allows the end user to quickly compare the spikes and drops across months; this value-add is made possible through Tableau table calculations.

CHAPTER 14

An Introduction to Parameters

As you make your way through *Practical Tableau*, and especially Part III, there is one functionality that you will hear about over and over again: parameters. Parameters are user-generated values that are not attached to a dataset, and due to their flexibility, are the solution to several of the handiest tricks in Tableau. Other than filters, parameters are also one of the most powerful tactics in Tableau for transferring control from the author to the end user. As discussed in Part IV, providing this type of user interaction not only improves the engagement with your dashboards, but it improves the retention of insights and improves the likelihood that they will be shared.

This chapter will use a simple algebra example to illustrate how to create a parameter, how to allow end users to control the parameter you've created, and how parameters work.

An Introduction to Parameters in Tableau

For this tutorial, imagine that you want to set up a simple equation for 2 multiplied by X, where X is the parameter, and the end user gets to choose the value of X. Tableau will then display the answer of 2 multiplied by X based on the parameter selection.

For this introduction, it does not matter what dataset you are following along with, but for consistency with the rest of *Practical Tableau*, I will be building a parameter in the Sample – Superstore dataset. There are several ways to create a new parameter in Tableau, including (a) clicking the down arrow in the top-right corner of the Dimensions area of the Data pane and choosing "Create parameter" or (b) right-clicking in a blank space on the Data pane Shelf and choosing "Create parameter." Once you have done this, you will be presented with a dialog box where you can design the parameter:

Instead of "Parameter 3," named that by default in the Sample – Superstore dataset because there are already two other parameters, I will change the name to "Algebra Parameter." By default, the data type for a new parameter is Float, which means any number including decimals, but there are five additional data types to choose from:

Integer
　　Any whole number (i.e., no decimals)

String
　　Text

Boolean
　　True or false

Date
　　Date without a timestamp

Date & Time
　　Date with a timestamp

The data type you choose for the parameter depends on your use case. For this 2 multiplied by X example, let's say that we eventually want the parameter to include only whole numbers, so I will change the data type from Float to Integer.

Within the parameter creation dialog box, you also have the ability to designate the allowable values for the parameter. The entries that you choose at this step will eventually determine what choices you and the end users have for the parameter in the final product. The choices are all or any integer, a specific list of integers, or a range of integers. I will choose Range so that I can set a minimum and maximum number as well as a step size, or multiple, for the parameter. After setting up the parameter to have a range of 1 to 20 with a step size of 1, my parameter looks like this and is ready to be saved by clicking the OK button:

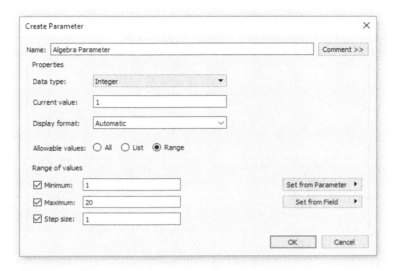

In order for a parameter to be useful, you must provide Tableau instructions for how to use it. This is accomplished through calculated fields. Being that the equation for our use case is 2 multiplied by X, or our algebra parameter, your first instinct may be to create a calculated field that says:

```
2*[Algebra Parameter]
```

Being that the current value of the parameter is 1, we would expect the answer to be 2*1 = 2. However, this calculation will be computed for every row in the data, which would not provide the answer we are looking for. Should we add this calculated field to the view, we would get an answer of 19,988, which is 2 multiplied by 1, multiplied by the number of records in the dataset (9,994 for the Sample – Superstore dataset).

To alleviate this, add an aggregation of MIN to the 2 so the Algebra Parameter is guaranteed to be multiplied by 2:

Now if I add my newly created Algebra Equation calculated field to the Text Marks Card to display the answer on a view, I see the answer I am looking for, MIN(2) multiplied by 1 equals 2:

Finally, to provide the power of selecting the value of X in our example to the end user, you must provide access to the parameter. To do this, right-click the newly created Algebra Parameter and choose "Show parameter control." A new selector will appear in the upper-right corner of the view that allows the user to choose from the allowable values that were set up when the parameter was created. Notice that the current value is 1, the maximum value is 20, and the numbers can be selected in multiples of 1, just like we set up. Here's what my final view looks like when I've shown the parameter control, moved the parameter control from its default location to below the Marks Cards, and changed the selection from 1 to 7:

In this example, the end user has chosen the number 7, which powered the underlying calculation of 2*7, to produce the answer of 14. Imagine all of the power that can be put into the hands of your end users through the use of parameters!

For just a few other possibilities, see the following chapters:

- Chapter 69, "How to Compare Two Date Ranges on One Axis"
- Chapter 66, "How to Change Date Aggregation Using Parameters"
- Chapter 48, "How to Make a What-If Analysis Using Parameters"
- Chapter 53, "How to Create and Compare"
- Chapter 64, "Allow Users to Choose Measures and Dimensions"

CHAPTER 15

An Introduction to Sets

Tableau sets allow you to isolate specific segments of a dimension, which can then be used in several different ways to find insights in your data. This chapter provides instructions on how to build sets as well as five different ways they can be used to enhance your analyses.

Sets can be thought of as custom segments, but unlike dimension fields, they are always binary. In other words, you are either in the set or not. Other than that one restriction, sets can be created for just about anything. You can pick individual dimension members to place in a set, have sets be based on quantitative thresholds, created with the top or bottom performing dimension members, and more.

How to Create a Set in Tableau

Similar to creating filters in Tableau, sets can be created in a couple of different ways. The first and most straightforward method is to simply select the dimension members on a view, then hover over one of the dimension members, click the Venn diagram icon that appears, and choose Create Set. Here's what that would look like if I wanted to create a set from the top 20 customers by sales in the Sample – Superstore dataset:

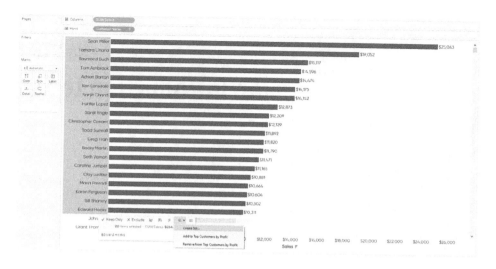

After clicking Create Set and giving the set a name, the set will appear in its own area on the Data pane. This set that tells us whether each customer name is in or out of the top 20 customers by sales is now available to use in our analyses. Note that sets created with this method are static, so the top 20 will not dynamically change should a new customer enter the top 20.

You can also create a set by right-clicking the dimension the set will be created from on the Dimensions area of the Data pane, hovering over Create, and clicking Set. After following the preceding steps on the Customer Name dimension, the following dialog box appears:

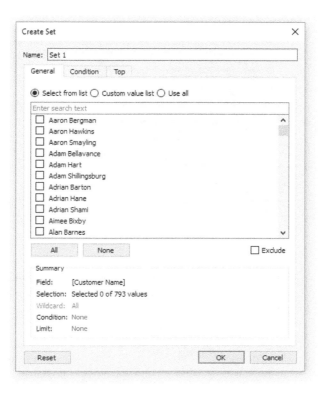

The first tab provides the ability to manually pick and choose the dimension members to be included in the set as we have done with the first method. The remaining two tabs can be used to base the set on a condition or Top N, respectively. Computed sets like this will dynamically change when the dataset is updated. Whichever method you choose to create your set, a new field will be created to use in the following examples.

Five Ways to Use Tableau Sets

As a filter

Sets can be used as a filter by right-clicking a set from the Sets area of the Data pane and choosing Show Filter. Sets are binary, so when you add them as a filter, you will only have the option to choose whether the marks on the view are in or out of the set. Here's how my bar chart of sales by customer name in descending order looks after showing the filter for Top 20 Customers by Sales and keeping only the names that are in the set:

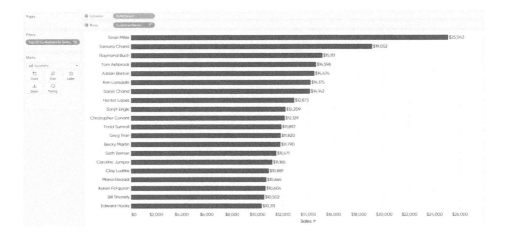

To encode marks

You can encode marks on a view by a set by dragging the set from the Sets area of the Data pane to the Color Marks Card. Here's an example where I've done this to make the top 20 customers by sales stand out on a scatter plot:

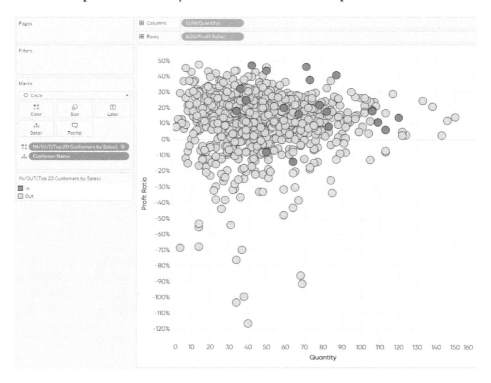

In calculated fields

Sets can be used in calculated fields just like dimensions or measures. This way you can treat dimension members differently based on whether or not they are in a set. Here is a simple example being used to rename the sets:

This formula is saying that if a customer name is in the set, name the set "Top 20 Customers"; otherwise call it "Other." Note that this example is used to show you that sets can be used within calculated fields, but this same renaming could have been accomplished by editing the aliases of the set.

As dimension fields

Sets can be used just like dimensions in that if you add a set field to the Columns Shelf or Rows Shelf, the view will be "sliced and diced" by that field. Here is how my scatter plot from earlier looks if I create two separate columns for in and out of the set by dragging the set from the Sets area of the Data pane to the Columns Shelf:

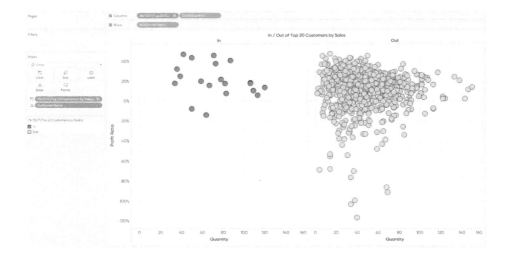

Within a custom hierarchy

Sets can be used as part of a custom hierarchy in Tableau, which allows you and your end users to easily drill down and back up across different dimensions. For example, you may want to create a hierarchy with customer names that starts with the Top 20 Customers by Sales set, then drills down to individual customer names, then to their segment.

Create a custom hierarchy by selecting the Customer Name and Segment dimensions, right-click, hover over Hierarchy, and choose Create Hierarchy. Once the custom hierarchy is created, you can drag the Top 20 Customers by Sales set into the hierarchy on the Dimensions area of the Data pane and rearrange them to the desired order of the drilldown. At this point, I see this hierarchy in the Dimensions area of the Data pane:

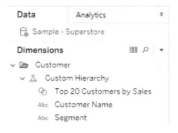

Now that the hierarchy is in place, if I replace the Customer Name dimension with the Top 20 Customers by Sales set dimension in the preceding bar chart example, I will be able to drill down from the top 20 set, to customer name, to segment. This is accomplished by clicking the "+" symbol on the field(s) on the Rows Shelf.

Here's how the view looks when the bars are aggregated at the highest level of the hierarchy. This view shows sales generated from customers in the set versus sales generated from customers out of the set:

Here's how the same view looks after clicking the + symbol on the blue pill on the Rows Shelf. We now see sales by whether or not the customer is in our set, but also the names of individual customers:

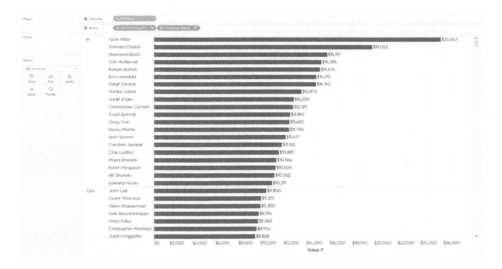

Lastly, because we built a third level of the hierarchy in for the Segment dimension, we can drill down one more time by clicking the + symbol on the Customer Name pill. This view first breaks sales down by the set that we created, then Customer Name, then Segment:

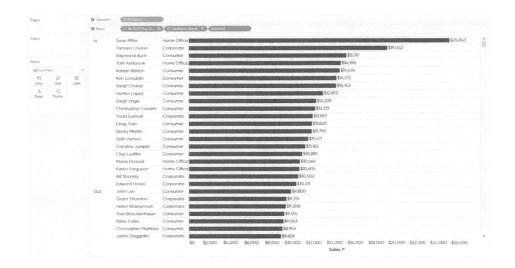

CHAPTER 16

An Introduction to Level of Detail Expressions

Tableau level of detail expressions (LODs) allow you to change the most granular place where an analysis takes place. An analysis such as AVG(Sales) by State includes the dimension that you are using to break down the measure by as well as the aggregation of the measure. Prior to Tableau version 9.0, and without some clever technical hacking such as duplicating a data source or leveraging table calculations, you were stuck using the same level of detail for an entire view. Now that you can alter the level of detail for specific measures, you can compare and contrast numbers at different granularities within the same chart.

With level of detail expressions in Tableau, you can now compute things such AVG(Sales) by State minus AVG(Sales) for the entire dataset to see how the sales per state compare to the overall average.

This unlocks a great deal of flexibility in your analyses because you can explicitly define the level of detail for different numbers in your view. Here are just 15 (*http://www.tableau.com/about/blog/LOD-expressions*) of limitless ways to take advantage of Tableau LOD expressions. I will also share a couple of resources that show you how I've used level of detail in my own Tableau workbooks at the end of this chapter, but this chapter mainly serves as an introduction to what level of detail is and the syntax needed to control it.

An Introduction to Tableau Level of Detail Expressions

In Chapter 10, we introduced the idea of level of detail and how you can make a visualization more granular by adding dimensions to the Detail Marks Card. Here is another example to help illustrate what a Tableau visualization's level of detail is:

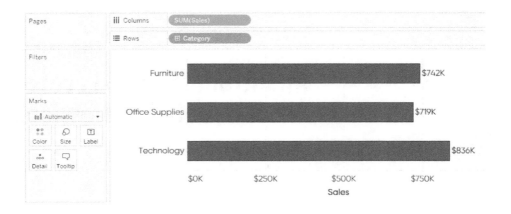

In this simple Sales by Category bar chart from the Sample – Superstore dataset, the most granular level of detail in the analysis is Category. Since we are only slicing and dicing the Sales measure by the Category dimension, there are only three marks; one for each category. We can make this analysis more granular by adding an additional dimension to the view. Here's what the bar chart looks like if I add the Sub-Category dimension to the Rows Shelf:

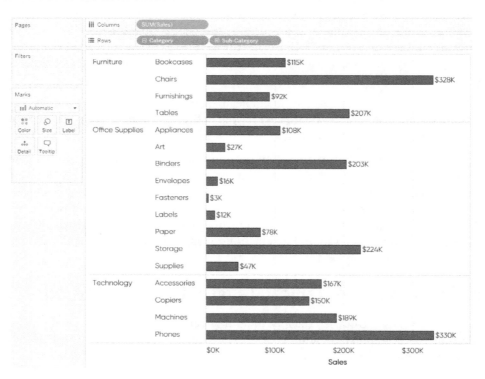

We are now slicing and dicing the Sales Measure by both the Category and Sub-Category dimensions. We have changed the level of detail for this view and made our analysis more granular.

But what if we wanted to look at it both ways? Perhaps we want to show the sales per sub-category in one column, the sales per category in a second column, and even divide the two by each other to determine how much each sub-category is contributing to its respective category.

That's where Tableau's level of detail expressions come in. level of detail expressions have their very own syntax in Tableau, which looks like this:

- An open curly bracket "{"
- Followed by one of three level of detail expressions: FIXED, INCLUDE, or EXCLUDE
- Followed by zero or more dimensions you want to be fixed, included, or excluded from the computation
- Followed by a colon ":"
- Followed by an aggregated measure
- Followed by a closing curly bracket "}"

The three level of detail expressions—FIXED, INCLUDE, and EXCLUDE—are fairly intuitive names for what they're going to do (i.e., fix the measure at a certain level of detail, include dimensions that are not on the view, or exclude dimensions that are on the view, respectively). As with many things in Tableau, there are multiple ways to get to the same answer, and there is not always a "best" way to go about a certain solution.

Your level of detail expressions may take some experimenting to get the result you want, but I have found the EXCLUDE expression to align best with the way I think about aggregations. The reason this works well for me is because I can make a view as granular as I'd like as I normally would, then "back out" to a comparison metric by excluding certain levels of granularity.

Take another quick look back at the last bar chart. I've made the analysis as granular as I'd like, slicing and dicing the Sales measure by the Category and Sub-Category dimensions. If I wanted to compare each row by the Sales at the Category level only, so excluding the Sub-Category dimension, I would create a calculated field with this formula:

```
{EXCLUDE [Sub-Category]: SUM([Sales])}
```

Now when I add my new calculation to the Columns Shelf, the left side shows my original analysis, while the right side "backs out" the level of detail to the Category level, excluding the Sub-Category dimension:

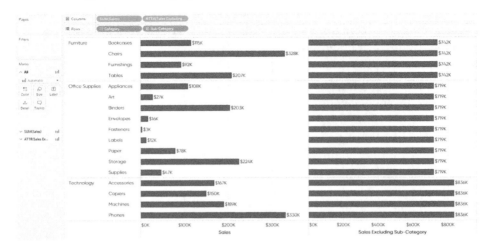

We're now displaying two different levels of detail on one view! This new measure can now be used for further analysis. If I want to calculate the contribution of each sub-category to its respective category, I can create another calculated field that divides SUM(Sales) by the newly created SUM(Sales Excluding Sub-Category):

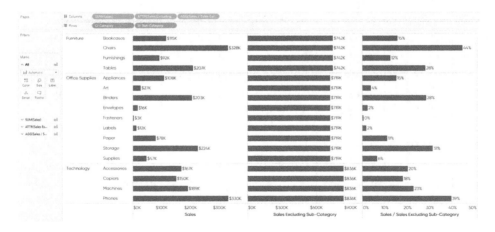

This third column could have been computed using a Tableau table calculation, as covered in Chapter 13, that took the percent of total per pane, but using level of detail expressions provides several benefits including:

- You can "show your math"; in the preceding example, we would not have been able to show the first and second column together without LOD expressions. You could have also used a different table calculation called WINDOW_SUM, but with LOD expressions.

- You no longer need to worry about setting and maintaining the direction and scope of a table calculation; set the level of detail once in the LOD calculation and don't worry about it again.

- You can definitely get creative with table calculations in Tableau, but LOD calculations are even more flexible, allowing you to specify the precise level of detail and aggregation for a measure.

We have barely scratched the surface on arguably the most powerful feature to ship with Tableau version 9.0, but this example should have provided a good foundation about what level of detail is and how it can be changed to benefit your analysis. You will have to experiment with your own use cases and LOD calculations, but in addition to the 15 uses of Tableau LOD expressions linked to at the beginning of this chapter, here are a couple more from *Practical Tableau*:

- Chapter 59, Using Level of Detail Expressions to Create Benchmarks
- Chapter 70, How to Compare Unequal Date Ranges on One Axis

CHAPTER 17

An Introduction to Dashboards and Distribution

Individual worksheets in Tableau can lead to powerful insights that help your business, but many times, it makes sense to combine the worksheets into a single dashboard. By combining varying visualizations into a dashboard, you and your audience are able to analyze different aspects of the data in context of each other. This is a much more intuitive experience than viewing the visualizations individually.

In addition to this one obvious benefit, Tableau comes with several technical features that allow you to control the user experience and even the ability to have the individual components of the dashboard interact with each other. This chapter offers an introduction to dashboards in Tableau and several ways to distribute the dashboard after it has been created.

An Introduction to Dashboards in Tableau

For this introduction, we will re-create this dashboard in Tableau:

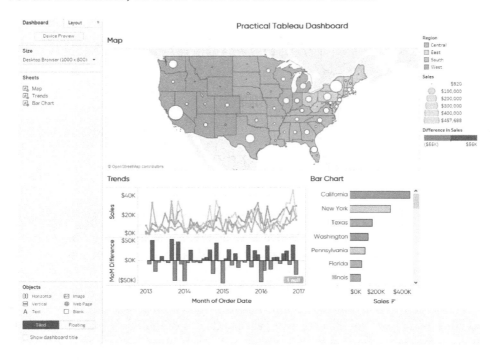

To create a new dashboard in Tableau, either click Dashboard in the top navigation and then New Dashboard or click the New Dashboard icon at the bottom of any worksheet. The New Dashboard icon is the second icon immediately following the existing worksheets in the workbook.

Upon creating a new dashboard, you will be provided a blank slate that looks like this:

Here's a quick overview of all the different dashboard options in the left navigation:

Dashboard and Layout tabs

By default, you will be working on the Dashboard tab, which allows you to set most aspects of the dashboard. The Layout tab allows you to set the dimensions and location of individual dashboard components. All sizes on the Layout tab are in pixels.

Device Preview button

The Device Preview button allows you see what the dashboard will look like on different devices and you can even save different versions of the dashboard so that it looks different depending on what device it is displayed on. For more, see Chapter 60.

Size

This is where you can set the height and width of the dashboard in pixels. There are several preset size options or you can set an exact size of your choosing. If you choose the Automatic option, the dashboard will change to fill all available space on the screen it is being displayed on and resize the individual components of the dashboard accordingly. While this option sounds good on the surface, beware that it is not truly "responsive," and the display can be somewhat unpredictable.

Sheets

These are the individual worksheets in your workbook that can be added to the dashboard. Note that to create the example pictured, there are three sheets in the workbook: Map, Trends, and Bar Chart. It helps to give the worksheets good names so you can easily find them, but you can also get a thumbnail preview of the worksheet by hovering over the name in the left navigation.

Objects

Horizontal

Adds a horizontal layout container that additional objects can be added to.

Vertical

Adds a vertical layout container that additional objects can be added to.

Text

Opens a mini word processor where you can add and format any text you wish.

Image

Adds an image from your computer to the dashboard.

Web Page

Embeds a web page in the dashboard (requires an internet connection to display the web page).

Blank

Adds blank space to the dashboard, which can be helpful when dashboard elements are too close to each other and in a tiled layout.

Tiled or Floating

When dashboard elements are tiled, they fill all available space in their respective tiles. When dashboard elements are floating, you control their exact size and location on the dashboard. Each of these layouts comes with their own pros and cons and the choice is largely dependent on your specific use case. Most Tableau users prefer the automatic resizing that comes with a tiled layout; I personally prefer the predictability and precision that comes with floating elements.

The dashboard pictured is tiled in the Desktop Browser size, which is 1000 pixels wide by 800 pixels tall. To create the dashboard, I first ensured the size was 1000 by 800 by clicking Size in the left navigation, choosing Fixed Size, then choosing the preset Desktop Browser option.

Tiled is the default layout option, so I am ready to go ahead and add individual sheets to my view. I will add the map first, and when there is nothing else on the dashboard, it will fill all the available space on the view:

To add a worksheet to a dashboard, left-click and drag the worksheet name from the left navigation to the dashboard. When you drag new objects onto the view, you will see gray shading that represents where the object will be placed. You can always move an object after it has been placed by hovering over it, and dragging and dropping the gray icon that appears at the top-middle of the object.

Note that when I added a worksheet that has legends, the legends were added for me automatically. The color legend can be used as a highlighter by simply clicking a color in the legend. To learn how to create the map pictured, see Chapter 32.

I will then add the Trends worksheet in the space below the map by dragging it toward the bottom of the dashboard. To learn how to make a line graph, see Chapter 9. To learn how to calculate the month-over-month difference pictured, see Chapter 13.

I will then add the Bar Chart worksheet by dragging it near the lower-right corner of the dashboard. To learn how to make a bar chart in Tableau, see Chapter 8.

Lastly, I added a title to the top by dragging a text object to the top of the dashboard, and ended up with this view:

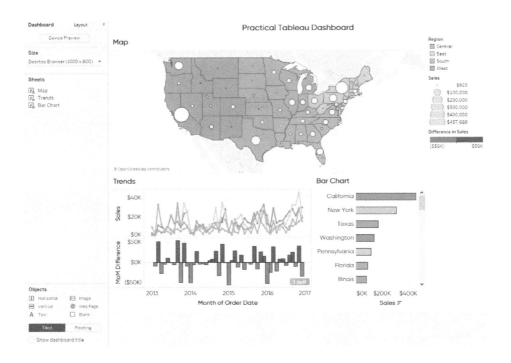

This is a more than serviceable dashboard that we were able to make in a matter of minutes in Tableau. You can add even more value by building in some user interactivity. Perhaps you want the trend lines and bar chart to update when a region is clicked on the map. To learn how to do this, see Chapter 56. Another option would be to add filters that allow the end user to filter the three worksheets. For more on filters, see Chapter 11.

Distributing Tableau Dashboards

After you've created a dashboard in Tableau, there are several ways the dashboard can be distributed.

Packaged Workbooks

If you have created a dashboard using Tableau Desktop, you can package the workbook for offline distribution. To package a workbook, navigate to File in the top navigation and click Export Packaged Workbook. This will package the data with the instructions for how to visualize the data. Anybody with Tableau Desktop or Tableau Reader can open the file and interact with the visualizations you have created. Note that packaged workbooks do not automatically update so the data within the workbook will only be as recent as the last update.

Tableau Public

Any dashboard built in Tableau Desktop or Tableau Public can be published to the web for public consumption. This is not a realistic option for sensitive business data, but if you are able to make your data public, this is the perfect solution for distributing your dashboard to the widest audience possible. To publish a dashboard from Tableau Desktop to Tableau Public, navigate to Server, hover over Tableau Public, and choose Save to Tableau Public As.

Tableau Server/Tableau Online

You can also distribute your workbooks privately on-premise or in the cloud by using Tableau Server or Tableau Online, respectively. Tableau Server requires incremental licenses for you and your end users, but is the most scalable Tableau solution for distributing your business-related workbooks. Publishing to Tableau Server is very similar to publishing to Tableau Public, but you will be presented with several additional options, including where to publish the workbook within Tableau Server, who has permission to view and interact with the workbook, and if/when you want the data in the workbook to update. To publish a workbook to Tableau Server, navigate to Server in the top navigation, and choose Publish Workbook. Tableau Online works similarly, but it is hosted by Tableau in the cloud.

PART II

Chart Types

CHAPTER 18

A Spreadsheet Is Not a Data Visualization

Like the movie *Groundhog Day* (but without its Certified Fresh 96% score on Rotten Tomatoes) there is one conversation I find myself having over and over again in my career as a data visualization consultant. It typically goes something like this:

Excel fan: "Thanks for this—looks great. Would it be possible to take your world-class data visualization and turn it into an unreadable wall of numbers?"

(OK, the "world-class" part is an exaggeration—no one has ever said that.)

Ryan (me): "But Excel fan, look how much easier it is to gain valuable business insights more accurately and efficiently when the numbers are visualized! Isn't that really cool?"

Excel fan: "Steven, my stakeholders are more comfortable seeing the exact numbers."

Ryan (me): "It's Ryan, actually. Let me just show…"

Excel fan: "Brian, please provide a text table of this information. Also, if there's room along the bottom, please add at least one pie chart."

At least this is how I sometimes feel the conversation goes when I'm having these discussions. I admit it can be discouraging, but mostly because I feel I have let my stakeholders down by my own failure to educate them on a better way of looking at data. It can also be encouraging, because it reminds me there is still a long way to go before best practice techniques are widely adopted and that I have a long career in data visualization ahead of me. (That means I have quite a bit of time to earn money that I can use to purchase barbecue.)

Scott Klein of ProPublica gave an inspiring talk (*http://tabsoft.co/2p5OF4V*) on the history of data journalism at the 2016 Tapestry Conference, sharing several fascinating examples of early data visualization. What I found most interesting was that William Playfair, inventor of the bar chart and line graph, was not celebrated in his time. In fact, most people did not understand the value in visualizing quantitative information and were critical of not using tables.

In other words, data visualization practitioners have been fighting this same fight since, quite literally, *the beginning of data visualization time.*

A Spreadsheet Is Not a Data Visualization

Spreadsheets are extremely valuable in business. They can be used in accounting, to store information, or to do calculations, just to name a few purposes.

However, a spreadsheet or text table view of data is not a data visualization. In my opinion, putting one or more of these text tables in one place does not make for a dashboard. To me, dashboards and data visualizations help users interpret data by leveraging the power of visualization. Further, once there is more than just *one* number in a report, I firmly believe that a text table is the worst possible choice for analyzing the data.

Consider this example of just two numbers: 23.4K versus 3.42M. Even when the numbers are in different units, you can likely tell that the first number is smaller than the second number, but it is challenging to consider the scale of the difference. Take a look at the same two numbers visualized as a bar chart:

The values can still be included as labels on the bars if the end users need those in order to sleep at night, but now they have a much better insight into what is happening with the numbers. Not only is the bar chart easier to interpret than the raw numbers, it is more memorable, and thus, effective.

I am not saying that raw numbers provide no value, but I am saying that visualizing raw numbers always provides additional value. If this is clear even when comparing two numbers, think about how much more value a visualization adds when we're looking at a tableful of numeric information.

Are Text Tables or Crosstabs Ever the Best Choice?

While my immediate reaction to tables in data visualization is *"Don't!"* we should nevertheless consider the times when it is appropriate to use crosstab views in Tableau:

Crosstabs can be used to export raw data

Sometimes there are legitimate reasons to get to the raw data. If end users are more comfortable using a tool like Excel and want to add their own calculations, for example, it would be nice to provide the data in an Excel-ready format. Fortunately, any view in Tableau can easily be duplicated as a crosstab. The crosstab view can then be opened in Excel. Here are the steps:

- From any view in Tableau, hover over Worksheet in the top navigation and select Duplicate as Crosstab.
- Once the crosstab view is generated, hover over Worksheet again, hover over Export, and choose Crosstab to Excel.

Crosstabs can be used to create "Callout Numbers"

In Chapter 95, I encourage data designers to use "callout numbers" to clearly communicate the most important points of the story. These numbers are stand-alone, which makes them descriptive in nature (typically with no prescriptive value), but they can help engage the viewers so they can immediately see what KPIs are prioritized by the designer. From here, hopefully the end users will continue exploring your dashboard so they can help answer why a callout number is the value that it is.

Callout numbers are created by making a crosstab view, filtering it down to one number, and formatting the number so that is oversized (think a minimum of 36-point font). These numbers are then typically placed along the top or left side of a dashboard to provide a natural starting point of an analysis.

Crosstabs can be used to create dashboard filters or navigation

Another clever application of text table views in Tableau is to use the view as a dashboard filter or navigation. This approach has an added advantage of making your data process more efficiently.

For example, if you wanted to create a dashboard filter for Region out of a crosstab, you would first make a crosstab view that displayed the four regions: North,

East, South, and West. You would then place this view on a dashboard and add a dashboard action that filters the rest of the dashboard when a Region selection is made.

Not only does this type of dashboard action process more quickly than a filter in Tableau, but it can be used for other purposes. Perhaps you want to add a dashboard action to the table view that takes end users to interior pages of your workbook or even conducts an online search.

For more dashboard action ideas, see Chapter 56.

CHAPTER 19

How to Make a Highlight Table

In Chapter 87, I demonstrate an exercise for "Smoothing the Excel Transition" by introducing the value of data visualization. In the example, we simply encode the values in a large text table of data by color—the higher the sales values, the darker the green. The result is called a highlight table.

Highlight tables are one of the simplest chart types to create, but are also among the most powerful. When compared to a crosstab (a.k.a. text table) view, this basic data visualization helps reduce the time to insight and improve the accuracy of insights. Highlight tables are definitely worth making a part of your chart type toolbelt, right alongside bar charts and line graphs. They are best used for:

- Quickly identifying highs and lows or other points of interest in your data
- As a means of enhancing a crosstab
- As a tactic for helping smooth the Excel transition

Highlight tables consist of one or more dimensions and exactly one measure (the color). Let's take a look at how they're made.

How to Make a Highlight Table in Tableau

Before we begin, let's see how the final product will look:

	January	February	March	April	May	June	July	August	September	October	November	December
Accessories	$5,478	$5,369	$8,735	$7,984	$9,613	$8,858	$17,177	$12,376	$24,900	$12,927	$25,957	$28,007
Appliances	$3,176	$4,933	$6,734	$6,042	$7,526	$7,479	$3,540	$13,345	$10,193	$9,152	$18,970	$16,443
Art	$966	$1,006	$1,413	$2,407	$2,231	$2,182	$2,102	$1,690	$3,660	$1,911	$3,966	$3,584
Binders	$12,412	$4,237	$13,889	$13,357	$9,160	$13,294	$8,557	$20,430	$37,342	$18,079	$20,858	$31,798
Bookcases	$5,352	$1,650	$7,352	$4,720	$6,290	$7,881	$9,856	$5,622	$22,849	$8,771	$23,561	$10,977
Chairs	$11,285	$7,583	$21,016	$18,855	$25,703	$21,714	$23,016	$18,340	$51,577	$21,905	$49,636	$57,819
Copiers	$3,960		$25,590	$3,880	$18,400	$900	$9,780	$5,730	$10,320	$37,020	$15,150	$18,800
Envelopes	$750	$669	$1,657	$945	$1,096	$514	$1,200	$701	$2,177	$1,403	$2,907	$2,458
Fasteners	$88	$159	$150	$258	$109	$116	$182	$243	$406	$326	$550	$438
Furnishings	$3,980	$2,316	$5,159	$7,404	$6,996	$5,956	$7,336	$4,307	$11,805	$5,447	$16,783	$14,218
Labels	$207	$300	$940	$430	$863	$1,207	$1,692	$876	$1,496	$1,248	$1,850	$1,376
Machines	$7,215	$8,990	$35,052	$18,190	$11,268	$12,183	$4,065	$6,262	$26,386	$10,613	$33,807	$15,210
Paper	$2,287	$2,813	$6,286	$3,964	$6,184	$6,751	$4,180	$6,523	$10,690	$4,965	$12,563	$11,274
Phones	$13,772	$8,984	$28,163	$17,890	$24,182	$26,493	$23,128	$28,413	$37,775	$26,472	$56,185	$38,551
Storage	$9,374	$6,125	$14,793	$15,806	$14,670	$18,606	$12,491	$17,719	$29,511	$15,822	$37,945	$30,983
Supplies	$4,403	$289	$10,637	$6,216	$1,154	$1,267	$8,816	$866	$6,436	$816	$1,372	$4,402
Tables	$10,952	$4,218	$16,913	$9,913	$9,288	$16,405	$9,299	$17,752	$19,626	$20,223	$33,182	$39,193

You can create a highlight table with any combination of one or more dimensions and one measure. You can also create a highlight table using Show Me, but I prefer to learn by creating chart types manually so I understand how Tableau is generating the data visualization:

1. Make a crosstab of data.

    First, make a basic text table. In my example, I'm looking at the measure of Sales by the dimensions of Sub-Category and Month of Order Date (Discrete). At this point, my view looks like this:

2. Color the numbers by sales.

Second, color the displayed sales values in the text table by dragging the Sales measure from the list of measures to the Color Marks Card. Note that the Sales measure is now on the Marks Shelf twice: once for text and once for color. At this point, my view looks like this:

3. Create a **highlight** table by changing the mark type.

While more helpful than a raw table of numbers, the view we have created so far can still be improved. While the numbers themselves are encoded by color, which helps us recognize highs and lows in the data more quickly than we could with a crosstab, there is a lot of whitespace around each number.

The final step in converting this view to a highlight table is to simply change the mark type from Automatic (which at this point is Text) to Square. When you convert the mark type from Text to Square in a crosstab view, the "Square" mark type fills each cell, creating a highlight table. When building highlight tables, I also like to add a white border around each cell; this can be accomplished by clicking the Color Marks Card and changing the border.

My final **highlight** table looks like this:

| Columns | ⊞ MONTH(Order Date) | | | | | | | | | | | |
| Rows | ⊞ Sub-Category | | | | | | | | | | | |

	January	February	March	April	May	June	July	August	September	October	November	December
Accessories	$5,478	$5,369	$8,735	$7,984	$9,613	$8,858	$17,177	$12,376	$24,900	$12,927	$25,957	$28,007
Appliances	$3,176	$4,933	$6,734	$6,042	$7,526	$7,479	$3,540	$13,345	$10,193	$9,152	$18,970	$16,443
Art	$966	$1,006	$1,413	$2,407	$2,231	$2,182	$2,102	$1,690	$3,660	$1,911	$3,966	$3,584
Binders	$12,412	$4,237	$13,889	$13,357	$9,160	$13,294	$8,557	$20,430	$37,342	$18,079	$20,858	$31,798
Bookcases	$5,352	$1,650	$7,352	$4,720	$6,290	$7,881	$9,856	$5,622	$22,849	$8,771	$23,561	$10,977
Chairs	$11,285	$7,583	$21,016	$18,855	$25,703	$21,714	$23,016	$18,340	$35,377	$21,905	$46,636	$57,119
Copiers	$3,960		$25,590	$3,880	$18,400	$900	$9,780	$5,730	$10,320	$37,020	$15,150	$18,800
Envelopes	$750	$669	$1,657	$945	$1,096	$514	$1,200	$701	$2,177	$1,403	$2,907	$2,458
Fasteners	$88	$159	$150	$258	$109	$116	$182	$243	$406	$326	$550	$438
Furnishings	$3,980	$2,316	$5,159	$7,404	$6,996	$5,956	$7,336	$4,307	$11,805	$5,447	$16,783	$14,218
Labels	$207	$300	$940	$430	$863	$1,207	$1,692	$876	$1,496	$1,248	$1,850	$1,376
Machines	$7,215	$8,990	$33,652	$18,190	$11,268	$12,183	$4,065	$6,262	$26,386	$10,613	$35,807	$15,210
Paper	$2,287	$2,813	$6,286	$3,964	$6,184	$6,751	$4,180	$6,523	$10,690	$4,965	$12,563	$11,274
Phones	$13,772	$8,984	$29,163	$17,890	$24,182	$26,493	$23,128	$28,413	$37,775	$26,472	$56,184	$58,551
Storage	$9,374	$6,125	$14,793	$15,806	$14,670	$18,606	$12,491	$17,719	$29,511	$15,822	$37,962	$30,983
Supplies	$4,403	$289	$10,637	$6,216	$1,154	$1,267	$8,816	$866	$6,436	$816	$1,372	$4,402
Tables	$10,952	$4,218	$16,913	$9,913	$9,288	$16,405	$9,299	$17,752	$19,626	$20,223	$53,302	$39,193

CHAPTER 20

How to Make a Heat Map

Heat maps are a visualization where marks on a chart are represented as colors. As the marks "heat up" due their higher values or density of records, a more intense color is displayed. These colors can be displayed in a matrix/crosstab, which creates a highlight table, but can also be displayed on a geographical map or even a customized image—such as a web page used to show where users are clicking.

Density plots are coming in Tableau version 11, but in the meantime, heat maps are defined somewhat differently in Tableau. This chapter shares how to create a Tableau heat map. If you are interested in creating a traditional heat map using a custom image, see Chapter 35.

To first get more specific about how Tableau defines heat map, let's take a look at the requirements to draw a heat map under Tableau's Show Me options:

"For heat maps try 1 or more dimensions and 1 or 2 measures"

This is very close to the requirements for drawing a highlight table with Show Me:

"For highlight tables try 1 or more dimensions and 1 measure"

The key distinction between the two chart types is that with a heat map, you are able to encode the marks by one additional measure. With a highlight table, your only option is to color the marks by one measure. Since you can only color marks by one thing at a time, your encoding is limited to exactly one measure. With a heat map in Tableau, you can color the marks by one measure, but also size the marks by a second measure. Depending on your analysis, this additional encoding can add value to your visualization.

How to Make a Heat Map in Tableau

Let's say we've been tasked with evaluating the product sub-category sales in the Sample – Superstore dataset by Month of Order Date to see if we can identify any seasonal trends in the data. The element of time (Month of Order Date) may give you the instinct to go with a line graph for this analysis, which would look like this:

As you can see, this graph is a bit of a mess. The 17 lines are causing a lot of overlap and several of the sub-categories at the bottom are on a much smaller scale than the rest, making it challenging to gain insights. In this case, a heat map may be a better option.

To create a heat map in Tableau, start by laying out the rows and columns that will serve as the grid for the visualization. I would like the months in this analysis to be listed along the top of the view. Since the months will create columns, I know that I should put the Month of Order Date dimension on the Columns Shelf. Conversely, I would like each sub-category to have its own row, so I will place that dimension on the Rows Shelf:

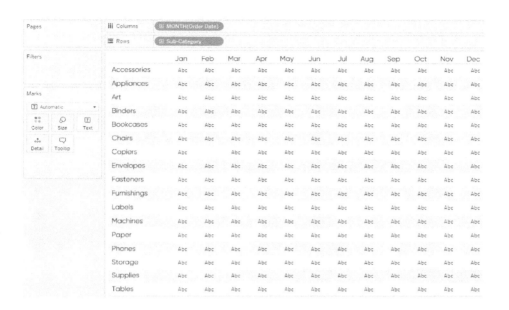

By default, the mark type is set to Text. I personally prefer my Tableau heat maps to be created with circles, so I will change the mark type to Circle to lay the foundation for the view. The Shape or Square mark types are also good choices:

Now that I have a mark at each intersection of Sub-Category and Month of Order Date, I can encode them by two measures; one that will determine the size of the marks and one that will determine the color intensity of the marks. This encoding is produced by placing the measures we want to encode the marks by onto the Size Marks Card and Color Marks Card, respectively. For my first analysis, I will size and color the circles by the same measure—Sales:

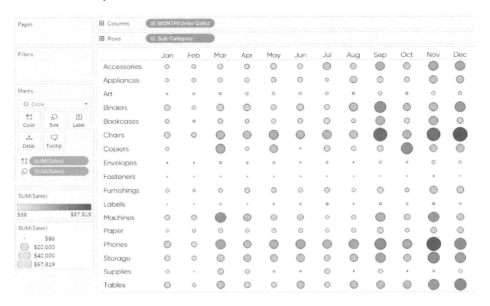

When the Sales measure—which always has a positive value—is used for color, we get a sequential color palette by default. If you were to place a measure such as Profit—which has both negative and positive values—on the Color Marks Card, you would see a diverging color palette by default with 0 at the center (i.e., one color for negative values; a different color for positive values).

This visualization uses the exact same fields as the line graph from before, but it is now much easier to compare sub-categories within a specific month (reading the chart vertically) or compare the seasonality across each sub-category (reading the chart horizontally). The "double-encoding," where the size and color are both based on the same field, are meant to help the insights "pop." However, you have the option to use one measure for the size, and a different measure for the color. For example, here is what the heat map looks like if I size the circles by the Quantity measure instead of Sales:

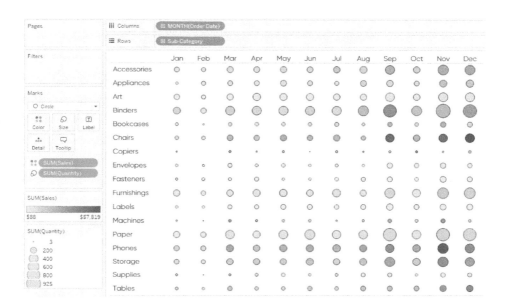

With this analysis, large and light circles would mean that a sub-category sold a relatively large quantity but made a relatively low amount of revenue: low sales per item. Conversely, small and dark circles would mean the sub-category sold a relatively small quantity, but generated a relatively high revenue: high sales per item.

Beware that this type of mixed encoding can be confusing for end users unless you explicitly state what the size and color represents. Despite some of their limitations, Tableau heat maps provide a viable alternative to a line graph or highlight table if you need to compare dimension members with varying scales across multiple measures.

CHAPTER 21

How to Make a Dual-Axis Combination Chart

Dual-axis combination charts, or Combo Charts, are an effective chart type for showing related information while saving real estate by combining views. This chart type is created with one shared axis, such as an x-axis for date, and two separate axes, such as y-axes for two different measures. This chapter will show you how to make a dual-axis combo chart in Tableau that looks at Sales and Discount by Year and Product Category.

How to Make a Dual-Axis Combo Chart in Tableau

Before we begin, let's take a look at how our final product will look:

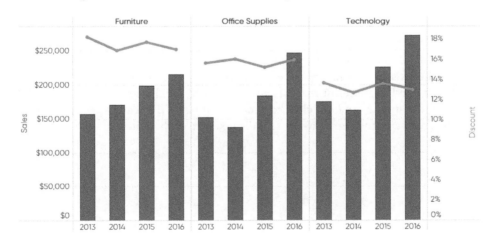

1. Make a graph of one of the measures.

    The first step is to make a graph for one of your measures. It doesn't matter too much which of your two measures you begin with, but the first measure you select will always form the lefthand y-axis or bottom x-axis (depending on the chart's orientation). Let's start by making a line graph for sales by year. To create the first graph, drag the Order Date field to Columns Shelf with an aggregation of Year Continuous. Then drag the Sales field to the Rows Shelf. At this point, the view looks like this:

    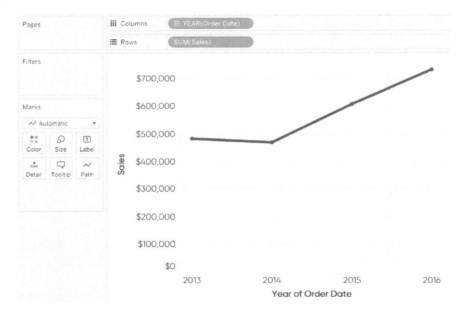

2. Drag the second measure onto the opposite axis.

    In order to create a dual-axis chart, you will drag the second measure onto the opposite axis from your first measure. In my case, Sales is on the left y-axis. I want to add the Discount measure to the view, so I will drag it to where the right y-axis will appear. As I get close to the opposite axis, Tableau is giving me a hint of where I can drop the measure as indicated by a dashed line:

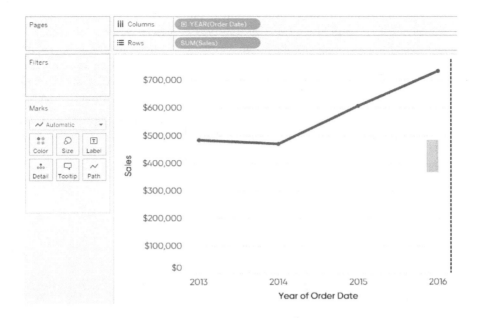

Once I drop the field on the opposite axis, Tableau generates a dual-axis chart. Note that this is a dual-axis chart at this point, but not a dual-axis *combination* chart. The name combination chart comes from using a combination of mark types, and so far, we only have one mark type (line):

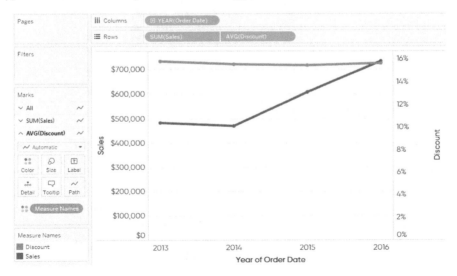

3. Create a dual-axis combination chart by changing one of the mark types.

When the second measure was dropped onto the view, not only did the field appear on the Rows Shelf, but two new Marks Shelves were generated. The first new Marks Shelf, "All," affects all of the marks on the view, and the second new Marks Shelf is for the marks on the right y-axis. The marks for each measure can now be edited independently of each other, allowing you to display a *combination* of mark types on your view.

Let's change the mark type of the Sales field to Bar and leave the mark type for Discount as Line. This is accomplished by clicking the Marks Shelf for SUM(Sales) and changing the mark type from Automatic to Bar. At this point, the view looks like this:

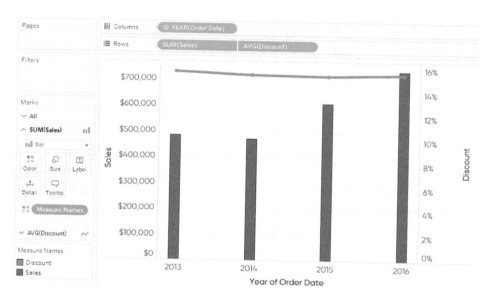

Some Additional Thoughts

- I decided to make the first graph, Sales by *continuous* Year, because it was meant to be a continuous (i.e., chronological) trend over time. Many people ask why the bars are so skinny (prior to version 10) and so fat (with version 10) when Year is continuous. You can get a better look by changing the Year field from continuous to discrete by right-clicking the field on the Columns Shelf and choosing Discrete. The catch with discrete date dimensions is that the dates can now be sorted out of chronological order. If you decide to make this change for formatting purposes, be careful not to sort the view in an unintended way.

- A mark type of Line should only be used when connecting dots between continuous dates. This is because a line implies that there is a chronological relationship between points. This works well for our example, where discount is being connected by years in chronological order. However, dual-axis combination charts do not necessarily need to use a date as the shared axis, so choose your mark types wisely.

- You can create small multiples, or comparison views, by dragging another dimension onto the Rows Shelf or Columns Shelf.

- If your axes should be on the same scale, you can synchronize the axes by right-clicking either axis and choosing Synchronize Axis.

Here is my final view after changing Year to Discrete, adding the Category dimension to the Columns Shelf, and cleaning up the formatting:

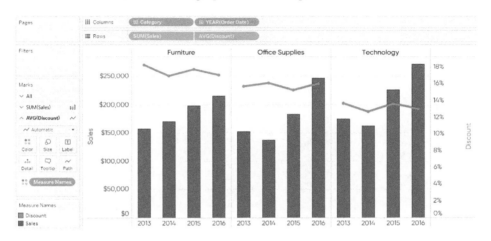

CHAPTER 22

How to Make a Scatter Plot

After the bar chart and line graph, I find the scatter plot to be one of the most effective visualization options for analyzing data. A scatter plot displays data points at their respective intersections of two measures, and displays every data point on the same view. The marks can then be further encoded by up to three additional measures and/or dimensions by leveraging the Color and/or Size and/or Shape Marks Cards.

 While scatter plots allow you to use several combinations of dimensions and measures, each new encoding increases the cognitive load on your end users. In other words, it makes it harder for them to process the view.

This ability to slice and dice data points in several ways within a condensed space provides an effective means for identifying patterns. Not only that, scatter plots provide a natural way to segment the marks into four quadrants by simply adding a reference line to each of the two axes. You can even take this a step further in Tableau by creating sets for each of the four segments to use for deeper analysis later. This chapter shares how to create a scatter plot in Tableau and use the results to create segments.

How to Make a Scatter Plot in Tableau

For this walkthrough, we'll be evaluating all of our products across the Sales and Profit Ratio measures. When you build a scatter plot, one measure will form the y-axis and one measure will form the x-axis. The marks on the view will then be plotted at the intersection of the values on the two axes. It is typically best to put the most dependent metric on the y-axis and the explanatory metric on the x-axis.

To create a scatter plot, drag and drop the Profit Ratio measure to the Rows Shelf and the Sales measure to the Columns Shelf. Scatter plot is the default chart type in Tableau when two measures are used, so you could have got to this same point by just double-clicking Profit Ratio, then double-clicking Sales to add them to the view. At this point, your view should look similar to this:

So far, we have just one point that represents the intersection of Profit Ratio and Sales for all of the records in our dataset. This is because we have yet to specify a level of detail for our analysis. For more on this topic, you can review Chapter 10. Our analysis is going to look at products, so change the level of detail by dragging the Product Name dimension to the Detail Marks Card. The view has now been changed to this:

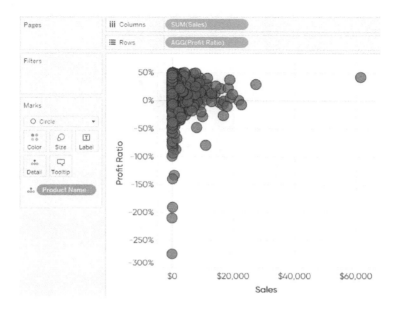

What's powerful here is that we are looking at all 1,850 of our products at once, which helps us evaluate them quickly in context of each other. You can see outliers, unprofitable products, and segments are beginning to emerge (i.e., high sales/high profit ratio, high sales/low profit ratio, etc.). One way to make the segments more apparent is to add reference lines to each axis. Here's what the view looks like when I add a reference line for the average of each axis by right-clicking each axis and choosing "Add reference line":

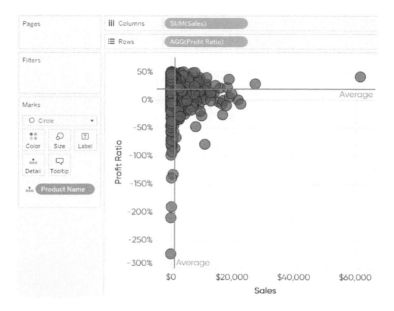

These reference lines create four quadrants on the view that can be used to segment the data:

- **Top-left quadrant:** High Profit Ratio & Low Sales
- **Top-right quadrant:** High Profit Ratio & High Sales
- **Bottom-left quadrant:** Low Profit Ratio & Low Sales
- **Bottom-right quadrant:** Low Profit Ratio & High Sales

This provides some areas to focus on. For example, we don't want to have high sales of products that are causing us to lose money. Also, are there opportunities to increase the sales of our most profitable items? This example created segments using the averages of each measure, but you can easily change the reference lines to the thresholds of your choice for segmentation.

Lastly, these segments or products of interest can be made more permanent by placing them into sets. In this example, our two highest-selling products are also above average in profitability. Let's put these two products into a "positive-outlier" set by selecting them on the view (either through multi-select or dragging a box around them), right-clicking, and choosing "Create set." Once in a set, these positive outliers can be highlighted in different visualizations, which can lead to valuable insights for the business.

CHAPTER 23

How to Make a Tree Map

A tree map is a visualization that nests rectangles in hierarchies so you can compare different dimension combinations across one or two measures (one for size; one for color) and quickly interpret their respective contributions to the whole. When used poorly, tree maps are not much more than an alternative pie chart. When used well, they provide at least two big benefits:

- Depending on the analysis, some portions of the tree map will be composed of large rectangles where additional context can be added as labels. This is beneficial when the visualization will not be interactive and you still want the written information represented.
- In addition to the scatter plot, tree maps are one of the only visualization types that allow you to reasonably communicate and consume hundreds of marks on a single view. This makes it easier to spot patterns and relationships that you would not otherwise be able to see.

For this tutorial, we will be making the following set of tree maps:

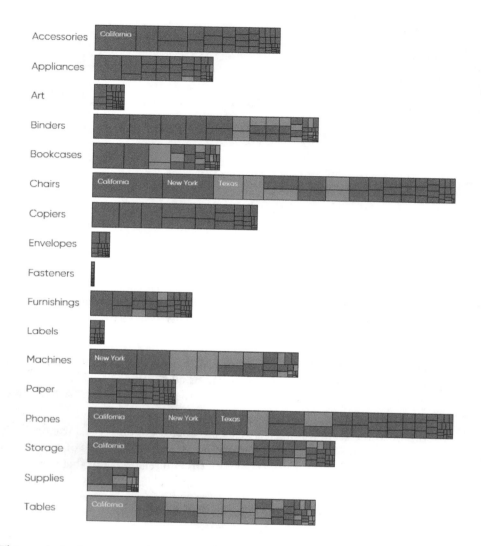

This analysis shows not only the sales amount by sub-category, but the sales contribution of each US state per sub-category and whether or not those states were profitable within each sub-category.

By changing the level of detail to make our analysis more granular and encoding the marks by a second measure of Profit Ratio provides more context to the view and helps us avoid the dreaded question, "So what?"

How to Make a Tree Map in Tableau

Tree maps are one of the out-of-the-box Show Me options, but as with most charts in Tableau, I find building them from scratch helps me not only understand how they work, but also helps me get to my desired output faster.

To make a tree map in Tableau, begin by changing the mark type for a view from Automatic to Square. Then drag the primary measure that you want to evaluate to the Size Marks Card and the secondary measure to the Color Marks Card. Just as it sounds, the primary measure will control the size of the squares on the view, and the secondary measure will control the color of the squares. In our case, I've dragged Sales to Size and Profit Ratio to Color:

At this point, we've simply laid the foundation of the tree map. There is no detail, so we just see one square colored by the overall profit ratio in the Sample – Superstore dataset. To create a square for each state, drag State to the Detail Marks Card:

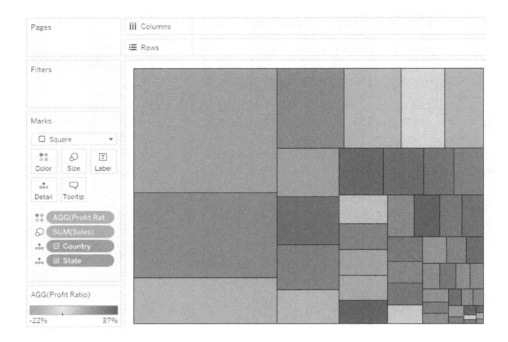

At this point, we have a tree map and a solid analysis. You can see there is quite a bit of real estate to add information to the Label Marks Card and have it displayed on the view (the first benefit mentioned in the introduction).

If I wanted to see this same analysis done at the Sub-Category level as just pictured, I would drag the Sub-Category dimension to the Rows Shelf. This will create a row with the sales and profit ratio by state tree map for each sub-category:

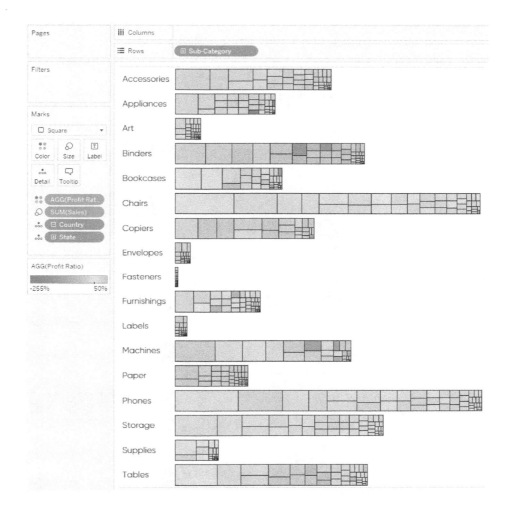

The final steps required to match the example would be to drag the State dimension to the Label Marks Card and double-click the color legend to choose the colors and steps. I changed the steps to 2 and changed the colors so that any state with a negative profit ratio per sub-category would be colored red and any state with a positive profit ratio per sub-category would be colored navy:

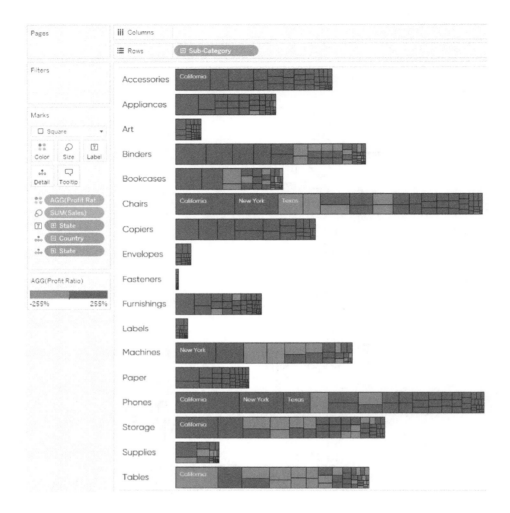

This tree map provides several insights, including:

- The overall sales are strongest in the Chairs and Phones sub-categories. This is the main insight we would see when looking at a simple sales by sub-category bar chart.

- The Tables sub-category is largely composed of unprofitable states, and two out of the top three highest selling states are unprofitable.

- The overall best-selling state and sub-category combination is Phones in California, which was profitable.

I also see that California is the highest-selling state in all sub-categories except for Machines and Binders. Note that I was not able to see that insight in the screenshot alone, but by hovering over marks in the interactive version of the workbook. You can also simply provide a filter that looks at one sub-category at a time and add even more context to the mark labels:

These are just a few examples of the insights gleaned from this visualization, and a couple of the limitless applications of tree maps.

CHAPTER 24

How to Make Sparklines

Sparklines are condensed graphs or charts that can be used in-line with text or grouped to show trends across several different measures. The term sparkline was introduced by Edward Tufte, a data visualization pioneer, and proponent of the chart type. Sparklines are typically so small that the chart itself usually does not contain familiar context that you would find in a full-size chart, such as axes. Despite this limitation, I find sparklines to be one of the most effective corporate chart types for quickly communicating trends across KPIs. After all, you can always provide context in the surrounding text, and if you are using Tableau, context can be added through other approaches such as tooltips (the information that appears when you hover over a data point).

It is very common for sparklines to be a foundational piece of the corporate dashboards I create. I think they are a great place to guide an end user to start, so I usually place sparklines in a prominent area of my dashboards, such as down the left side. For more on dashboard layout and design, see tip five in Chapter 90.

How to Make Sparklines in Tableau

Sparklines are easy, and (dare I say?) fun, to create in Tableau. To get started, you will leverage two special fields in your data, *Measure Names* and *Measure Values*. These fields are automatically generated in your data by Tableau so they will be available to use even though they do not exist in your underlying data:

1. PlaceMeasure Names, then Measure Values on the Rows Shelf:

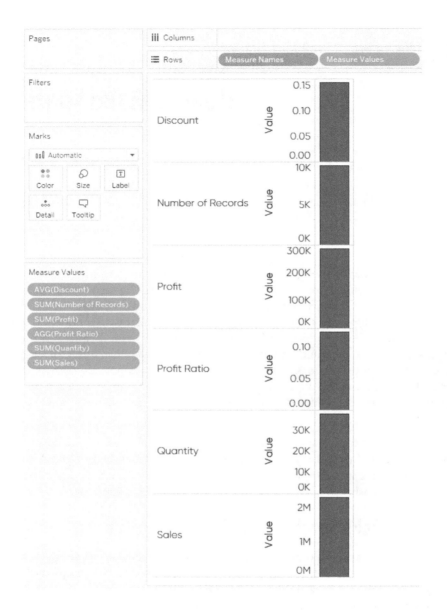

Notice that *every* measure name appears in your chart, whether it is relevant to your analysis or not—more on filtering out specific measure names later. Since you placed Measure Values on your view as well, each measure name has an accompanying value, shown by default as a bar in each measure's default aggregation (i.e., SUM, AVG, etc.). I have also changed the view's fit to Fit Height so that I can see all of the measure names and values without scrolling.

This is a good start, but now we need an element of time to trend the measure values.

2. Place a date field on the Columns Shelf.

By right-clicking and dragging my Order Date field onto the Columns Shelf, I was given an extra option to select the date part (i.e., Year, Month, Week). To get the view to look as it does here, I chose the MONTH option preceded by a green icon. The green indicates that the date will be continuous:

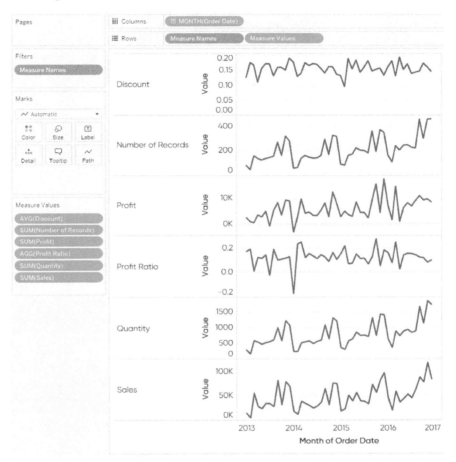

We have now essentially made a series of line graphs, but they are not very "sparky," making it difficult to quickly glean insights. This is an easy fix in Tableau by clicking and dragging the right side of the graph to the left to reduce the width of the view.

3. Reduce the width of the sparklines view to make the trends pop:

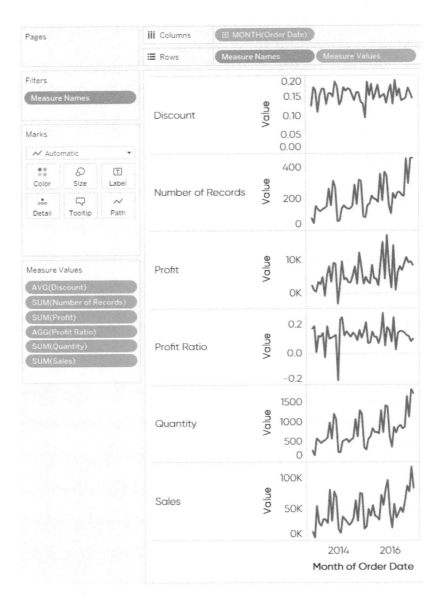

You can see at this point that the sparklines are coming together, but as previously mentioned, we have an irrelevant measure name that is not adding much to our analysis.

4. Remove irrelevant measures from your view:

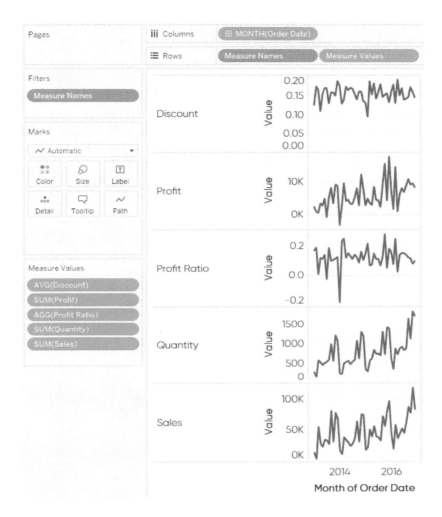

For the purposes of this analysis, I removed the Number of Records measure by dragging its green "pill" from the Measure Values Shelf. Number of Records is a generated field and not needed for this analysis.

We're getting even closer now, but notice that Discount is not providing much insight because this measure has very little fluctuation. For this reason, I typically remove zero from my axes in sparklines. There is much debate around whether it is ever appropriate to exclude zero from your axes because it is easy to mislead your audience when an axis starts anywhere but zero. In the case of sparklines, and measures with little to no volatility, I recommend either excluding zero on the axes, or removing these types of measures completely from your view. Remember: if you cannot gain any insight from these measures in your sparklines, they are not adding any value. There may be times when you expect to see little to no volatility, in which case control charts (covered in Chapter 43), may be a better choice.

5. Exclude zero from your axes or remove measures that have little to no fluctuation.

If you're comfortable excluding zero from your axes, right-click any of the axes in your sparklines and choose Edit Axis. You will see a box specifically created to give you the option to include or exclude zero in your axes. By default, the box to "Include zero" is checked. To exclude zero, uncheck this box:

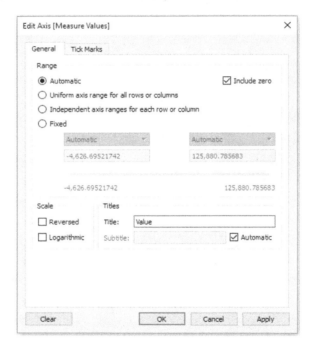

You can now see the fluctuation in Discount:

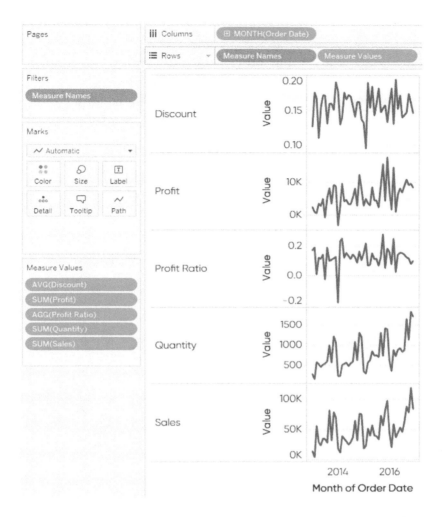

From here, all that's left is to format the sparklines to your preference. Remember, sparklines are not quite like regular charts or graphs in that they are meant to provide quick trends at a glance. They don't usually contain typical context, such as the axis values.

6. Hide axes and format your view:

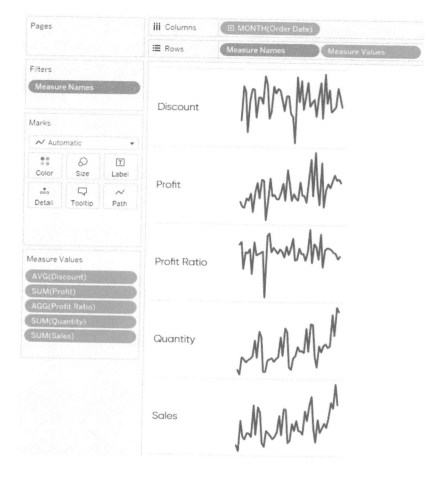

Formatting changes I made to finalize this view include:

- Hid the y-axis by right-clicking the axis and deselecting Show Header.
- Hid the x-axis. Some prefer to keep the axis that shows the date range. I personally exclude this from my sparklines, but if you need to show it, I recommend only showing the start and end points.
- Removed the gridlines.
- Removed the column separators.
- Softened the row separators by choosing a dotted line instead of a solid line.

Final Considerations

The sparklines pictured in this chapter can definitely stand on their own and provide a great deal of insight and a starting point for any dashboard. That being said, Tableau allows you to customize from here in many different ways. For example, you may choose to show labels for the minimum and maximum values for each sparkline. This approach provides an alternative to showing the y-axis because it shows the end user how low and high the axis goes. You can also customize the tooltips to provide additional context such as the exact values and dates that the end user is viewing.

CHAPTER 25

How to Make Small Multiples

Small multiples are a group of charts or graphs that share the same axes and scales, which allows the user to compare trends across dimensions in a single view. They have been praised for their ability to provide a great deal of context, reducing the need for end users to ask the dreaded, "So what?" The term "small multiples" was popularized by Edward Tufte, who puts it best in his book, *Envisioning Information*:

"At the heart of quantitative reasoning is a single question: *Compared to what?*"

While smaller series of small multiples can work well on an executive summary dashboard, I typically like to use them as a second layer in an analysis. My executive level view, or "first layer," may provide higher-level information about a particular measure, such as the overall sales trend and progress toward goals. This is a "descriptive" view of the data answering the question, "What is happening with sales?" From here, I may provide an option to view sales across different dimensions and sub-categories as a series of small multiples in a second layer of the dashboard (often located away from the first view). While small multiples is still a "descriptive" view, it helps answer the question, "Compared to what?"

In this chapter, we will be re-creating the following small multiples view:

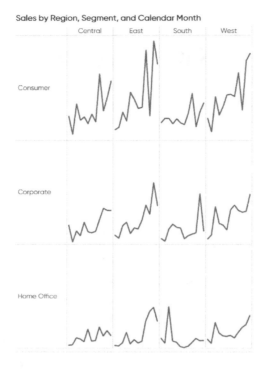

Sales by Region, Segment, and Calendar Month

How to Make Small Multiples in Tableau

Small multiples can come in several different forms, but for the purposes of this tutorial, I am going to show you how to compare a single measure across two different dimensions. To get started, select two dimensions and a measure. I have chosen the dimensions of Segment and Region and the measure of Sales for the view to follow:

1. Place one dimension on the Columns Shelf and the other dimension and your measure on the Rows Shelf.

   By default, Tableau has created a bar chart for you. By placing Segment on the Rows Shelf, performance for each segment is read left to right, in rows. By placing Region on the Columns Shelf, each region is represented vertically, in columns:

Small multiples may be a series of bar charts, but we still need to add an element of time to trend the Sales measure.

2. Place a date field on the Columns Shelf.

Let's pretend that we would like to evaluate the seasonality of sales to answer a question such as, "Is there a certain month that I can expect a spike in sales?" For this type of analysis, we will use a discrete date field with a monthly aggregation, which will always show us the performance per distinct calendar month. By using discrete months, I know that I will always have twelve data points per small multiple, one for each calendar month (January, February, March, etc.). The Superstore sample dataset contains four years of data, so if we used a continuous date field with a monthly aggregation, we would have up to 48 data points per small multiple (4 years × 12 months = 48 points).

By right-clicking and dragging the Order Date field onto the Columns Shelf, I was given an extra option to select the date part (i.e., Year, Month, Week). To get the view to look as it does here, I chose the MONTH option that was colored blue. The blue indicates that the date will be discrete:

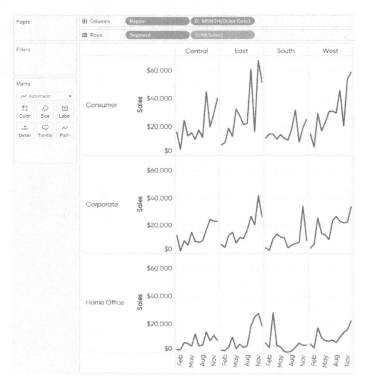

3. Format the small multiples to your preference.

From here, all that is left to do is format the view to your liking:

Formatting changes I made to finalize this view include:

- Hid the field labels for columns by right-clicking Region/Order Date.

- Hid the field labels for rows by right-clicking Segment.

- Hid both the x- and y-axes by right-clicking them and deselecting Show Header. This is a personal preference of mine. You may choose to keep the axes in the view for additional context. To keep the view as clean as possible, I opted to provide this context in the form of a title, and would typically provide additional information in the tooltips that appear when an end user hovers over different data points.

- Increased the font size in the headers.

Final Considerations

In this tutorial, we have laid a strong foundation for using small multiples, but Tableau makes it easy to build on this view by customizing it in many different ways. For example, instead of using lines, you can change the mark type to bars, which are particularly useful for measures that can be positive or negative, or areas—which provide a beautiful design alternative. I have also seen small multiple views that display year-over-year data nicely and Ben Jones of Tableau has shown how to create small multiple *maps* in Tableau (*http://bit.ly/2FPcJTj*). So get creative, and build small multiples that help provide the answer to "Compared to what?"

CHAPTER 26

How to Make Bullet Graphs

Bullet graphs are a variation of the bar chart invented by Stephen Few. Bullet graphs are one of my go-to chart types and are often featured prominently throughout my dashboards because I find that when I use them, I hear the question "So what?" less often. As powerful as bar charts are at communicating data, when viewed in a vacuum—or without additional context—their comparisons are limited to only the dimension members that are displayed in the chart. Bullet graphs improve on the bar chart by providing additional points of comparison. For example, in addition to showing a bar for widget sales, a bullet graph would also include a point of comparison that shows either last year's sales or a target sales amount. Further, bullet graphs can include shading to illustrate how close your sales number is to last year's number or your target.

While I find this to be one of the most powerful visualization types, it took me some time to wrap my head around how to make them when I was getting started with Tableau. Bullet graphs are a "Show Me" option in Tableau, but I found that this option was not always providing the results that I expected. Once I figured out that bullet graphs are simply a combination of bars and reference lines, it was much easier for me to create them. The good news is that if you can create a bar chart in Tableau, you can create bullet graphs!

In this chapter, we will re-create the following chart:

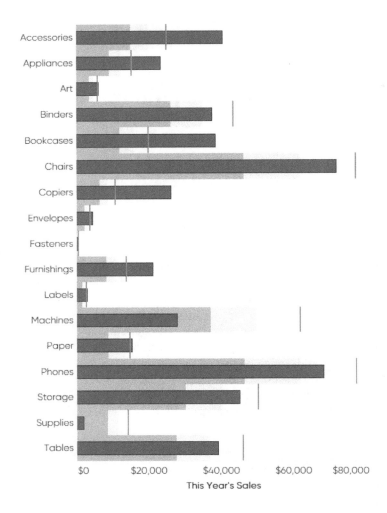

This Year's Sales

How to Make Bullet Graphs in Tableau

Bullet graphs are only an appropriate chart type to use if you have a point of comparison, such as last year's performance or annual performance goals. The Sample – Superstore dataset does not contain goal information, so my point of comparison will be last year's performance.

1. Break out this year's performance and last year's performance.

   For this bullet graph, I am going to look at sales by sub-category. In order to create a bullet graph, I will need to break out this year's sales and last year's sales.

The Superstore dataset currently runs through 2017, but for the purpose of illustration, I am going to use 2015 as "this year" and 2014 as "last year."

The isolation of sales for these two years is achieved through calculated fields. To create a field that contains only 2015 sales, right-click the Sales measure and select Create Calculated Field. This approach provides a small shortcut because sales is already part of your formula when the Calculated Field dialog box opens. Once the dialog box is open, enter a formula like this to isolate the current year's sales:

```
IF YEAR([Order Date]) = 2015 THEN [Sales] END
```

Repeat this step to isolate last year's sales (in this case, 2014).

2. Create a bar chart that will serve as the foundation for your bullet graph.

Create a bar chart as you normally would by placing the current year's sales on the Columns Shelf and a dimension on the Rows Shelf. I am looking at sales by sub-category, so I have placed the Sub-Category dimension on the Rows Shelf. I have also fit the height for more visibility:

3. Add a reference line for' last year's sales.

In order to use last year's (2014) sales as a reference line, the isolated calculation that you created in Step 1 needs to be a part of your view. Even though it is not yet visible, you can make Last Year's Sales part of your view by dropping the field on your Detail Marks Card. Notice that when you place Last Year's Sales on the Detail Marks Card, your view does not change, but now that data is available to use as a reference line.

To create a reference line, right-click the x-axis and select Add Reference Line. Change Value to SUM(Last Year's Sales) and Label to None. The most important change is to toggle the Scope radio button from Per Pane to Per Cell. This will give you a reference line for each distinct sub-category. You may also choose to make the line a bolder color and heavier weight to make it stand out on your view. After the appropriate selections, your reference line dialog box should look something like this:

At this point, your view should look like this:

4. Add a reference distribution for last year's sales.'

At this point, you have already added a comparison point to your bar chart that shows whether each category is outperforming or underperforming last year's sales. To take this a step further, you can add a reference distribution to show how close this year's sales are to last year's for the underperforming sub-categories.

This reference type is slightly more complicated, but still easy to do in Tableau. To create a reference distribution for your bullets, do the following:

5. As you did before, right-click the x-axis and select Add Reference Line.

6. Select Distribution at the top.

7. Change the Scope from Per Pane to Per Cell.

8. This is the trickiest part. You need to change the Computation Value from This Year's Sales to Last Year's Sales. You can do this by clicking the down arrow on the Computation → Value box. Then where it says "Percent of:", make the appropriate selection. Notice that the default percentages are 60% and 80%. This means that it will show shading for 0%–60% of last year's sales and 61%–80% of last year's sales.

9. Change Label to None.

10. Check the box that says Fill Below. This will provide the correct shading when you apply the reference distribution.

After hitting OK, you should see a well-done bullet graph that looks like this:

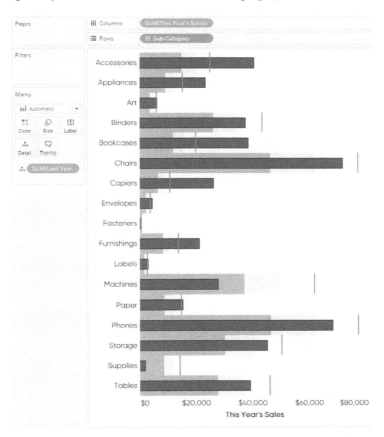

Now that you have a reference distribution, you can quickly determine not only whether or not each category is on pace with last year, but you can see how far behind pace underperforming sub-categories are relative to a year prior.

Another great application of bullet graphs is to use them to show progress toward goals. In that case, the bars would be current year's sales, and the reference lines and distributions would be your goals. By using year-end goals, you can track movement throughout the year and determine which sub-categories are progressing the fastest. This type of context may be enough to help you pivot resources to help underachievers catch up—actionable insight that may not have come from a bar chart alone.

CHAPTER 27

How to Make a Stacked Area Chart

A stacked area chart "stacks" trends on top of each other to illustrate how a part-to-whole distribution changes over time. Combined with a table calculation that computes the percent of total for each dimension member in the visualization, stacked area charts are an effective way to evaluate distributions. In this chapter, we will be re-creating this visualization:

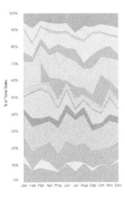

To create a stacked area chart, I will start with this line graph showing Sales by Sub-Category by discrete Month of Order Date in the Sample – Superstore dataset:

To create a stacked area chart in Tableau, simply change the mark type from Automatic, which is currently set to Line, to Area:

As stacked area charts are one of the foundational Show Me options and are extremely easy to create in Tableau, this chapter will focus more on the best applications of this chart type and a trick for using them most effectively.

As you can see in the previous image, when the mark type was changed from Line to Area, the values for each of the dimension members for Sub-Category were stacked on top of each other. This provided a new insight to us that was not available when the mark type was Line: the monthly total across all 17 sub-categories. If it was more important to know the monthly total versus the exact contribution of each sub-category, the stacked area chart is the right tool for the job.

However, if it is more important to know the individual trends of each sub-category, that becomes difficult to assess with a stacked area chart. The reason is that after the trend on the bottom of the stack, each subsequent trend inherits the trend below it. So by the time you get to the slice on top, the value equals the value of the first 16 slices combined, plus the value of the 17th and final dimension member. You can turn off the stacks by navigating to Analysis → Stack Marks and choosing Off, but at that point, you're better off with the line graph we started with.

One other big word of caution if you are using stacked area charts: never use them to stack rates, such as a click-through rate, open rate, or another type of conversion that divides a numerator by a denominator. This is again because the trends are stacked on top of each other, so if you have three dimension members, each with a conversion rate of 5%, the top slice would display the value of the first two stacks combined (10%) plus the value of the third and final dimension member (5%). In this scenario, the slice on top would display a value of 15%, far from its true 5% performance.

So when is a stacked area chart a good choice?

I like to use stacked area charts when the total axis equals 100% and each individual dimension member is displayed as a percentage of the total. This can be achieved by adding a quick table calculation for "Percent of total" to the measure being displayed. For a refresher on table calculations, see Chapter 13.

By default, Tableau calculates table calculations across the table. So if I were to add a quick table calculation for percent of total to the stacked area chart in the previous image, I see this:

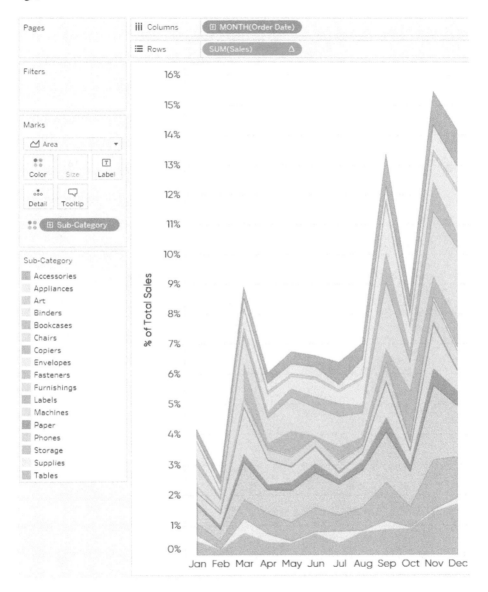

With this view, the trends look exactly the same, but the axis is being displayed as a percent of total instead of the raw revenue values. To change the view so that the axis totals 100% and the areas represent each dimension member's contribution to each month's total, the table calculation needs to be changed to compute using Table (down). This is changed by clicking the measure with the table calculation for percent of total, now designated with a delta symbol, hovering over Compute Using, and selecting Table (down):

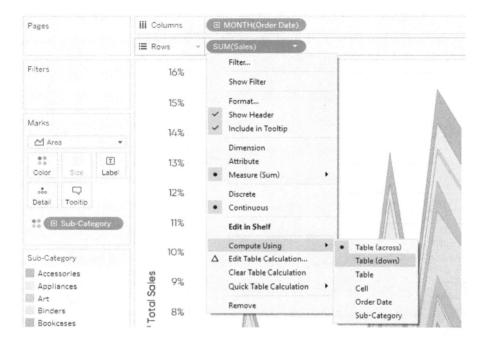

After changing the direction of the table calculation, it is easier to see the monthly contribution for each individual dimension member:

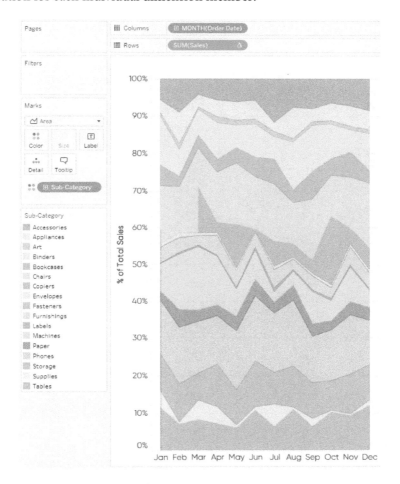

Unless the slice is on the top or the bottom, it can still be challenging to evaluate the trends for individual dimension members with a great deal of precision. At the very least, it should be easier to evaluate which dimension members are gaining or losing share from month to month. As with most analyses in Tableau, the chart selection should be informed by the business question at hand. Stacked area charts, especially when combined with table calculations, are a good visualization to have in your toolbelt to display how distributions in your business are changing over time.

CHAPTER 28

How to Make a Histogram

Histograms are one of the most effective chart types for showing a distribution of quantitative data at one point in time. Similar to a bar chart, the important distinction is that histograms are used to plot continuous, numerical data while the bar chart is used to plot discrete, categorical data. When you create a histogram, bins are created to group equally sized numerical ranges. Despite being continuous and quantitative, these bins can be thought of as the dimension that you slice and dice the count of records by to create the histogram.

In this chapter, we will re-create the following visualization:

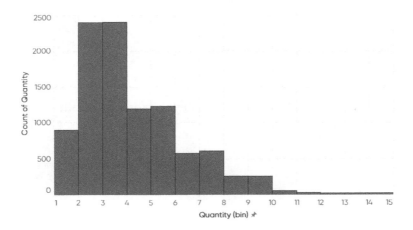

How to Make a Histogram in Tableau

Histograms are one of the 24 chart types in Tableau that can be created using the Show Me tool in the upper-right corner of the Tableau Desktop interface. I've mentioned I usually like to explain how a visualization is created manually in Tableau instead of relying on Show Me, but histograms are one of my few exceptions. Histograms are created in Tableau using just one measure. To create a histogram, pre-select the measure that you want to visualize the distribution for by clicking it in the Measures Shelf. Then navigate to the Show Me options and choose "histogram":

Here's how a histogram looks if you follow the steps for the Quantity measure in the Sample – Superstore dataset:

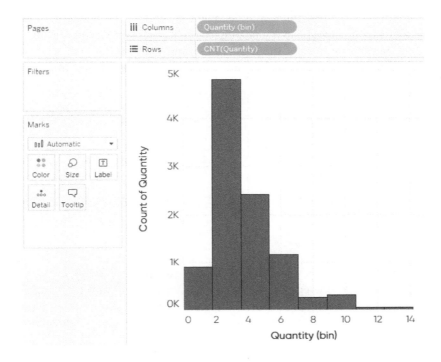

When this chart was created, Tableau conveniently created the dimension for Quantity (bin) to provide the equally sized ranges that are required to create a histogram. The bars then represent the count of records within each of these ranges. Notice that the bars have no space between them; this is how some authors like to differentiate the bars with continuous data in a histogram from the bars with categorical data in a bar chart.

Depending on how the distribution looks, you may choose to change the size of the bins. This is easy to accomplish by locating the newly created Quantity (bin) dimension in the Dimensions area of the Data pane, right-clicking the field, and choosing Edit. A new interface will appear that shows you the current bin size and allows you to change the equal ranges:

Here, you can either type in a number, or click the drop-down arrow to have the bin size be based on a parameter. Let's say for simplicity that we want to change the bin size for the quantity measure to one. This analysis would show the end user how many records (i.e., sales) included one item, two items, three items, and so on. Here's how the histogram looks after editing the bin size:

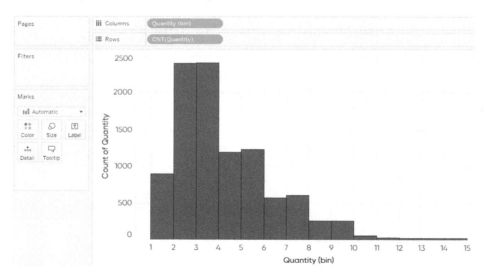

Lastly, because the bin ranges are continuous, we have a continuous axis that begins at zero and ends at one bin past our maximum bin size. If you need to change the axis range, right-click the x-axis and choose "Edit axis." Here is how my final histogram for quantity looks after fixing the axis range from 1 to 15:

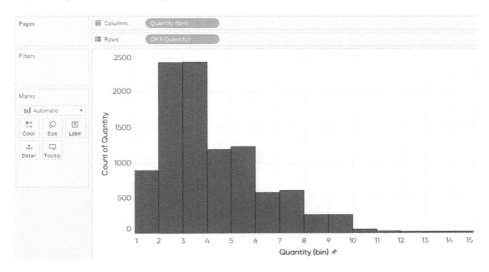

CHAPTER 29

How to Make a Box-and-Whisker Plot

The box-and-whisker plot, or box plot, is another effective visualization choice for illustrating distributions. Along with histograms and stacked area charts, box-and-whisker plots are among my favorite chart types used for this purpose. They work particularly well when you want to compare the distributions across two different dimension members side-by-side, where one set of dimension members makes up the x-axis, and the other dimension member is used as the visualization's level of detail. To help illustrate, here's the box-and-whisker plot we will create with the Sample – Superstore dataset during this tutorial:

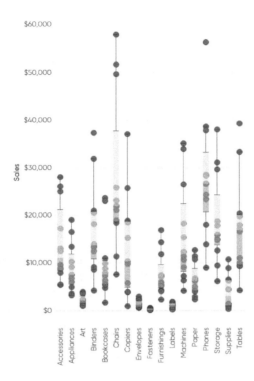

As you can see, each set of circles corresponds to the dimension members on the x-axis for the Sub-Category dimension. The level of detail, or most granular level of the analysis, is Month of Order Date. Since the level of detail is Month of Order Date, each Sub-Category column has 12 circles, one for each month of the year.

In short, this visualization is showing how the distributions of monthly sales vary between product sub-categories. While I can easily find several insights in this visualization and believe box-and-whisker plots to be among the most effective ways to communicate distributions, I find them to be one of the most misunderstood chart types when I attempt to share them with an external audience.

For this reason, this chapter shares not only how to make box-and-whisker plots in Tableau, but how to read them. You may need to teach your users how to make sense of a visualization, an effort that can pay off when building a dashboard or other viz that they will refer to on a regular basis. Putting in this effort can also be useful if you're doing a live presentation, but it may not be the best choice if you're putting data out for a general audience.

How to Make a Box-and-Whisker Plot in Tableau

Box-and-whisker plots are one of the out-of-the-box Show Me options in Tableau, but they are actually created with reference lines—which is what I'll show here. To create a box-and-whisker plot, start by creating a bar chart with the dimension and measure of interest (in the preceding example, we are looking at Sales by Sub-Category):

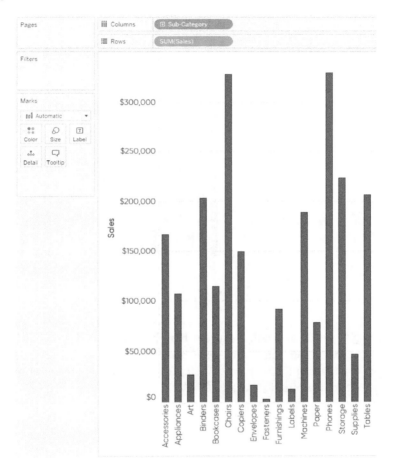

Next, add the distribution that you care about to the Detail Marks Card. In this case, we are looking at how Sales are distributed by Sub-Category, by Month of Order Date. So in this example, Month of Order Date is added to the Detail Marks Card:

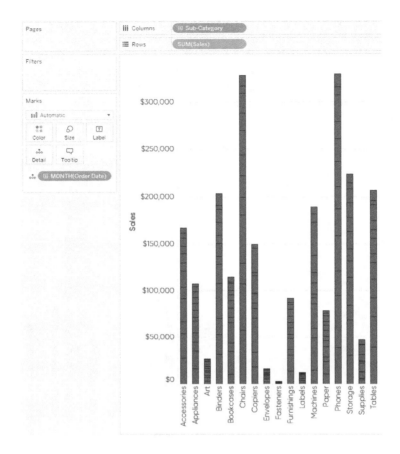

By increasing the level of detail, a stacked bar chart is created, with each stack per sub-category representing one of the twelve months of the year. To set the foundation of the box-and-whisker plot, convert this stacked bar chart to a dot plot by changing the mark type from Automatic (Bar), to Circle:

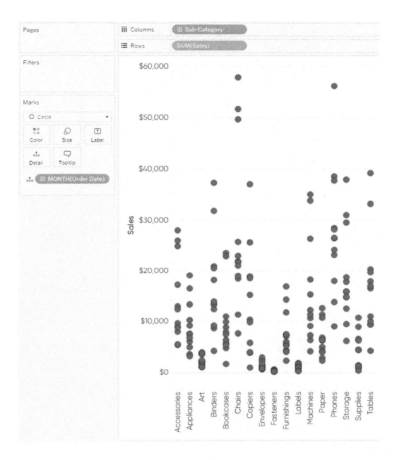

Lastly, to create a box-and-whisker plot, right-click the y-axis, and choose Add Refer-ence Line. When the add reference line dialog box appears, click the choice for Box Plot. There are some formatting options available, but the default settings are usually best:

IQR stands for Interquartile Range, which are the data points between the first and third quartile. So the default options are telling Tableau to make all of the data points on the box-and-whisker plot fit into 1.5 times the IQR; anything outside of that range is an outlier. This sounds confusing and is probably why I don't see this chart type getting much traction, but this chart type provides a lot of helpful context and is easy to read once someone explains it to you. Let's take another look at the final box-and-whisker plot from this tutorial:

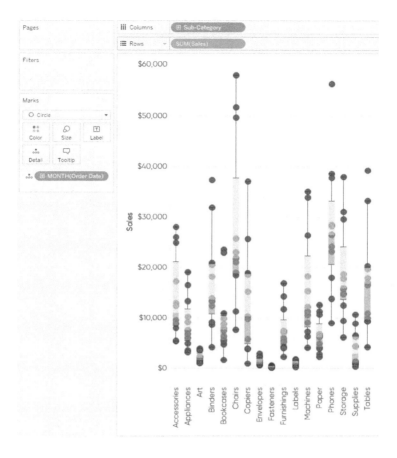

Each line on the box-and-whisker plot provides a piece of statistical context. The most important line is the one right in the middle of each "box," which represents median. With median displayed, you can quickly look across the dimension members and compare medians, regardless of how big or small the range of values is within each column.

That alone is very useful for an analysis, but the rest of the lines also have a meaning. Working out from the median, the next set of lines is showing plus or minus one quartile from the median.

Lastly, the upper whisker is 50% higher than the IQR, or "middle fifty," which are the data points within the first and third quartile. The lower whisker is 50% lower than the IQR. Any data points outside of the box-and-whisker are considered outliers.

Now not only can you make a box-and-whisker plot in Tableau, you know how to use them to get the most out of your analyses!

CHAPTER 30

How to Make a Symbol Map with Mapbox Integration

Maps, which were introduced with Tableau 4.0 in August 2008, are one of the most powerful visualization types available. The power of maps comes from their inherent ability to leverage schemas that your users have been building up for many years. In Chapter 98, I'll show how an image of a map helps you decode dozens of latitude/longitude pairs almost instantly.

The next several chapters cover different map types you can create with Tableau and their purposes. The first shares how to harness this power by creating symbol maps and how to take your maps a step further by integrating Tableau with Mapbox maps.

First, let's take a look at how my final map example will look:

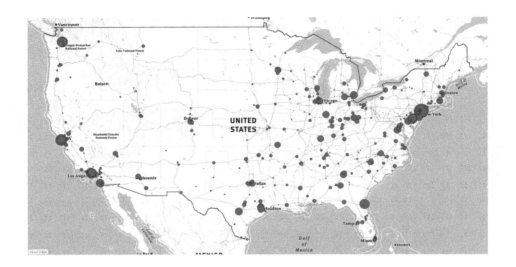

How to Make a Symbol Map in Tableau

The easiest way to start a symbol map in Tableau is to double-click a geographic dimension from the Dimensions area of the Data pane on the left side of the interface. You know that Tableau recognizes your geographic fields as map-compatible if there is a globe icon next to the dimension. In my example, I am going to double-click Postal Code in the Sample – Superstore dataset to start the view:

Notice that Tableau put Longitude on the Columns Shelf and Latitude on the Rows Shelf, and each circle represents the intersection of each pair. At this point, I technically already have a symbol map, but there are several ways I can add value to the visualization. You may want to change the "symbol" from the default circle to a square or other shape. Perhaps you want to size and/or color the symbols by a measure such as sales by placing measures on the appropriate Marks Cards.

I personally like the default circles because you can add a border and they look nice with transparency (which is controlled on the Color Marks Card), so I am going to stick with that. I will change the color to something that pops more by clicking the Color Marks Card and size the bubbles by sales by placing that measure on the Size Marks Card. At this point, my view looks like this:

This is a solid symbol map at this point, but you can also add additional data layers or choose from three map styles by navigating to Map → Map Layers.

How to Add Mapbox Maps

Tableau provides three map styles out of the box, but starting in Tableau version 9.2, it is very easy to integrate your Tableau workbooks with Mapbox, a custom map designing service, to access 14 additional map styles. Mapbox is a free service as long as you get fewer than 50,000 map impressions per month. Once you grow past that, there are paid plans available. To access the new styles, follow these simple steps:

1. Go to mapbox.com.
2. Sign up via the button in the upper-right corner.
3. Once you're signed up, navigate to the Home tab, and copy your access token on the right side.

4. From within your map view in Tableau, navigate to Map → Background Maps → and click Map Services.

5. From the new dialog box, click Add and select Mapbox Maps.

6. This is where you give your custom map a name, paste your access token, and choose one of the styles:

For my example, I chose the high contrast Mapbox style, but there are 13 additional styles to choose from! After clicking OK and closing the dialog box, I am left with a nice-looking Tableau symbol map with an integrated Mapbox style:

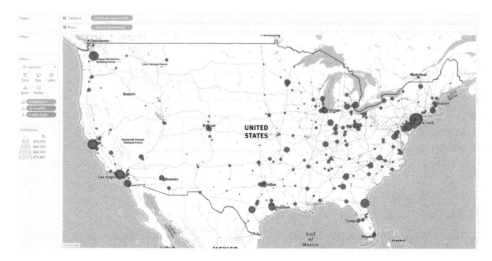

CHAPTER 31

How to Make a Filled Map

In the previous chapter, I shared how to create symbol maps in Tableau with custom Mapbox maps, and how mapping in Tableau leverages schemas that you are familiar with to help you rapidly decode latitude and longitude pairs. Maps in Tableau can be thought of as scatter plots, with a background image of a map to help you orient yourself almost instantly to the geographic territories being displayed.

Filled maps in Tableau are similar to symbol maps, but they include many more data points. While a symbol map draws a symbol at the intersection of each latitude and longitude pair, filled maps draw a polygon around the entire border. Here's one example of a filled map colored by region in Tableau:

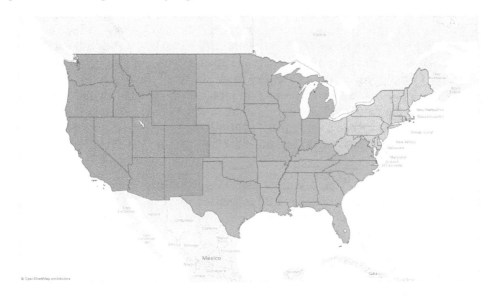

How to Make Filled Maps in Tableau

Filled maps are one of the easier chart types to create in Tableau using Show Me. Just click a geographic dimension (identified by a globe icon) from the Dimensions area of the Data pane and choose "maps" under Show Me. That being said, in the spirit of learning, we will build a filled map from scratch. To create a filled map manually, I will first double-click the geographic dimension for State in the Sample – Superstore dataset:

By default, Tableau generates a symbol map, placing a circle at the intersection of Longitude and Latitude for each state. In keeping with the "looking under the hood" theme of not relying on Show Me, take a look at the location of each dimension and measure. First, Longitude is on the Columns Shelf, which can also be thought of as the x-axis. Conversely, Latitude is on the Rows Shelf, or the y-axis. On the Marks Shelf, we can see that State is the most granular level of detail in the view. Even without seeing the map in the view, we should be able to guess what Tableau will display just by seeing the geographic fields on the Columns Shelf and Rows Shelf, the level of detail on the Marks Shelf, and the mark type of Automatic (which is Circle by default).

In order to change this from a symbol map to a filled map, change the mark type from Automatic to Map. By selecting this special mark type in Tableau, you will see that the single circles on each state have been converted to nice, smooth polygons that trace the entire border of each state.

From here, you can encode the filled map by color by placing a field on the Color Marks Card. Perhaps you want to color the territories by a measure such as Sales or Profit. You can also color the marks by a dimension, as is the case in this example, where the states are colored by the Region dimension. The map view ends up looking like this:

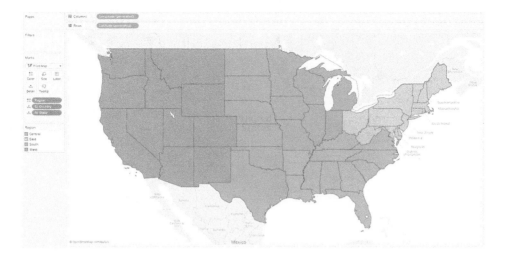

CHAPTER 32

How to Make a Dual-Axis Map

In the previous two chapters, you've read how to make a symbol map with Mapbox maps and how to make a filled map in Tableau. This chapter provides a step-by-step tutorial on how to combine the two into a single, dual-axis map. The final view in this example will display sales by city as a symbol map and US States colored by region as a filled map:

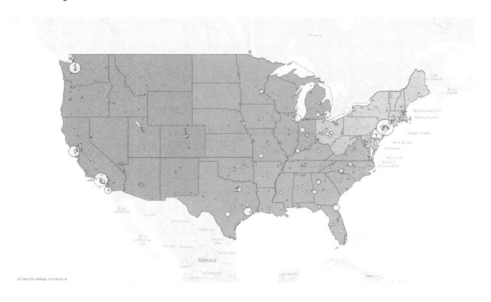

This type of map is useful any time you want to combine two maps into one to help provide additional context that would not be available when showing only one map or the other. One of the best real-life use cases I have seen for a dual-axis map in

Tableau was when an analytics partner wanted to see how the sales of their product by territory compared to the brick and mortar locations of a competitor.

To create a dual-axis map in Tableau, start by creating one of the two maps that you want to combine. I will start this example by creating a symbol map for sales by city:

Once the first map is created, you can create a duplicate of that map in one of two ways:

- While holding the Control key, left-click and drag the Longitude field on the Columns Shelf or the Latitude field on the Rows Shelf right next to itself. This is a shortcut for duplicating fields that works with any blue or green pill in Tableau.

- Drag Longitude from the Measures area of the Data pane to the second position on the Columns Shelf, or drag Latitude from the Measures area of the Data pane to the second position on the Rows Shelf.

Whichever method you select, the key is that by placing a second pill on the Columns or Rows Shelf, a second Marks Shelf for the geographic field is generated. Now that there are two separate Marks Shelves, one for each map, the maps can be edited independently. That means a symbol map can exist on the first Marks Shelf, and the second Marks Shelf can be changed to a filled map. In this example, I will leave the first map as is, but change the second map to be a filled map by region. To format the map for my example, follow these steps:

- Navigate to the second Marks Shelf by clicking it or clicking the pill associated with it.

- Remove the Sales measure.

- Remove the City dimension.
- Add the Region dimension from the Dimensions area of the Data pane to the Color Marks Card.

I've now got two distinct maps in my view:

To combine the maps, click the second geographic measure on the Rows or Columns Shelf (depending on whether you duplicated Longitude or Latitude) and click Dual-Axis. If you want to change the float order of the maps, drag the second geographic measure on the Rows or Columns Shelf to the first position. My final map looks like this:

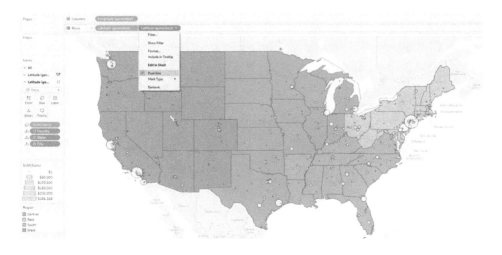

CHAPTER 33

How to Map a Sequential Path

As with most features in Tableau, maps are flexible enough to meet many different analysis needs. One of the most popular uses of maps in Tableau that I have seen involves evaluating traffic through a certain travel hub, such as an airport or train station. These powerful visualizations are created using hub and spoke paths, with the airport or train station acting as the hub, and the paths to the destinations acting as the spokes. See the Tableau Path Mapping article on Knowledge Base (*http://tabsoft.co/2GAWjMk*) if you are interested in creating this type of map.

This is a great application of path maps in Tableau, but I had a need to display multiple destinations in sequential order instead of from a single origin to multiple destinations. My wife and I make it a priority to travel as much as we can, and I wanted to create a visualization to document our travels between stops. This tutorial walks you through how to create sequential paths on a map in Tableau.

How to Map Paths in Tableau

Before we get started, let's take a look at the visualization that inspired this chapter:

Notice that within each trip, a path is displayed not only from our hometown of Kansas City to each destination, but from each stop in between. Here are the steps required to get this effect:

1. Prepare your data.

   Create your dataset so that each stop has a latitude, longitude, and path order. By looking up the latitude and longitude sets, you will have more flexibility when you create maps than you would if you use the automatically generated coordinates that Tableau applies to geographic fields. The path order is what tells Tableau how to connect the dots. Here's how my underlying data looks for one of our trips ("Stop" = Path Order):

Trip Name	Stop	Latitude	Longitude	City	Country
A. DeVos SBM Reunion in Orlando - October 2011	1	39.0997	-94.5783	Kansas City	United States
A. DeVos SBM Reunion in Orlando - October 2011	2	28.538	-81.379	Orlando	United States
A. DeVos SBM Reunion in Orlando - October 2011	3	29.8947	-81.3144	St. Augustine	United States
A. DeVos SBM Reunion in Orlando - October 2011	4	30.3369	-81.6614	Jacksonville	United States
A. DeVos SBM Reunion in Orlando - October 2011	5	28.538	-81.379	Orlando	United States
A. DeVos SBM Reunion in Orlando - October 2011	6	39.0997	-94.5783	Kansas City	United States

When you open this data for the first time in Tableau, your Stop field will be classified as a measure because it is quantitative. Make sure you change this field to a dimension by either dragging and dropping it from the Measures area of the Data pane to the Dimensions area of the Data pane, or by right-clicking the measure and choosing Convert to Dimension.

2. Start your map.

Using the dataset from step 1, begin your map in Tableau by placing your Longitude field on the Columns Shelf and your Latitude field on the Rows Shelf. It is important in this step to use the coordinates that you added to your dataset instead of the generated latitude and longitude in Tableau. You can always tell the difference because generated fields in Tableau are italicized.

3. Change the map type.

At this point, you should see a map with a single point. That single point represents the average for all of the coordinates in your data. Change the mark type from Automatic, which is set to circles by default, to Line. This change will reveal a new Marks Card called Path. The final step is to add the Stop (or path order) dimension to the Path Marks Card. This should connect the dots in the proper order, creating a sequential path.

Using the sample dataset from before, your final product should look like this:

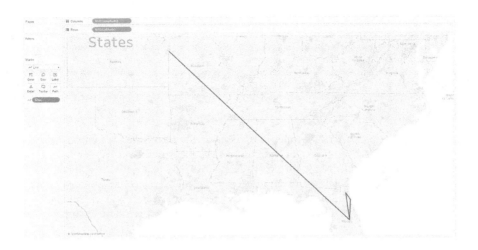

Remember, many Tableau Public authors allow you to download their workbooks by clicking in the lower-right corner of an embedded Tableau Public viz. This is a great way to reverse engineer techniques that you want to incorporate into your own work.

CHAPTER 34

How to Map Anything in Tableau

The out-of-the-box Tableau symbol and filled maps are some of the most powerful visualization types available in the software. As illustrated in Chapter 98, maps provide a means of decoding hundreds of latitude/longitude pairs almost instantly—all with a single image. Not only that, Tableau does a lot of the heavy lifting for us by providing the geographic coordinates of locations all over the world—this way we get to enjoy making maps instead of looking up longitudes and latitudes. Maps became even better in Tableau 9 with lasso and radial selections.

But wait—there's more! You can create custom maps in Tableau for just about anything. This tutorial will walk you through how to map *any* background image in Tableau.

Maps in Tableau can be thought of as scatter plots with a background image. Tableau will plot a point at each combination of the latitude on the y-axis and longitude on the x-axis. To help illustrate the scatter plot concept, take a look at the following two images. First, the latitude and longitude plotted with no background image:

And here, the same data points plotted with a background image of the United States:

Due to the way maps function in Tableau, as long as you know the coordinates of a point on the vertical y-axis and horizontal x-axis, you can map anything you would like! This provides some unique possibilities. So let's build one of these. For this tutorial, I will use this image of a baseball diamond:

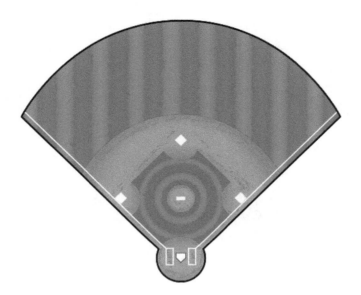

Building Custom Background Maps in Tableau

Let's imagine that we want to visualize different baseball statistics by player position. To create this visualization, we first need to plot the nine positions on the field.

1. Locate image and image dimensions.

   First we will need an image. If you want to follow along, download an image of a baseball diamond. For best results, pre-size the image in the desired dimensions and take note of the height and width of the image in pixels. The baseball diamond image just shown is 500 pixels wide by 500 pixels high.

2. Create dataset with fields for x and y coordinates.

   The next step is to create a dataset that has at least three fields:

   a. Each point you want to plot (in our case it's player position)

   b. x position

   c. y position.

   For the first row, just put an arbitrary name in the cell for the point you want to plot, such as Lookup. The x value will be the width of the image, and the y value will be the height of the image. At this point, my dataset looks like this (the player position coordinates still need to be looked up):

	A	B	C
1	Position	X	Y
2	Lookup	500	500
3	Pitcher		
4	Catcher		
5	First Base		
6	Second Base		
7	Shortstop		
8	Third Base		
9	Left Field		
10	Center Field		
11	Right Field		

3. Add the background image.

   Start a new workbook in Tableau and connect to the data from step 2. Navigate to Map → Background Images, and click the data source. This will open a new dialog box where you can choose Add Image in the lower-left corner. This is where you can choose which image will act as the background. If you're following along with the baseball example, navigate to the image that you downloaded earlier.

   All that is left in this step is to put the maximum value for the x and y coordinates. If our image is 500 px wide by 500 px high, we would make the following entries:

   - X Position: 0 Left, 500 Right
   - Y Position: 0 Bottom, 500 Top

   Also be sure to change the Y Field from X to Y. At this point, your screen should look like this:

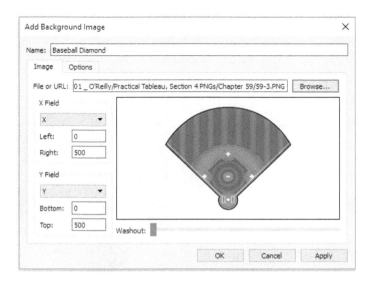

Click OK to apply your changes.

4. Look up x and y position for each coordinate.

   Start your new custom map by placing the x measure on Columns Shelf and the y measure on the Rows Shelf. Ensure both axes are fixed at the maximum X and Y values; which are 500 for both in our case. If you need to change an axis, simply right click the axis, choose Edit Axis, and fix the range at 0 to 500.

   In order to look up the x and y coordinates for each position player (or whatever you are plotting), right-click the view, hover over Annotate, and click Point. If the X and Y measures are the only fields on your view, the annotation will show you the X and Y values by default. This is what we want, but you may want to make the font larger so that it's easier to read.

   Now drag the end point of the annotation to each location you want to plot, and see how the X and Y values change. For best results, format the annotation so the line end is a circle; this way you can precisely drag the circle to the exact location you want plotted. Here is one example showing the coordinates for the Catcher:

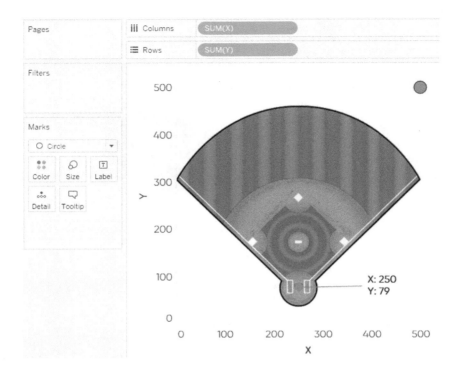

Drag the annotation to each point you want to plot, and record the coordinates in your dataset. Note that you don't need to record the decimals. Here is a look at my data with the *x* and *y* coordinates for each player position:

	A	B	C
1	Position	X	Y
2	Lookup	500	500
3	Pitcher	249	173
4	Catcher	250	79
5	First Base	344	173
6	Second Base	250	268
7	Shortstop	180	256
8	Third Base	155	173
9	Left Field	113	344
10	Center Field	250	400
11	Right Field	380	344

5. Refresh your map.

   After all coordinates have been recorded in your dataset, save your data and refresh the data source in Tableau.

   Drag the field you are plotting, such as position in the baseball example, to the Detail Marks Card. You should now see a circle at each position, like this:

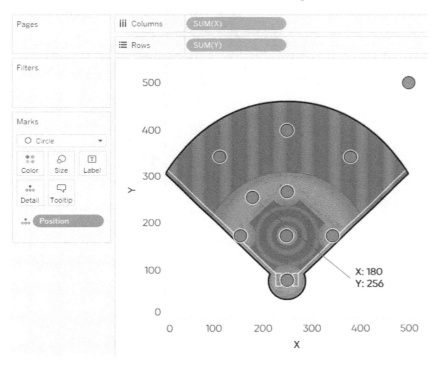

6. Finalize your map and/or add metrics.

   There are just a few items you can do to finalize your custom Tableau map:

   - Remove the annotation by right-clicking it and selecting Remove.
   - Hide the axes by right-clicking each one and deselecting Show Header.
   - Format your marks; my favorite is a filled circle with a custom color and white border.
   - Filter out the Lookup *x* and *y* coordinates. You will notice a mark in the upper-right corner of your new custom map. You can filter this out by either right-clicking it and choosing Exclude, or for better longterm results, remove this row from your underlying data and refresh your view.

- Optional: You can now add measures to your underlying data for each position to visualize different metrics on your customized view (i.e., size the circles by fielding %).

The final custom Tableau map will look like this:

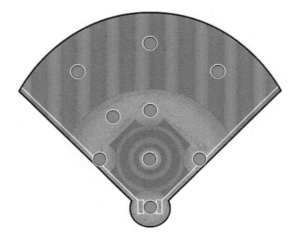

CHAPTER 35

How to Make Custom Polygon Maps

In the last two tutorials about mapping, we have discussed path maps (in Chapter 33) and custom symbol maps (in Chapter 34). There is a third type of map in Tableau called a polygon map that allows you to map custom shapes. These types of visualizations are what we're making anytime we're making a filled map. Imagine a map of sales by US state where each state is colored by their respective sales volumes, something we've done before. With these filled maps, Tableau is essentially looking up the latitude and longitude coordinates all the way around the border of each state, and plotting a custom polygon for each territory. With custom polygons, we're not limited to a prepared set of polygons like state borders—we can define shapes for anything we can imagine from custom geographic dimensions, to your favorite theme park, to your local dog park, to grocery store shelves, or anything else!

This tutorial will use one of my most asked-about visualizations, The Cost of Attending the Baseball Championship Series (*http://tabsoft.co/2FWpknH*), to illustrate how you can create custom polygon maps with any shapes—including stadiums!

First, let's take a look at the screenshot of the original viz:

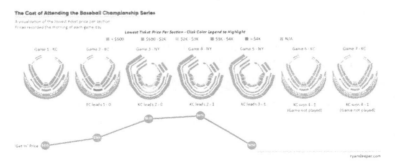

Polygon maps in Tableau are created by looking up the coordinates of the shape you want to draw, and then connecting the dots by drawing a path between them. I encourage you to read the first two chapters in this series mentioned in the opening paragraph if you are not familiar with these concepts. The main difference between a polygon map and a path map is that you "close the loop" around the dots by choosing a polygon mark type instead of a line mark type. Here are the steps for making custom polygon maps in Tableau:

1. Find an image of what you want to draw in Tableau. Being a visualization about the 2015 Baseball Championship Series, I used Kauffman Stadium in Kansas City and Citi Field in New York.

2. Follow the steps in Chapter 34 to set up your map in Tableau and record the coordinates for your shapes.

3. Similar to mapping a sequential path (see Chapter 33), each combination of coordinates should be given a *point order*. This is a field in your underlying data that tells Tableau what order the dots are connected. At this point, my underlying data for one section of Kauffman Stadium looks like this:

	A	B	C	D	E
1	Stadium	Zone	Point Order	X	Y
2	Blank	None		1000	1000
3	Kauffman Stadium	State Farm Neighborhood	1	268	720
4	Kauffman Stadium	State Farm Neighborhood	2	273	731
5	Kauffman Stadium	State Farm Neighborhood	3	317	776
6	Kauffman Stadium	State Farm Neighborhood	4	324	767
7	Kauffman Stadium	State Farm Neighborhood	5	289	731
8	Kauffman Stadium	State Farm Neighborhood	6	277	715

4. Once you have the x and y coordinates for each point of each shape you want to plot, we are ready to build the polygon map in Tableau. To start, put your x measure on the Columns Shelf and y measure on the Rows Shelf; both with an aggregation of AVG.

5. Change the mark type from Automatic to Polygon, and place your Point Order dimension on the Path Marks Card.

6. Place the Section dimension (and/or the dimension with the most granular level of detail) on the Detail Marks Card. Note that my maps are actually plotted by Zone and Zone Section (which was required when the same zone name existed in two places in the stadium) so I had to add both of these to the Detail Marks Card. If your granularity isn't reflected on both sides of your polygon, you would just

place the most granular dimension on the Detail Marks Card. At this point, my map looks like this:

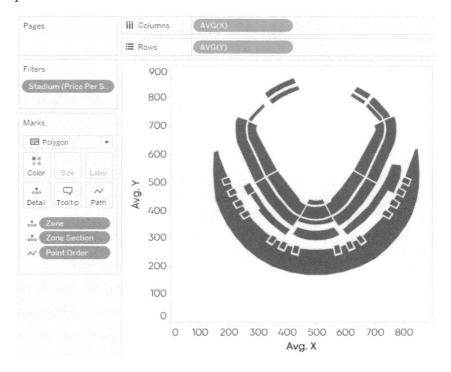

7. This can now be made into a small multiples view by *slicing* the map coordinate measures by a dimension. In my case, I was looking at the maps for each game of the series, so I put "Game" on the Columns Shelf to create a column for each game with a stadium in each cell.

From here, you can hide the axes and encode each section by putting a measure on the Color Marks Card. Here's what my final product looks like under the hood:

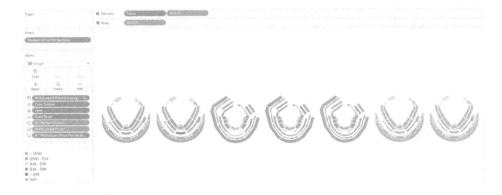

I admit that this map creation process requires painstaking attention to detail, but this step only has to be done once. The map coordinates can then be used over and over in future analyses and the results are great!

The approach provided in this chapter requires no additional software or resources (outside of Excel and some elbow grease). I would be remiss if I did not mention that there are other paid programs including Adobe Illustrator and Alteryx that can help make this process more efficient.

CHAPTER 36

How to Make a Gantt Chart

Gantt charts are traditionally used for visualizing project schedules. They are effective for illustrating task durations and dependencies in context of the larger business operation. As with several visualizations that can be built with Tableau, the fact that "Gantt Bar" is a mark type option unlocks some flexibility that allows you to use this chart type in many other ways. To start demonstrating the usefulness of the Gantt Bar mark type, we will build a Gantt chart with a traditional application of illustrating project schedules. The final product will look like this:

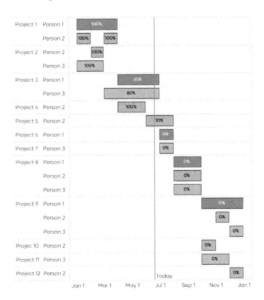

This is one of the few examples that cannot be illustrated using the Sample – Superstore data source, so I will be using the following dataset:

	A	B	C	D	E
1	Person	Project	Start Date	End Date	Percent Complete
2	Person 1	Project 1	1/1/2018	3/31/2018	1
3	Person 2	Project 1	1/1/2018	1/31/2018	1
4	Person 3	Project 2	1/1/2018	2/28/2018	1
5	Person 2	Project 2	2/1/2018	2/28/2018	1
6	Person 2	Project 1	3/1/2018	3/31/2018	1
7	Person 3	Project 3	3/1/2018	6/30/2018	0.8
8	Person 1	Project 3	4/1/2018	6/30/2018	0.65
9	Person 2	Project 4	4/1/2018	5/31/2018	1
10	Person 2	Project 5	6/1/2018	7/31/2018	0.1
11	Person 1	Project 6	7/1/2018	7/31/2018	0
12	Person 3	Project 7	7/1/2018	7/31/2018	0
13	Person 1	Project 8	8/1/2018	9/30/2018	0
14	Person 2	Project 8	8/1/2018	9/30/2018	0
15	Person 3	Project 8	8/1/2018	9/30/2018	0
16	Person 1	Project 9	10/1/2018	12/31/2018	0
17	Person 2	Project 10	10/1/2018	10/31/2018	0
18	Person 3	Project 11	10/1/2018	11/30/2018	0
19	Person 2	Project 9	11/1/2018	11/30/2018	0
20	Person 3	Project 9	12/1/2018	12/31/2018	0
21	Person 2	Project 12	12/1/2018	12/31/2018	0

For the purposes of this illustration, let's pretend that we are a manager with three employees and we are plotting out their schedules across twelve projects for the year. We have created the schedules in Excel, but want to leverage data visualization to (a) get a better sense of how our projects and employees line up, (b) track progress to completion for each project, and (c) provide a visual schedule for our employees to use. All three of these features can be provided through a Gantt chart.

Gantt charts are created with one date, one or more dimensions, and zero to two measures. The date provides the axis; the dimensions provide the breakdowns we want to visualize and/or the encoding of the Gantt bars; the measures create the length of the Gantt bars and/or their encoding.

For this Gantt chart, I would like to have a continuous axis running left to right, so I will put the Date dimension (being used as a continuous field) on the Columns Shelf. Looking at the final product shown before, there are rows for each combination of Project and Person, which tells us those breakdowns reside on the Rows Shelf. Gantt Bar is the default mark type in Tableau for this combination of dimensions and measures, so placing the fields on the view results in this foundation of a Gantt chart:

What Tableau has done is place a Gantt mark at the start date of each combination of Project and Person. To extend the Gantt bars to illustrate task duration, we need to size each mark by the number of days in each respective project/person combination. You may have a field for duration in the underlying dataset, but it can also be created in Tableau with a calculated field. In this case, duration simply equals [End Date] – [Start Date]:

Placing the duration on the Size Marks Card will extend the Gantt marks so that project/person combinations with longer durations will be longer bars and project/person combinations with shorter durations will be shorter bars:

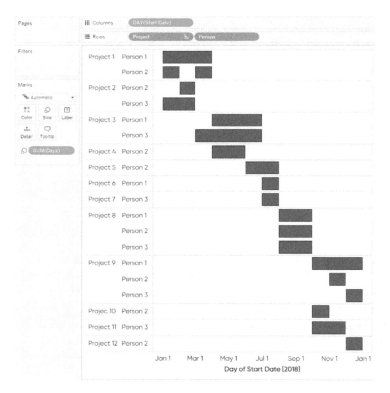

At this point, we have a usable Gantt chart, but there is still room to add a lot of value in Tableau through formatting, encoding, and reference lines. This step is flexible based on your own requirements, but as just one example, I have done the following:

- Colored the bars by employee by adding the Person dimension to the Color Marks Card. One of my goals was to provide a visual schedule to my team and by doing this, they can quickly view their own schedule and even highlight themselves in Tableau by clicking their name on the color legend.
- Added a reference line for "Today" (pretending it's June 20, 2018) to show each project in context of today's date.
- Added percent complete to the Label Marks Card to help determine if we are ahead or behind pace for each project. This number was hardcoded in my underlying dataset but in the real world it may also come from a time-tracking system. Another good use of color would have been to color the Gantt bars by progress to completion.

Here is my final Gantt chart after making these changes and cleaning up the formatting:

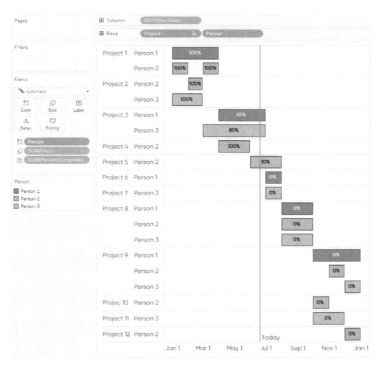

In the next chapter, I will illustrate one special use of the Gantt mark type: waterfall charts.

CHAPTER 37

How to Make a Waterfall Chart

This chapter shares how to make a waterfall chart in Tableau—a visualization that helps understand how positive and negative values of dimension members are contributing to a cumulative total. What makes waterfall charts different from a simple running total calculation is that they illustrate how each dimension member with a positive value adds to a running total and each dimension member with a negative value detracts from a running total. For this tutorial, we will build the following waterfall chart in Tableau, which visualizes how each Sub-Category in the Sample – Superstore dataset is contributing to total profit:

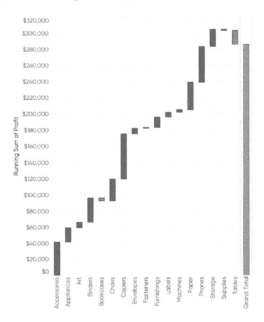

To start a waterfall chart in Tableau, create a vertical bar chart showing the measure, Profit, by the dimension, Sub-Category:

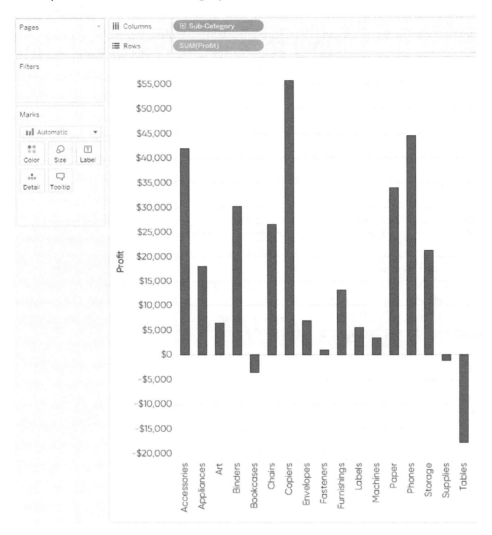

Next, add a table calculation to the Profit measure so that it calculates a "Running total" on Table (Across). For a refresher on table calculations, see Chapter 13. After adding the quick table calculation, the view looks like this:

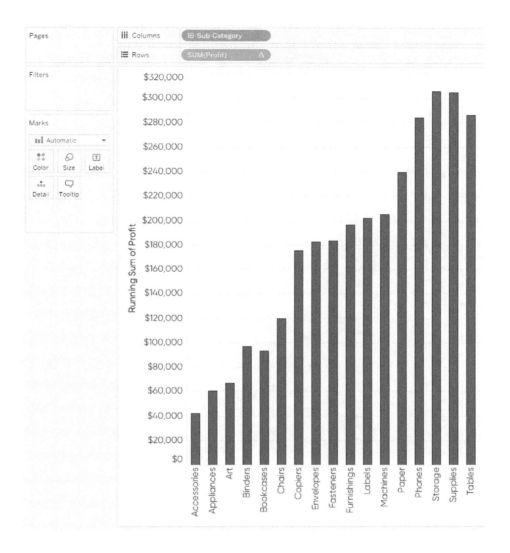

As mentioned in the introduction, while at this point we see how the running total has accumulated across our different sub-categories, it is not easy to determine the positive or negative contribution of each individual dimension member. To make this easier, we will convert this bar chart showing running total to a waterfall chart with a couple of additional steps.

First, change the mark type from Automatic, which is currently Bar, to the Gantt Bar mark type:

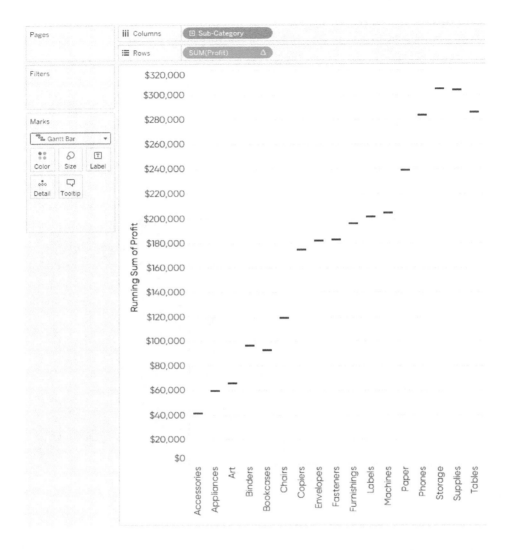

To get this view to look like the first image in this chapter, we need the tops or bottoms of each bar to line up at the same points on the y-axis. To accomplish this, we have to size the Gantt bars by something in order to extend them. While your first instinct may be to size the Gantt bars by the Profit measure or even the Profit measure on the view that includes a table calculation for running total, there is a trick involved with this step to get the desired effect. In order to get the Gantt bars for each dimension member to properly line up, you first have to create a new calculated field that takes the measure in the waterfall chart multiplied by negative one. This example is using the Profit measure, so I will create a new calculated field that equals –[Profit]:

Once this calculated field has been created, this is the measure that you drag to the Size Marks Card to create the waterfall effect:

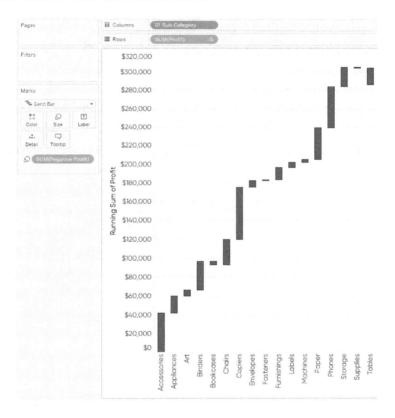

In Chapter 13, I mentioned that double-clicking a measure on the view gives you a kind of "x-ray vision" showing the underlying syntax of the measure. This technique can also be used to change a measure in the flow of your analysis. Another way to convert the Profit measure to negative is to drag SUM([Profit]) to the Size Marks Card, double-click the Profit pill once it is on the view, type a negative sign (-) at the beginning, and hit Enter.

At this point, we have an effective waterfall chart, but there are a few things I did to polish the final product as shown at the beginning of this chapter:

- Cleaned up the axis formatting.
- Colored the Gantt bars by Profit by dragging the Profit measure to the Color Marks Card; this created the blue and red color coding, which represents positive and negative values, respectively.
- Added a total to the far right side of the visualization by navigating to Analysis → Totals in the top navigation and choosing Show Row Grand Totals.

Lastly, you may choose to sort the dimension members by the sequence in which they were introduced or their values by ascending or descending order. As with many uses of Tableau, there is a great deal of inherent flexibility. These types of choices will depend on your analysis, business requirements, and business questions. Now that you know how waterfall charts are constructed in Tableau, experiment with the sort order of the dimension members to get the visualization that works best for you.

CHAPTER 38

How to Make Dual-Axis Slope Graphs

Slope graphs, or essentially line graphs between two points, are one of my favorite Tableau charts when my analysis requires a comparison between two data points. They work so well, in fact, that they are the one chart I will use to connect lines between discrete categorical variables. In almost every scenario, lines should only be used to connect points in time, but with slope graphs, I am OK drawing a line between "Thing 1" and "Thing 2," as well as "Time 1" and "Time 2." I like the following approach so much because you can easily view changes of individual dimension members (i.e., sub-categories) in context of each other, and the dual-axis mark provides extra real estate to share additional context in your analysis.

This chapter shares not only how to make slope graphs in Tableau, but how to enhance them by leveraging a second axis to provide additional context. By the end of the chapter, we will have re-created this dual-axis slope graph:

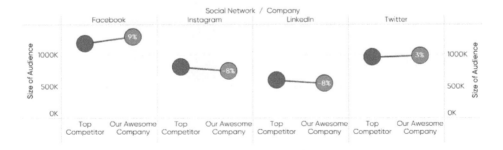

How to Make Slope Graphs in Tableau

First, let's knock out the traditional slope graphs using this data:

	A	B	C
1	Year	Category	Measure
2	2016	Category 1	1289632
3	2015	Category 1	1186461
4	2016	Category 2	989511
5	2015	Category 2	965035
6	2016	Category 3	551117
7	2015	Category 3	600718
8	2016	Category 4	748338
9	2015	Category 4	812562

1. Create a bar chart.

   Create a bar chart with your two-point time comparison on the Columns Shelf as a discrete dimension and your measure on the Rows Shelf:

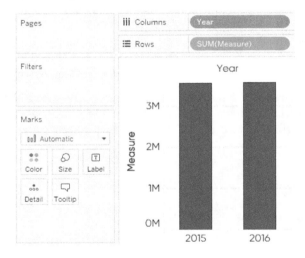

2. Add dimension to level of detail.

   Add the dimension you are wanting to compare to the Detail Marks Card. This will eventually create one line per categorical variable:

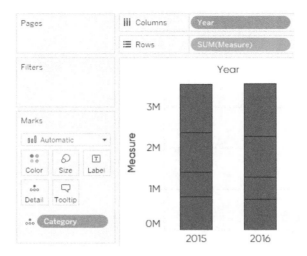

3. Change the mark type to Line.

   Change the mark type from Automatic (currently set to Bar) to Line to create slope graphs:

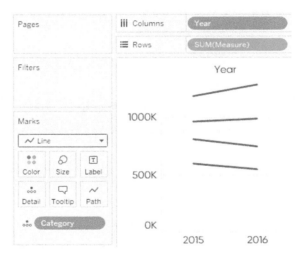

4. Format the lines.

   To finalize the view, add labels and markers to the line ends. To update the labels, place the fields you want on the view to the Label Marks Card, and edit the Label Marks Card to show labels on the line ends. The markers are added by editing the Color Marks Card:

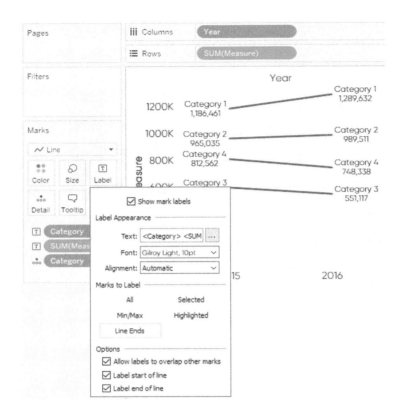

How to Make Dual-Axis Slope Graphs in Tableau

For the purposes of this exercise, the underlying data looks like this:

	A	B	C
1	Company	Social Network	Size of Audience
2	Our Awesome Company	Facebook	1289632
3	Top Competitor	Facebook	1186461
4	Our Awesome Company	Twitter	989511
5	Top Competitor	Twitter	965035
6	Our Awesome Company	LinkedIn	551117
7	Top Competitor	LinkedIn	600718
8	Our Awesome Company	Instagram	748338
9	Top Competitor	Instagram	812562

I'm using a Company A versus Company B scenario just to show a slightly different use case, but this same exact process is applicable if you are comparing two points in time.

Disclaimer before I let the genie out of the bottle: in the Thing 1 versus Thing 2 scenario I'm about to share, I only think this works well if you are comparing exactly two things. Once you get beyond two things, the visualization officially becomes a line graph, and should never be used to connect dimensions that are not elements of time. The best practice with more than two things is a simple bar chart.

1. Create a bar chart.

   As already mentioned, the first step to creating slope graphs is to get the columns set up with whatever dimensions we are comparing. Sometimes with traditional slope graphs, there can be overlapping points and labels if data points are too close together. In that case, and when comparing two things (versus times), I prefer to place the more granular dimension (in our case, social network) on the Columns Shelf first, followed by the dimension that includes "Thing 1" and "Thing 2" or "Time 1" and "Time 2." The measure we are analyzing goes on the Rows Shelf, to end up with a bar chart view like this:

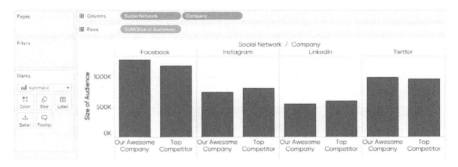

   Again, this chart type is best practice when we are comparing two discrete categorical variables such as Company A versus Company B, so stop here if you are feeling any discomfort with looking at this in a different way.

2. Change mark type to Line.

   From here, a bar chart is converted into a slope graph by simply changing the mark type on the view from Bar to Line:

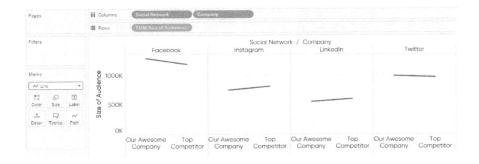

You can get a nice look from here by adding markers to the line ends:

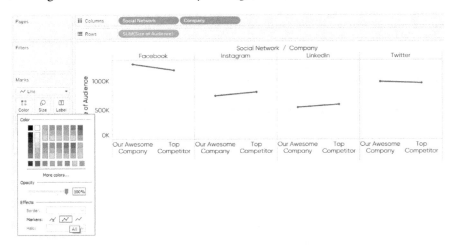

At this point, you already have slope graphs in Tableau. This is an awesome chart type. If you want an incredibly awesome chart type, keep reading.

3. Create a dual-axis combo chart.

   Create a dual-axis combo chart by dragging the measure you're interested in (in our case, Size of Audience) to the opposite axis, and change the mark type on the second Marks Shelf for SUM(Size of Audience) to Circle. If you are not familiar with building dual-axis combo charts, be sure to check out Chapter 21.

   For best results, also be sure to synchronize the second axis by right-clicking the right-axis and choosing Synchronize Axis. At this point, my chart looks like this:

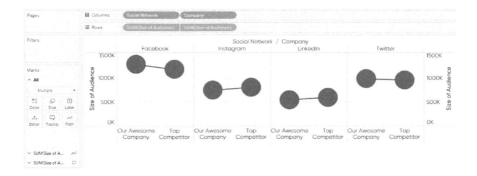

4. Customize the second view.

Now that we have two measures on the Rows Shelf, we have two Marks Shelves for those measures that we can edit independently of each other. This means we can keep the slope graph on one Marks Shelf, but change the size, colors, and context on the circles in the secondary Marks Shelf.

As just one example, I'll use the circles to display the delta between ourselves and our main competitor. I will also color both the slope graphs and circles to make our brand clear on the view. Here are the steps:

1. Change the sort order so the top competitor is listed first and Our Awesome Company is listed second. This is more intuitive when you are comparing things across a table. The sort order can be changed by clicking the Company dimension on the Columns Shelf.

2. Add the Size of Audience measure to the Label Marks Card.

3. Add a quick table calculation to the Size of Audience measure for Percent Difference.

4. Edit the table calculation to compute the percent difference along Pane (Across). This will execute the table calculation for each social network column.

5. Add the Company dimension to the Color Marks Card of both the Slope Graph and the Circles (which is actually a dot plot) Marks Shelves.

After some basic formatting, I end up with this:

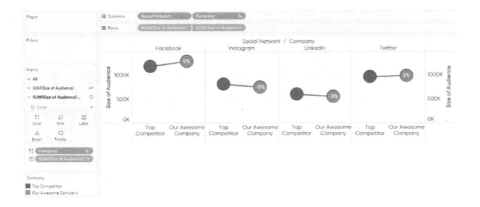

This is just one example, but you can use this approach with other mark types, to show different KPIs, and/or to color based on performance such as a stoplight index (discussed in Chapter 61). Slope graphs are an excellent choice for comparing two things—especially changes over two points in time—and they are made even stronger when additional context is added by leveraging a dual-axis in Tableau.

CHAPTER 39

How to Make Donut Charts

When used properly, donut charts can be an effective way to communicate comparisons in a unique way. When used improperly, they are the butt of jokes mentioned in the same vein as pie charts. In fact, donut charts are essentially pie charts with a circle in the middle, and in Chapter 93, I explain why you shouldn't use pie charts. The big reason charts like bar charts work better than pie charts is that the viewer is comparing the length of the bars; not comparing the area of the wedges of the pie—and our brains are much better at comparing length than area.

So what's the difference with donut charts?

One of my recommendations for practitioners that cannot quite let go of pie charts is to use five slices or fewer. Personally, I would not use more than two. When used for the specific purpose of showing a metric's progress to goal, with one "slice" being the current state of the KPI and one "slice" being the remainder to goal, I think a donut chart works well.

I admit, a bullet graph would be the most efficient way to communicate the progress to goal scenario. A bullet graph would be processed faster by end users than a donut chart and also take up less real estate on a dashboard. It also works better for showing progress above goal because a donut chart stops once you get to 100%. If you think a bullet graph may be a more appropriate choice for your data visualization, see Chapter 26.

That being said, I don't mind the extra real estate that a donut chart takes up because that space can be used to provide additional context in a visually appealing way. For example, you can place an icon that denotes what the donut chart applies to or a callout number that shows the percent your KPI has progressed to goal. Donut charts are an acceptable alternative chart type that can make your data visualization stand out. For more on making your work "remarkable," see Chapter 97.

How to Make Donut Charts in Tableau

For the purposes of this exercise, we will make a gauge showing how our sales are progressing toward goal.

1. The Sample – Superstore dataset contains a measure for Sales, but we will need to create one more field that calculates the sales goal minus the actual sales. The data you are working with may contain a measure for Sales Goal, but I am going to hardcode a goal of $8,000,000 into my calculated field: $8,000,000 – SUM([Sales]):

The reason we make this calculated field is so the two slices in our donut chart will always add up to the total goal, and actual sales will always by a correctly sized portion of the total goal.

2. You will now create a pie chart using two measures: Sales and the newly created Sales Goal – Actual Sales. Do this by first changing the mark type on your view to Pie. Now place Measure Names on the Color Marks Card and Measure Values on the Angle Marks Card. Finally, filter the view on Measure Names to only include Sales and Sales Goal – Actual Sales. At this point, your view should look like this:

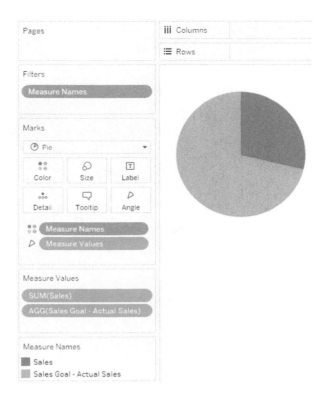

3. Format the donut chart (currently a pie) by increasing the size, adding a border, and most importantly, coloring the Sales measure to a color of your choice and the Sales Goal – Actual Sales measure white. This will eventually create the filling gauge effect we are going for:

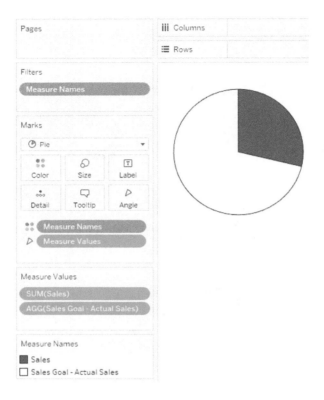

4. The final step in creating a true donut chart is to "poke a hole" in the chart we have created so far by adding a circle to the middle. I have two approaches for this final step:

Approach 1: Single Sheet

For most situations, this first approach will be the most elegant solution.

- Start by creating a calculated field called "Placeholder" that has this formula: MIN(0)

- Create a Dual-Axis Chart by placing this new calculated field on the Rows Shelf, then adding it again to the opposite axis. At this point, my view looks like this:

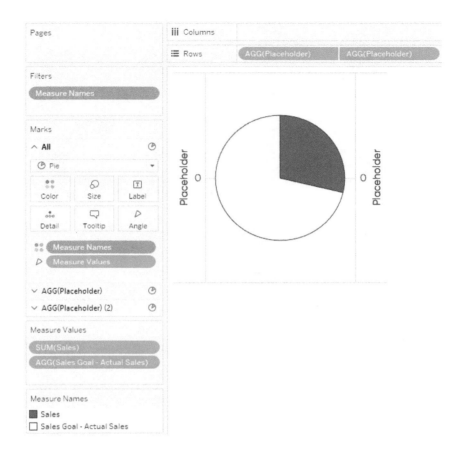

Notice that there are now different Marks Shelves for each of my Placeholder fields. That means that you can now edit the marks for each field independently of each other. On the Marks Shelf for the first placeholder, leave the settings as is with a mark type of Pie—this is our original chart and we don't want to change it. On the Marks Shelf for the second placeholder field, change the mark type to Circle, which will become the hole in the donut chart. Reduce the size and change the color of the circle as desired. You can also modify the marks for the second placeholder further by adding a label to provide additional information. At this point, my view looks like this:

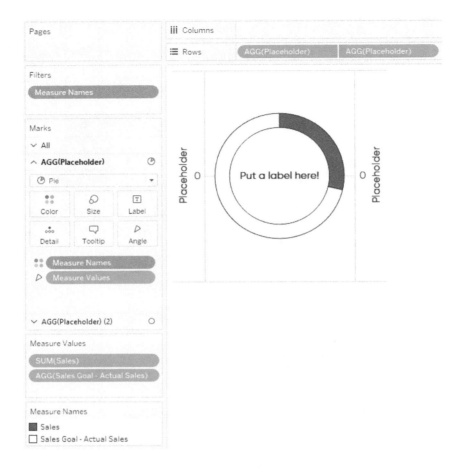

Finally, clean up the view by doing some simple formatting such as hiding zero lines and headers. You now have a donut chart that is comparing Sales to Sales Goal. You can take this a step further by adding a dimension to the Columns Shelf to create a small multiples view that compares performance across several different dimension members (i.e., Region, Segment, etc.):

Approach 2: Floating Sheets

If your visualization requires icons or additional graphic design, as is the case in my Your Salary vs. a MLB Player's Salary viz (*http://tabsoft.co/2tOGhve*), I recommend you float a *.png* image over the chart. It is very important that you use a *.png* file so that your corners are transparent and you will be able to see the underlying chart:

Sales Progress to Goal

Finally, I mentioned earlier that I don't mind donut charts because the real estate available in the inner circle can be used to communicate additional context either through icons or text.

If you're using approach 1, you can create a calculated field that determines the percentage of sales goal obtained, and then add this calculated field to the label of the placeholder 2 Marks Shelf.

If you're using approach 2, you can enhance the *.png* image being used with your own icons or other design elements. If you would like to use a calculated field to show progress to goal, you can create a sheet with that metric and float it over the chart and *.png* image.

In either approach, your final product will end up looking like this:

Sales Progress to Goal

CHAPTER 40

How to Make Funnel Charts

The Odds of Going Pro In Sports viz (*http://tabsoft.co/2tQxXeF*) has generated more questions around how it was created than any other viz I have put together during my career with Tableau. With its one dominant funnel chart and icon-based navigation, the viz tells the story about the share of high school athletes progressing to the college and pro levels across several sports for each gender.

The most common question I receive: *That was made in Tableau?* I would be lying if I said that question doesn't make me want to stand up a little taller, but the secret is, the viz was one of the easiest dashboards I have ever put together. In fact, I put it together in a couple of hours on a Sunday afternoon. Funnel charts are one of the simplest chart types you can create, but they have proved to be incredibly effective in a corporate setting—think conversion rates and customer flows. This chapter will walk you through multiple approaches to creating funnel charts.

First, let's take a look at the full version of *What are the odds of going pro in sports?*

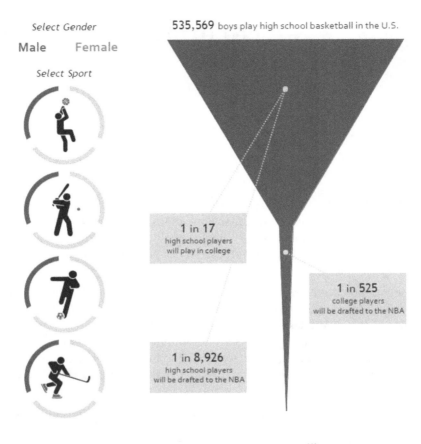

WHAT ARE THE ODDS OF GOING PRO IN SPORTS?
An analysis of high school, college, and pro sports in the United States by gender.

Select Gender

Male   Female

Select Sport

535,569 boys play high school basketball in the U.S.

1 in 17
high school players
will play in college

1 in 525
college players
will be drafted to the NBA

1 in 8,926
high school players
will be drafted to the NBA

Data from | www.scholarshipstats.com   Data visualization by | ℞yan**Sleeper**

How to Make Funnel Charts in Tableau

Option 1: The Step Dimension

Going into this project, I knew that I wanted the main view to be a funnel chart. For this reason, I was able to plan ahead and put the data in an optimal format for Tableau. Here is a sample of the underlying data:

▲	A	B	C
1	Gender	Step	Players
2	Female 1	1	371393
3	Female 2	2	35490
4	Female 3	3	36
5	Male 1	1	412351
6	Male 2	2	36741
7	Male 3	3	77

Note that there is a dimension called Step, which is just an arbitrary, intuitive name for each of the three levels of high school, college, and pro. The measure is then the corresponding number of players that reached each step. This is the easiest way to build a funnel chart. Here are the steps:

1. Create a horizontal bar chart by dragging your Step dimension onto the Rows Shelf and your Players measure to the Rows Shelf:

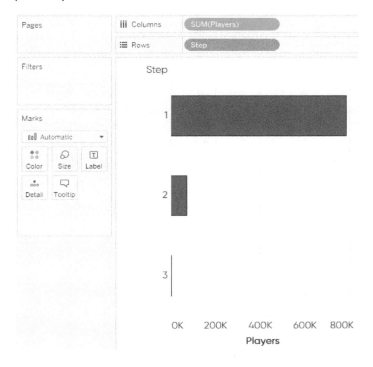

2. Here is where the magic happens. Simply change the mark type from Automatic (which is currently Bar) to Area. You are left with the right side of the funnel:

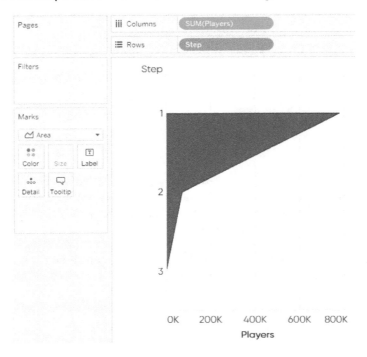

3. If your data is in a format outlined in the table just shown, there is a simple solution to mirroring the right side of the funnel onto the left side. To do this, you will create a calculated field by right-clicking the Players measure and selecting Create Calculated Field. Name your calculated field Negative Players and add a "-" in front of [Players]. Your entire formula will look like this:

4. The final step in creating a symmetrical funnel chart is to drag and drop your new Negative Players measure in front of the Players measure on the Columns Shelf:

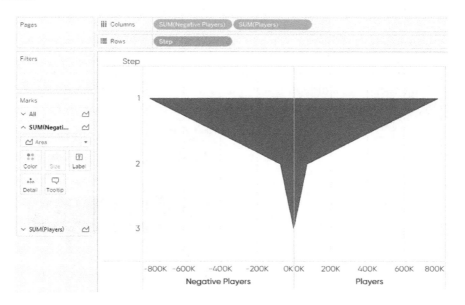

From here, your funnel chart can be used like any other chart in Tableau. Encode it by color (in my case, it's colored by gender), add filters, and add tooltips/labels/annotations to make the data in the chart clear to the end user.

Option 2: Separate Measures

It is likely that your corporate data is not in the layout of the preceding table by default, and you may not be in a position to easily change this on your own. This solution is not as flexible or optimal for Tableau, but it is functional. Let's assume that instead of the layout in the table from before, your data looks more like this, with each Players measure broken out by level, causing your layout to be more horizontal instead of vertical:

	A	B	C	D
1	Gender	Step 1 Players	Step 2 Players	Step 3 Players
2	Female	371393	35490	36
3	Male	412351	36741	77

In this case, because you no longer have a dimension of Step, the approach is slightly different:

1. To create the right side of the funnel, you will need to add the measures to the view individually. The easiest way to do this is to double-click each of your three measures (Step 1 Players, Step 2 Players, and Step 3 Players) to add them to the view. Double-clicking each measure will create a small multiples chart, so you will have to use the Show Me button to change the chart type to a bar chart. While the setup is different, you should now see the beginnings of the right side of your funnel, just like in Step 1 from the first approach:

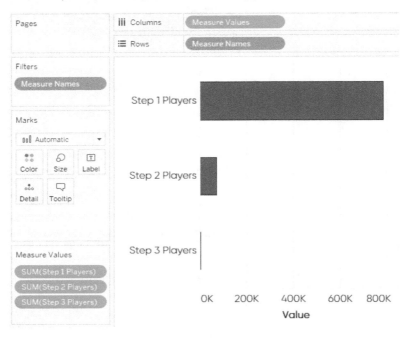

2. Follow step 2 from the first approach, changing your mark type from Automatic to Area.

3. This is where the second approach gets tricky. The first thing you need to do is create a negative version of each of your three measures, much like creating a negative version of the Players measure in step 3 from the first approach. Once you have three new calculated fields, one negative version for each of your three measures (i.e., Negative Step 1 Players, Negative Step 2 Players, and Negative Step 3 Players), open a new worksheet and follow steps 1 and 2—this time using your newly created negative versions of each measure. You should end up with the left side of your funnel:

4. The final step to this approach is joining the left and right side of your funnel. This can be accomplished by floating each sheet on a dashboard and lining them up:

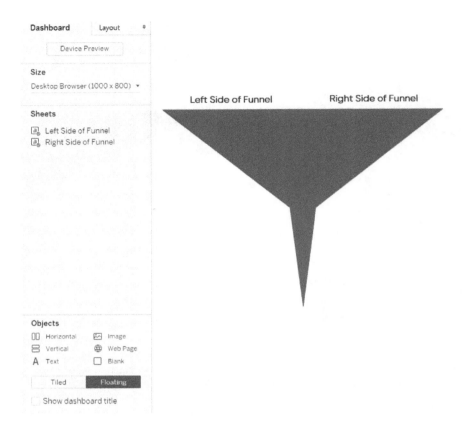

Admittedly, this second approach requires some hackish creativity, but it works with most data out of box without any reformatting.

So there you have it! Funnel charts in four steps, regardless of the layout of your funnel data.

CHAPTER 41

Introducing Pace Charts in Tableau

Pace charts are an alternative bullet graph (*http://bit.ly/2tW7wEt*) design that normalize progress to goal visualizations across KPIs, even if the KPIs have different data formats, scales, and/or seasonal trends. They are useful for providing an "apples to apples" pace to goal comparison in businesses that have KPIs that span different categories such as revenue, social media followers, attendance, and so on.

With KPIs such as revenue, social media followers, and attendance, not only are the metrics in different formats, but they are often on very different scales and have varying seasonality. For example, you may gain social media followers throughout an entire year, but if you are an NFL team, your attendance won't start until August. Further, your growth on social media might be on a scale of thousands, while revenue may be on a scale of millions.

Pace charts normalize KPIs by comparing them all on an axis that ends at 100% (the goal). In addition to showing how much progress each KPI has made toward the goal, a linear or seasonal pace is displayed to illustrate whether progress to goal is on pace to reach goal. To enhance the illustration, the marks can be colored to show how current progress to goal for each respective KPI compares to its pace to goal.

To illustrate how to create a pace chart in Tableau, I will start by re-creating this pace chart showing a variety of KPIs that are on a linear pace (i.e., they should all be at the same progress to goal at this point in the year):

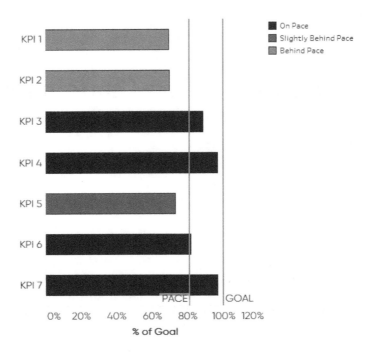

The underlying dataset used to create this pace chart looks like this:

	A	B	C
1	Measure	Current	Goal
2	KPI 1	26308469	37900000
3	KPI 2	12235114	17550000
4	KPI 3	7959	9000
5	KPI 4	28005548	29000000
6	KPI 5	6000000	8200000
7	KPI 6	7000000	8588000
8	KPI 7	3100000	3200000

Even though the KPIs are on very different scales, it is easy to compare them to determine which are on pace, slightly behind pace, or behind pace.

To affirm this point, here is the same data using a traditional bullet graph:

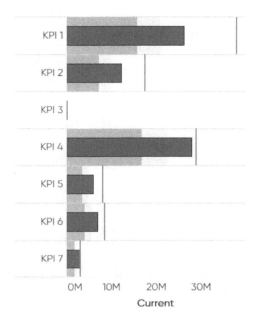

With this visualization, it is impossible to compare the progress to goal of KPI 3, which is on a much smaller scale than the other KPIs. It is also challenging to determine the progress to goal of KPI 7, because it is on the same scale as KPI 1, which has the largest goal and is extending the x-axis. While you could break up this graph into seven different parts to fix the scaling, there is a better way to normalize the data.

How to Create a Pace Chart with a Linear Pace in Tableau

To normalize the bars in a pace chart, create a calculated field that calculates the progress to goal. This is used to represent the bars instead of the current values. The formula for this calculation is SUM([Current Value])/SUM([Goal]):

After you have created the Progress to Goal calculated field, create a horizontal bar chart showing the progress to goal for each KPI:

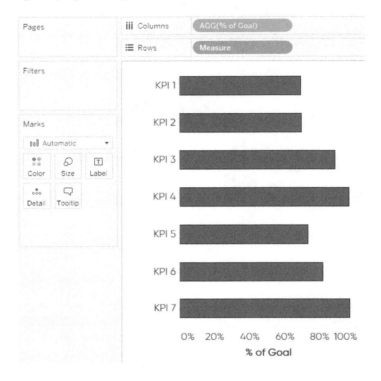

With a pace chart, the goal line is always normalized across every KPI at 100%. To add this reference to the visualization, simply add a reference line with a constant of 1 (which equals 100%):

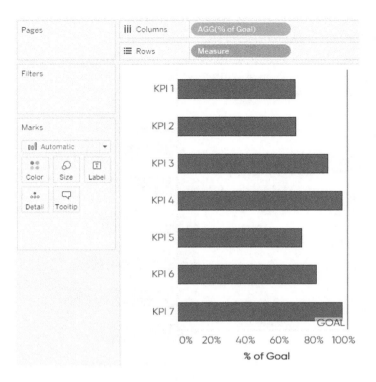

For this illustration, we will pretend that the pace to goal should be the same across all seven of our KPIs. When using a linear pace, a calculated field can be created to calculate how far to goal each KPI should be at the current point in the year. For example, if we are in week 42, the pace calculation would be:

    (1/52) * 42

This calculation is dividing the year into 52 equal parts (i.e., weeks), then multiplying that fraction by the number of weeks that have passed in the year:

In Tableau, you have the option to replace the 42 with a parameter that allows the end user to change the multiplier.

Once you have the Pace calculated field, add it to the Detail Marks Card so it can be used as a reference line. Then add a reference line that shows where the pace should be at this point in the year:

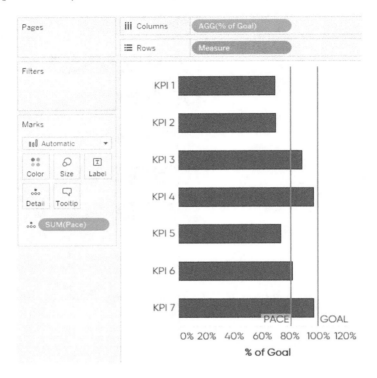

Lastly, to color the bars to illustrate whether each KPI is on pace, slightly behind pace, or behind pace, create a calculated field with the scoring logic. This will vary based on your own requirements, but as one example, I'll pretend that 100% or above is on pace, 90%–99.99% is slightly behind pace, and anything less than 90% is behind pace:

This pace score is then dragged to the Color Marks Card to color each bar by its progress to goal classification:

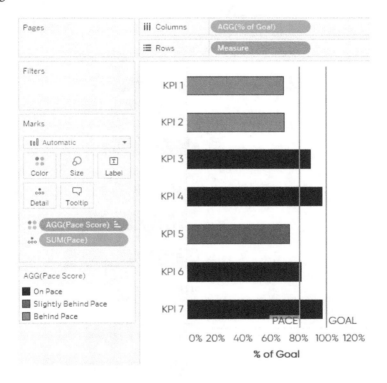

In this tutorial, we used a linear pace that was calculated by taking 1/52 of the year multiplied by the current week of the year. However, this pace can be replaced with a different metric such as the value for each KPI at this point last year, or a goal for each respective KPI at this point in the year. Here is one more example using a different expected pace for each respective KPI. In this example, I have the expected pace at this point in the year as an additional field in my underlying data:

	A	B	C	D
1	Measure	Current	Goal	Expected Pace
2	KPI 1	26308469	37900000	0.6
3	KPI 2	12235114	17550000	0.8
4	KPI 3	7959	9000	0.9
5	KPI 4	28005548	29000000	0.95
6	KPI 5	6000000	8200000	0.7
7	KPI 6	7000000	8588000	0.85
8	KPI 7	3100000	3200000	0.95

The seasonal pace chart using this data looks like this in Tableau:

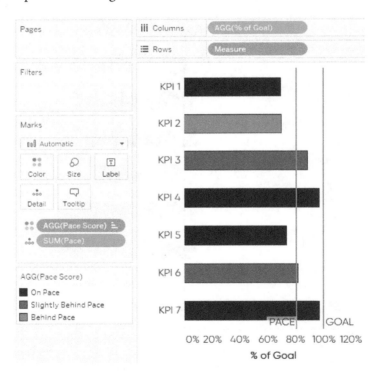

To create this version, I replaced the calculated linear pace reference line with a reference line for expected pace, which shows the expected pace for each respective KPI. I also replaced the linear pace calculation in the Pace Score calculated field with the Expected Pace measure from the underlying data:

Notice how this seasonal pace chart tells a different story regarding the progress to goal for each KPI than the pace chart with the linear pace. But in both cases, pace charts were used to normalize progress to goal calculations across KPIs to get a more effective visualization about the business.

CHAPTER 42

How to Make a Pareto Chart

A Pareto chart, named for Vilfredo Pareto (the 80-20 guy!), is a dual-axis combination chart used to highlight dimension members that are having the biggest impact to the measure in question. On the primary axis, bars are used to show the raw quantities for each dimension member, sorted in descending order. On the secondary axis, a line graph is used to show the cumulative total in percent format. While this chart type can serve a variety of purposes, it is part of the seven basic tools of quality control, and is traditionally used to identify the biggest contributors to a cumulative total and opportunities for improvement.

How to Make a Pareto Chart in Tableau

In sticking with a quality control scenario, this tutorial will use the Sample – Superstore dataset to look at which product sub-categories contribute the most returned items. The final chart will look like this:

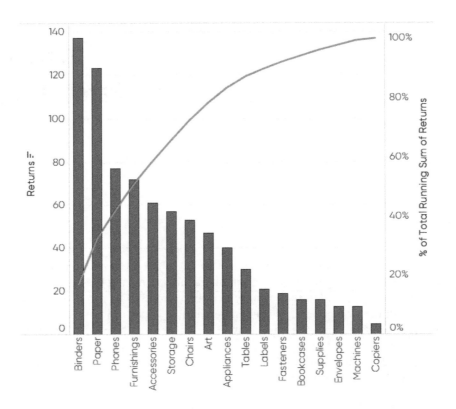

As with the rest of *Practical Tableau*, you can follow along using the Sample – Superstore data that comes with every download of Tableau. However, this tutorial required me to take two additional steps to prepare the data:

1. Left join the Returns table to the Orders table.

   To do this, right-click the Sample Superstore data connection and choose "Edit data source". A new interface will appear where you can drag the Returns table next to the Orders table and set up a left join on Order ID:

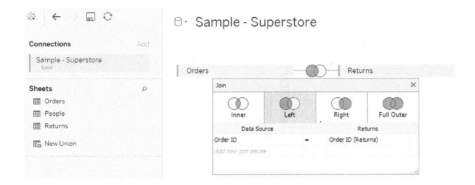

2. Create a calculated field to count the number of returns.

   The formula for this calculation is COUNT([Returned] = "Yes"):

We are now ready to build out the Pareto chart. First, create a bar chart that looks at the number of returns per product sub-category and sort it in descending order:

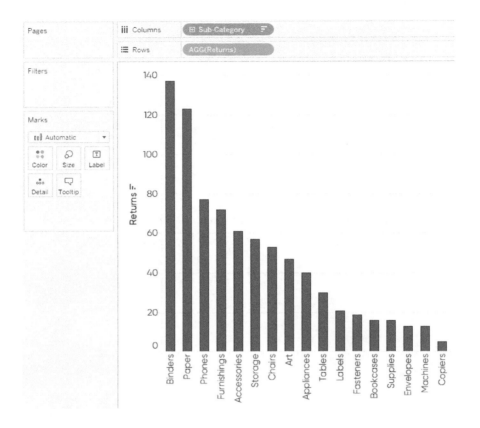

3. Next, create a dual-axis combination chart by dragging the Returns measure from the Measure area of the Data pane to the right axis, changing the mark type on the primary axis back to Bar, and changing the mark type for the secondary axis to Line. For a refresher on creating this type of chart, see Chapter 21. At this point, the visualization will look similar to this:

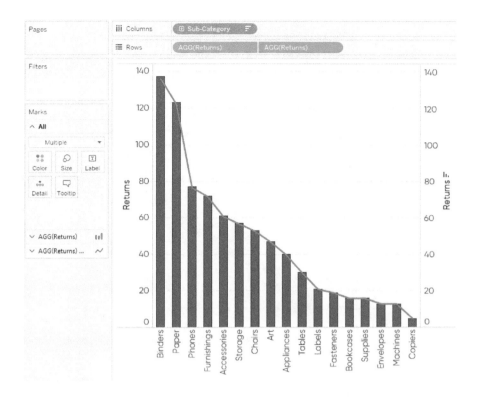

4. Now the step that makes this a Pareto chart. We will add a table calculation and a secondary table calculation to the second Returns pill to display the cumulative percent of returns across product sub-categories. To add the first table calculation, click the second Returns pill, hover over "Quick table calculation," and choose "Running total." With the table calculation for running total, you can add a second table calculation on the result. This is how we can calculate the raw running total number at each product sub-category, then add a secondary calculation to determine the cumulative percent of total. To add a secondary table calculation, click the second Returns pill again, choose "Edit table calculation," and check the box at the bottom of the interface that says Add Secondary Calculation. Changing the Secondary Calculation Type to Percent of Total will display the cumulative percent of total:

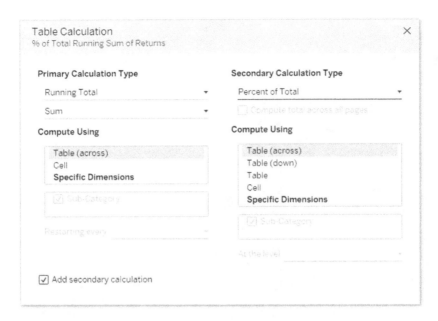

After changing the axis tick marks for a cleaner look, I am left with this Pareto chart:

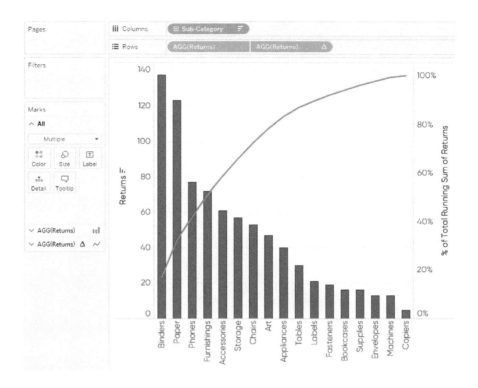

This chart can now be used for insights such as, "The business' three most returned product sub-categories are causing about 40% of the total returns." Pareto charts are an effective way to quickly highlight opportunities for improvement and provide a scale for how urgently a quality control problem should be treated.

CHAPTER 43

How to Make a Control Chart

Control charts, or Shewhart charts, were designed to evaluate whether production is in a state of statistical control. Along with Pareto charts, histograms, and scatter plots, they are one of the seven basic tools for quality control. Basic control charts show a time-series analysis with reference lines that show the average performance along with an upper control limit, typically three standard deviations above the mean, and lower control limit, typically three standard deviations below the mean.

Control charts were originally called Shewhart charts, named for Walter Shewhart, who invented the visualization type while working on a way to improve the reliability of the telephony transmission systems at Bell Labs in the 1920s. Control charts were born in, and are still primarily used for, evaluating manufacturing processes. For example, a factory may use this type of analysis to predict production levels and have a statistical indicator for when corrective action needs to be taken.

How to Make Control Charts in Tableau

While designed for manufacturing, I find control charts to be useful for any measure in which historical data can be used to predict performance and provide visual cues for when a statistically significant change is occurring in the business. In that vein, and so we can all follow along using the same data, this tutorial will create a basic control chart that evaluates the Profit Ratio measure in the Sample - Superstore dataset.

To create a control chart, start by creating a continuous line graph that looks at Profit Ratio by week:

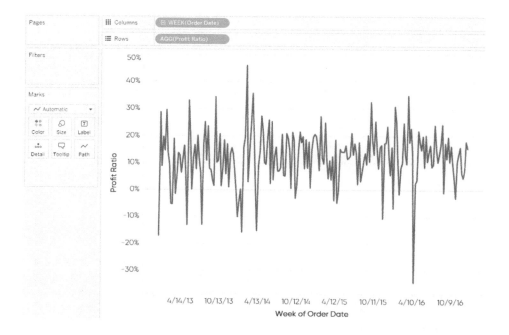

It may be concerning that we see several weeks with a negative profit ratio, but based on our historical data, is it a *statistically significant* cause for concern? The answer comes through control charts. Control charts start with a line that shows the mean performance for all of the data points. This is easily added in Tableau as a reference line. To add the reference line, right-click the axis for Profit Ratio, choose "Add reference line," and click OK. Here's how the view looks at this point after removing the label on the reference line and formatting the line for color and weight:

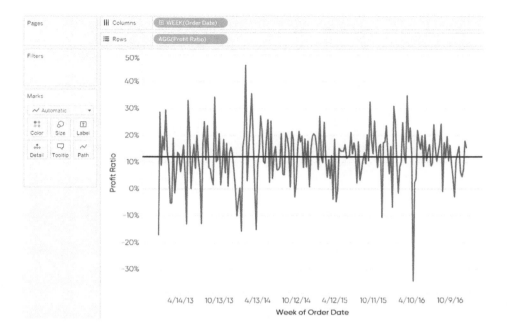

To finalize the control chart, we need to add the upper and lower control limits, which are typically three standard deviations from the mean. This step will also be accomplished through reference lines in Tableau. More specifically, a reference *distribution* will be used that draws two lines on the view, one for the upper control limit and one for the lower control limit. To do this, follow these steps:

1. Right-click the axis for Profit Ratio and choose "Add reference line."

2. In the reference line options listed at the top of the dialog box, choose Distribution.

3. In the drop-down for the distribution value, select the Standard Deviation option.

4. Change the factors to −3 and 3:

Here's how my final view looks after removing the line labels and doing some formatting to the reference distribution:

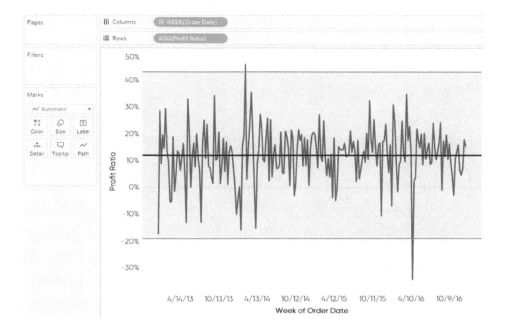

This final control chart shows not only the average profit ratio during the weeks in our analysis, but that the business can expect profit ratio to fall between −19% and 42%. In the current example, there was a week that fell outside of the lower control limit and deserves further investigation.

For more on this chart type, see Ben Jones' Tableau Public post, How to Make Control Charts in Tableau (*http://bit.ly/2tUwG6g*).

CHAPTER 44

How to Make Dynamic Dual-Axis Bump Charts

Bump charts are an effective way to show how dimension members are ranking across different measures over time. For example, you may want to see how specific product categories have ranked in sales for your company from year to year. Or maybe you want to use discrete months as your element of time to see if the rankings for product categories change based on seasonality. Or maybe you want to do something outside of work and see how your fantasy football players are ranking across different statistics from week to week!

Whatever the case may be, I've found bump charts to be an engaging and easy-to-interpret means of visualizing ranks over time. Fellow Tableau Zen Master, Matt Chambers, created one of the most popular Tableau Public visualizations of the year with a bump chart and provided his technique at his site, Sir Viz-a-Lot (*http://sirviza lot.blogspot.com*).

In addition to being engaging and easy to understand, this chart type is very easy to make in Tableau.

This tutorial will show you how to make bump charts in Tableau, but also how to leverage a dual-axis to provide additional context on the view, and how to allow the end user to choose the measure being ranked and the dimension members being compared.

How to Make Bump Charts in Tableau

For the first part of the tutorial, we will re-create this bump chart that shows us how the segments from the Sample – Superstore dataset rank between January and December for the SUM(Sales) measure:

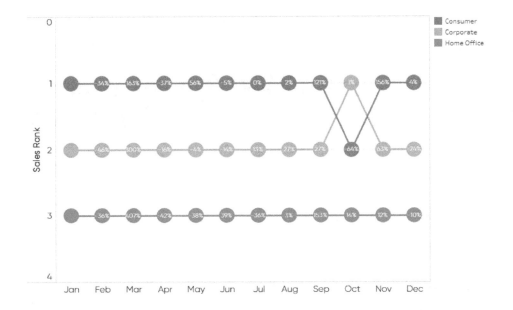

To create a bump chart, start by placing the element of time that you want to evaluate onto the Columns Shelf. To re-create the bump chart pictured, I placed discrete MONTH(Order Date) onto the Columns Shelf. I want to point out that by choosing the month date part, and because the dataset I'm working with here has four years of data, that each of the twelve months will have four years of data aggregated together. I'm doing this for illustrative purposes, but if you are using this chart type to show changes over time, make sure you choose the most appropriate date for your analysis.

On the Measures Shelf, I will place a calculated field for the measure that we want to rank; in this case Sales. The formula for my calculated field is RANK(SUM(Sales)). At this point, the view looks like this:

The RANK function acts as a table calculation in Tableau, so when it was added to the view, it was computed across the table from left to right. To rank the sales amounts by the Segment dimension, let's make the level of detail in the view more granular by dragging the Segment dimension to the Color Marks Card:

That got us closer, but we still need to change the RANK table calculation to compute for each segment. The delta symbol on the Sales Rank measure tells us that a table calculation is happening. To edit how the table calculation is being computed, right-click the Sales Rank measure, hover over Compute Using, and choose Segment:

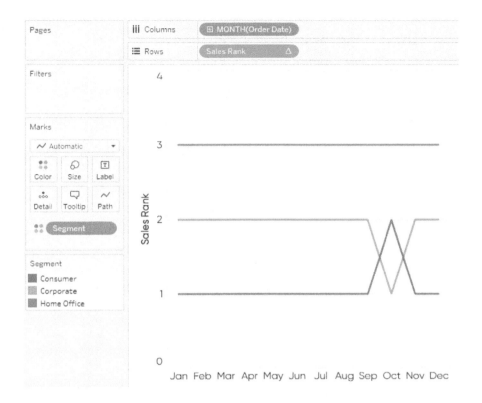

At this point, we've technically got a bump chart in Tableau. It may be more intuitive for the best rank (i.e., 1) to be on top, so I will reverse the axis by right-clicking the Sales Rank axis, clicking Edit Axis, and checking the box to reverse the scale:

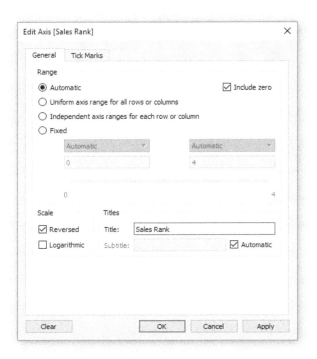

We have a bump chart, but wouldn't it be great to provide some additional value to the analysis? It's good to know that the consumer segment led the way for the first nine months of the year, but we don't know if the sales for that segment were going up or down throughout the year. To provide that context I will create a dual-axis combination chart. The first axis will be the bump chart that we just set up, and the second axis will be a dot plot that displays the percent change in month-over-month sales.

To make this bump chart dual-axis, duplicate the Sales Rank measure, place it on the opposite axis, and right-click the right axis to click Synchronize Axis.

At this point, we have the same line graph twice, with one laying on top of the other. Now that we duplicated the Sales Rank measure, we have two separate sets of Marks Cards for Sales Rank, and they can be edited independently. I will change the mark type on the second Marks Shelf for Sales Rank to Circle to make my bump chart look a little bit nicer:

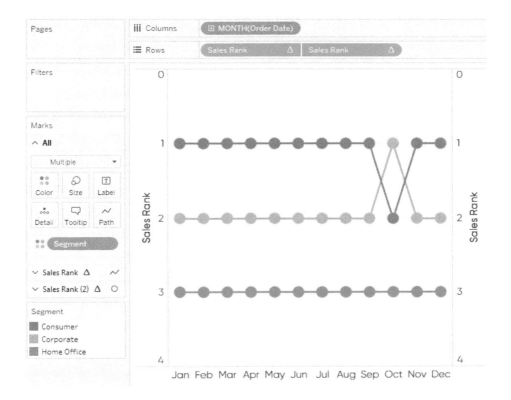

I now have some real estate to add some additional context to the marks. One possibility is to display the rank (1 through 3) for the mark on each circle. That may be a good use if you're dealing with many separate rows of marks, but with only three, that seems like a waste of valuable real estate. Instead, I will add the Sales measure to the Label Marks Card (for the circles only), then add a table calculation that computes the month-over-month percent change in sales for each segment. I also hid the right axis to finalize my bump chart:

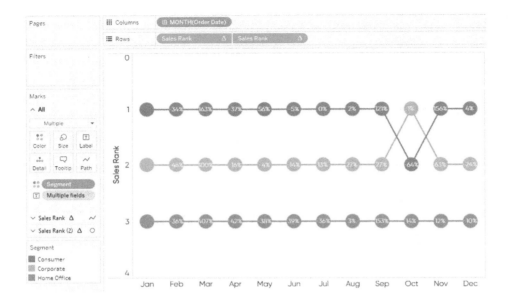

Our Tableau bump chart is now showing the month-over-month rank per segment, but also the month-over-month percent change in sales for each segment. This is turning out to be a solid static analysis, but why don't we add even more value in Tableau by allowing our end user to choose what dimension is used in the sales ranking.

To accomplish this, I will use this trick outlined in Chapter 64 to allow end users to choose measures and dimensions. For this example, I will allow my end users to choose from the Segment, Ship Mode, or Category dimensions. The first step is to create a string parameter with the choices of Segment, Ship Mode, and Category:

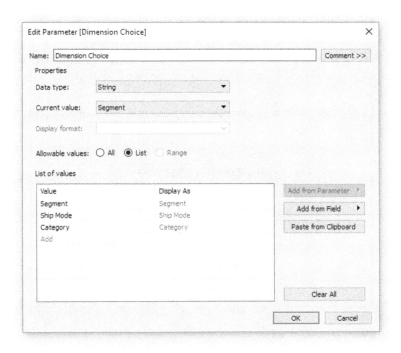

Then I will create a calculated field to give Tableau instructions on what to display for each parameter choice:

Now if I replace the Segment dimension on the Color Marks Cards of my bump chart with my newly created Dimension Choice field, the lines and circles will be colored based on what my end user selects in the parameter.

In addition to placing the Dimension Choice dimension on the Color Marks Card for both axes, there are two more small steps to get this working:

1. Ensure the table calculations on the Rows Shelf are now computing on Dimension Choice (they were previously computing on Segment).

2. Show the parameter control for Dimension Choice so the end user can change the selection (to do this, right-click the parameter and choose Show Parameter Control).

Now if I select Ship Mode in the parameter control, my bump chart rankings are based on Ship Mode:

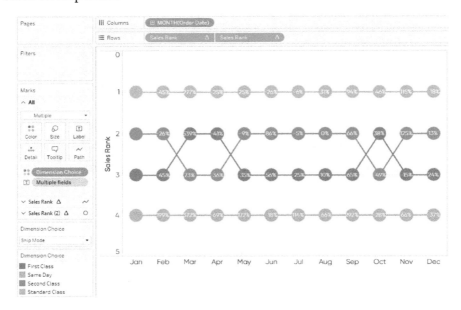

If I choose Category, my bump chart rankings are based on Category:

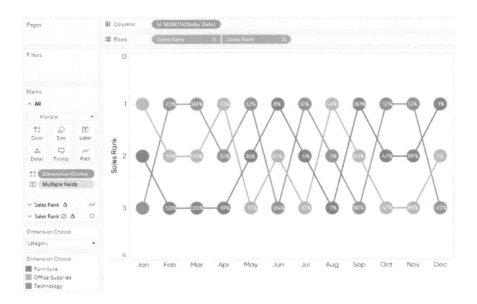

We now have a dynamic, dual-axis bump chart that is providing multiple layers of insight for our end users, and allows them to control the visualization. Your wheels may already be turning at the possibilities for your own analyses, and yes, you can also use the parameter selection approach to change the measure for the ranking!

CHAPTER 45

How to Make Dumbbell Charts

Tableau dumbbell charts, also known as DNA charts, are an alternative visualization choice for illustrating the change between two data points. Dumbbell charts get their slang name from their appearance, which look similar to weights, and sometimes strands of DNA, when they are in a horizontal orientation.

I personally love that there is an outside-of-the-box chart type that isn't named after a delicious food such as donuts or waffles. You may even say that dumbbell charts are a healthy alternative...

Names aside, this is another chart type that I find to be engaging, effective, and relatively easy to create in Tableau. This tutorial will illustrate how to make a dumbbell chart in Tableau in just a few steps.

How to Make Tableau Dumbbell Charts

Tableau dumbbell charts are actually dual-axis combination charts, where one of the axes has a mark type of Circle and the other has a mark type of Line. For this tutorial, we will re-create this visualization, which compares the year-over-year sales per sub-category in the Sample - Superstore dataset:

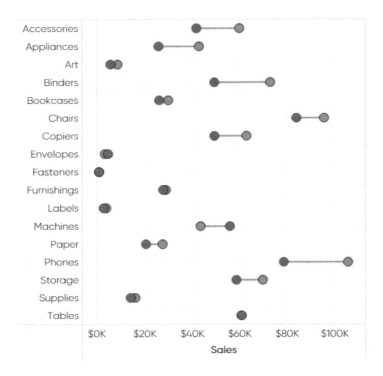

The first step to creating a dumbbell chart in Tableau is to create a dot plot with the measure and dimension you want to visualize. In this example, I will place the Sales measure from the Sample – Superstore dataset onto the Columns Shelf and the Sub-Category dimension onto the Rows Shelf. This creates a sales by sub-category bar chart that can easily be converted to a dot plot by changing the mark type from Automatic to Circle.

I will also filter the visualization to the last two years in the dataset so that I have only two comparison points per sub-category, and also color the marks by year to distinguish which year is which. At this point, my view looks like this:

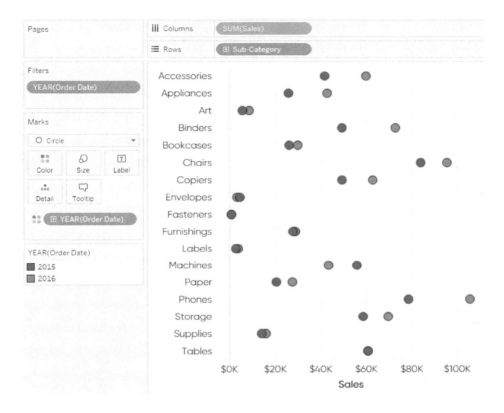

Note that this chart type can also be created with a vertical orientation by swapping the location of the fields on the Rows and Columns Shelves, but we will stick with the horizontal orientation for this tutorial.

The second, and actually final, step is to create a second axis with the Sales measure and change its mark type to Line. To turn this dot plot into a dual-axis combination chart, drag the Sales measure near the top of the chart, directly across from the sales axis on the bottom of the chart; when a dashed line appears, drop the measure on the view. Alternatively, you can place a second occurrence of the Sales measure onto the Columns Shelf, right-click the second pill, and choose Dual Axis. Ensure the axes always line up by right-clicking the top axis and choosing Synchronize Axis.

At this point, you have a set of Marks Cards for each occurrence of the Sales measure, and they can be edited independently. Navigate to the second set of Marks Cards for SUM(Sales), change the mark type to Line, then drag the YEAR(Order Date) dimension on the Marks Shelf to the Path Marks Card:

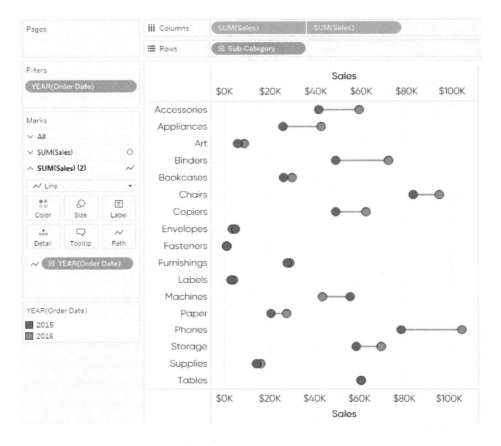

That's all it takes to get to a nice-looking dumbbell chart in Tableau. From here, you can format the size and color of the marks and hide the top axis by right-clicking it and deselecting Show Header.

CHAPTER 46

How and Why to Make Customizable Jitter Plots

"Jittering" is a technique for separating overlapping marks on a view. By giving marks some extra room by separating them into different columns, hidden data is often revealed and it is easier to visualize how the data points are distributed. The bad news is that Tableau does not provide an out-of-the-box option to jitter data points. The good news is that Tableau has an amazing community of very smart people who are willing to share their ideas. At least three Tableau Zen Masters that I know of—Steve Wexler (*http://bit.ly/2tSe3QB*), Mark Jackson (*http://bit.ly/2tUNytG*), and Jeffrey Shaffer (*http://bit.ly/2tRJo5V*)—have written about jitter plots.

If it's good enough for them, it's good enough for me. This chapter shares my favorite technique for creating jitter plots in Tableau, and also shows you how to put the intensity of the jitter into the hands of your end users.

Consider the following box and whiskers plot, which shows the sales distribution of all of the customers in the Sample – Superstore data source:

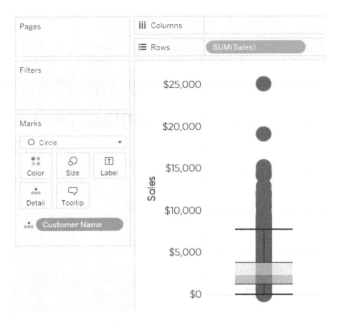

While the box and whiskers themselves are providing some valuable information about the distribution of the customers, it is impossible to get a good sense of how many customers are at each sales value on the y-axis. We are able to see a couple of outliers at the very top, but the view summary in the bottom-left corner of the authoring interface is telling me that there are 793 marks (i.e., customers) on the view. I cannot tell what is happening with the other 791 customers because they are all overlapping on a single column in the chart.

Jitter plots are created using the INDEX() function and changing the addressing to the most granular level of detail—which in our case is Customer Name. To get started with jitter plots, create a calculated field named Jitter that includes only the INDEX() function:

When this newly created calculated field is placed on the Columns Shelf, a new axis will appear, but all of the marks will still be lined up in one column. To apply the jitter, click the calculated field, hover over Compute Using and choose the most granular level of detail—Customer Name:

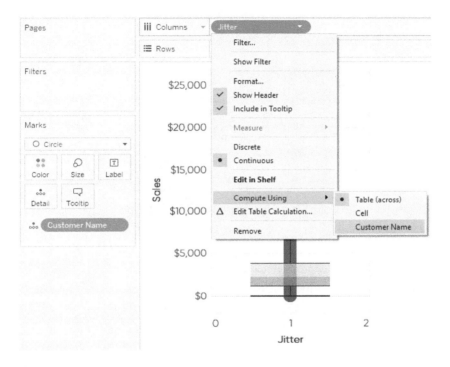

After changing the transparency and size of the marks, hiding the Jitter axis, and bringing the right side of the view in to make the chart skinnier, I am left with this jitter plot:

As you can see, it is now much easier to see how our customers are distributed on the y-axis. The horizontal position of each mark type does not mean anything to the analysis, but it separates the marks so they are not all lying on top of each other.

This is a perfectly usable jitter plot, but there may be times when you want to control the intensity of the jitter, or how many columns there are on the x-axis. To hardcode the number of columns used to jitter the marks, simply edit the Jitter calculated field and add %X, where X represents the number of desired columns, immediately after the INDEX() function. Here's how the same analysis from earlier looks when I edit the underlying formula to be "INDEX()%10":

This technique works particularly well if additional dimensions are going to be added to the Columns Shelf for the analysis because all of the columns will have the same jitter intensity specified in the previous step.

Instead of picking just one number to specify the jitter intensity, you can even replace the number in the Jitter calculated field with an integer parameter to allow the end user to quickly change it. Here's how my Jitter calculated field looks after building a parameter and replacing the "10" with the new parameter:

For this example, I set up my parameter to include integers from 10 to 100 with a step size of 10. After showing the parameter control, my end users can change the intensity of the jitter plot, picking any multiple of 10 between 10 and 100. Here's how my final view looks after some formatting to remove the vertical zero line and changing the jitter intensity to 50:

For more on parameters, see Chapter 14.

PART III

Tips and Tricks

CHAPTER 47

How to Create Icon-Based Navigation or Filters

Let's take another look at the *Odds of Going Pro* visualization. We discussed how to make funnel charts in Tableau using this as an example back in Chapter 40. Now I will show you how to install custom shapes and use the images to filter and navigate dashboards in Tableau. Here's the Tableau Public dashboard:

WHAT ARE THE ODDS OF GOING PRO IN SPORTS?
An analysis of high school, college, and pro sports in the United States by gender.

Select Gender

Male   Female

Select Sport

535,569 boys play high school basketball in the U.S.

1 in 17
high school players
will play in college

1 in 525
college players
will be drafted to the NBA

1 in 8,926
high school players
will be drafted to the NBA

Data from | www.scholarshipstats.com   Data visualization by | Ryan Sleeper

How to Make Icon-Based Navigation/Filters in Tableau

As I mentioned in Chapter 40, I attribute the success of this viz to its simplicity. Not only does it use just one chart to tell the story about the odds of going pro in sports, it uses a simple, intuitive navigation that allows the end user to filter the funnel by gender and sport.

You can easily create a similar navigation by placing the icons you want to use in your Tableau Repository. Every computer with Tableau has a folder called *My Tableau Repository*. On a PC, it's located at *C:Users/[Your User Name]/Documents/My Tableau Repository*. Among other handy Tableau files, the *Shapes* folder in your Tableau Repository holds custom shapes that can be used to create a custom navigation.

I recommend creating a new folder for each unique "shapes palette" that you want to create, and place the corresponding image files there. For example, the preceding viz uses a custom shapes palette I called "Odds of Going Pro" in *My Tableau Repository*. Here is how the folder structure looks behind the scenes on my computer:

› This PC › Documents › My Tableau Repository › Shapes			
Name	Date modified	Type	Size
Arrows	3/11/2017 2:03 PM	File folder	
Bars	3/11/2017 2:03 PM	File folder	
Bug Tracking	3/11/2017 2:03 PM	File folder	
Gender	3/11/2017 2:03 PM	File folder	
KPI	3/11/2017 2:03 PM	File folder	
☑ Odds of Going Pro	3/11/2017 2:04 PM	File folder	
Proportions	3/11/2017 2:03 PM	File folder	
Ratings	3/11/2017 2:03 PM	File folder	
Thin Arrows	3/11/2017 2:03 PM	File folder	
Weather	3/11/2017 2:03 PM	File folder	

For maximum flexibility with your custom shapes, it is important to use *.png* images with a transparent background. By using shapes with a transparent background, you can use shapes as icons or marks. If you do not have a transparent background, shapes may show up as a colored square instead.

Once the *.png* files are in the *Odds of Going Pro* folder in *My Tableau Repository*, they will be available to use as custom shapes when I reopen Tableau. To create the custom navigation used in the *Odds of Going Pro* viz, follow these steps:

1. On a new sheet, change the mark type from Automatic to Shape.

2. Drag the dimension that contains the names of the buttons you will be using in your navigation to the Shape Marks Card. In my case, the name of the dimension is Icon Name.

3. To adjust the navigation orientation from horizontal to vertical, drag the same dimension on the Shape Marks Card to the Rows Shelf.

   At this point, your view should look like this:

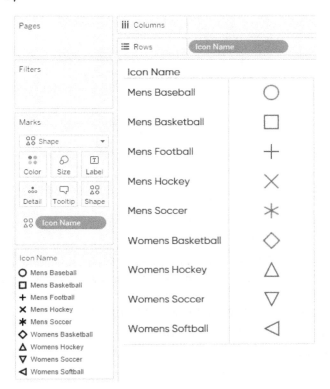

4. Notice that there is now a shape assigned to each of your button names, but these are the default shapes. To map your custom shapes, hover near the upper-right corner of the shapes legend, click the down arrow, and select Edit Shapes.

5. In the drop-down menu where it says Select Shape Palette, select the custom palette that you added to your Tableau Repository in the preceding steps. Note that you will not see your custom shapes unless you either reopen Tableau after saving your custom shapes in your Tableau Repository or select the option to Reload Shapes in the Edit Shape interface.

6. Map the correct shapes with their corresponding icon names by clicking each item name individually, then clicking the custom shape that is most appropriate:

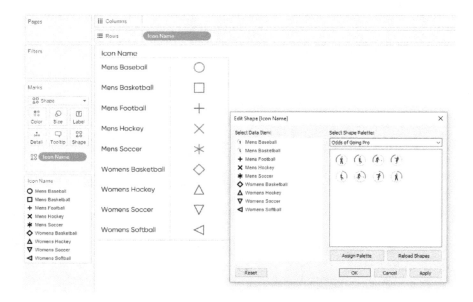

7. The last step in making your icon-based navigation functional is to add the sheet to your dashboard view, and add a dashboard action that will filter the rest of your dashboard based on the button that is clicked. From within your dashboard view, you can accomplish this by following these four steps:

   a. Navigate to Dashboard → Actions.

   b. Click Add Action.

   c. Choose a "Filter" based action.

   d. Set up logic that basically says "If you click my navigation sheet, I want the dashboard to filter every other sheet." This is how the logic looks on my dashboard:

You now have a fully functional and aesthetically pleasing icon-based filter in your dashboard. Be creative and use the combination of these icon-based filters and dashboard actions to filter the view, highlight insights in the data, navigate between worksheets or workbooks, and even open embedded web pages and videos (discussed in Chapter 56).

CHAPTER 48

How to Make a What-If Analysis Using Parameters

Parameters are one of the most powerful tools available in Tableau for exploring your data and providing interactivity to your end users. As discussed in Chapter 14, the best way to think of parameters is that they are user-defined values that are not tied to a specific dataset. In the simple formula 2 multiplied by X = 16, the value of X would be the parameter; in this case, equal to 8. The reason parameters are so powerful is that you or your end users can change the value of X from 8 to any number, which will change the results of a view.

In this chapter, we will use this concept to create a what-if analysis that will show us what would happen if we improved our sales from 0%–100%. Parameters come in many different forms, but for this chapter, we will be creating a parameter from *integers*, or whole numbers.

Let's start by creating a simple line graph showing sales over time:

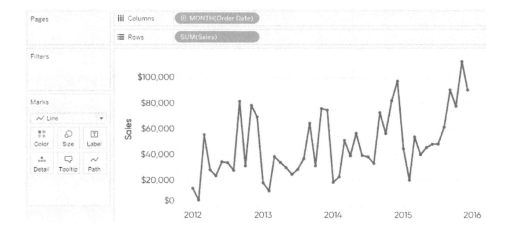

To create a parameter, right-click any white space in the Data pane and select Create Parameter. This is where you can choose from six different data types. We only want the ability to select nonfractional numbers, so choose Integer as the data type. There are some additional options available, including the current value (which will be the default value the first time you use the parameter), allowable values, and within "Range," minimum value, maximum value, and step size.

For the purpose of this what-if analysis, we will set the current value to zero, which will end up not changing our view at all the first time we use the parameter. We will also choose Range and set the range from zero to 100 with a step size of five. This means that the end user can select any number between zero and 100 in increments of five:

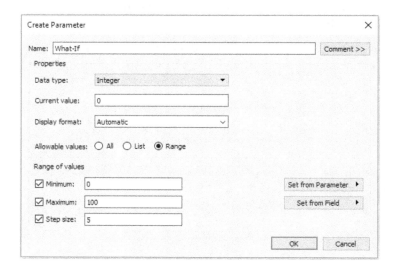

Parameters do little on their own because they are independent values that are not generated from the data, but controlled by the end user. To make the parameter useful, we will integrate the parameter's value in a calculated field that multiplies its value by something else. We are interested in creating a what-if analysis that shows how our sales would change if they improved by 0%–100%. There are a couple of ways to write this calculation; here is one:

Notice that parameters are colored purple and can be used in a formula just like any other field in your calculation.

Now that we have our parameter in a calculated field, we can use it in a view. To create two lines on the same axis, one for actual sales and one for what-if sales, we will drag our newly created calculated field onto the existing axis for sales. For this view, I have changed the colors of the measure names and placed the line for What-If Sales on top of actual sales by dragging What-If Sales up in the Measure Names color legend. At this point, your view should look like this:

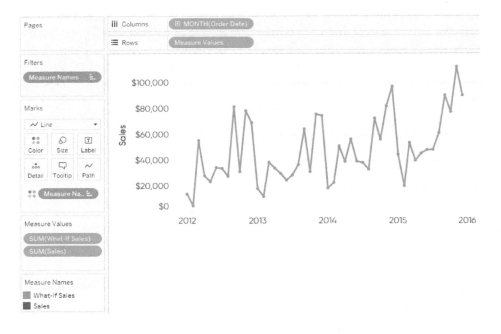

There is one last step needed in order to utilize your parameter. Right-click the What-If parameter and select Show Parameter Control. You now have a way to control the input for the What-If Sales Calculated Field. Notice that the inputs available are the ones that we set up when we first created the parameter; a range of 0–100 in increments of five:

For additional ways to provide interactivity to your end users, see storytelling tip 11 in Chapter 96.

CHAPTER 49

Three Ways to Add Alerts to Your Dashboards

One of the biggest advantages to using a tool like Tableau is that the software can do much of the "heavy lifting" for you. For example, you can build in logic to improve the usability of your dashboards once, and have it work for you or your end users from that point on. One application of this is to add alerts to your dashboards that help communicate notifications or insights.

You may want to use alerts to notify users or remind yourself that a certain filter is on. Perhaps you have specific performance thresholds that are tolerable to your business, but want to be alerted somehow if performance is ever higher or lower than expected. Adding alerts to your dashboards helps reduce the time to insight and elicit action that helps your business—the primary goal of analytics. This chapter will cover three different examples of dashboard alerts.

Alert 1: Date Settings

The first type of alert that I frequently use in my own dashboards communicates which dates are being displayed and, if I'm using a line graph, how finely the dates are aggregated (daily, weekly, monthly, etc.). This alert serves two key purposes: (a) it clearly communicates how current the dataset is, and (b) helps avoid confusion in the case that the dataset has not updated or a view doesn't look as expected due to the aggregation. Here is an example using the Sample – Superstore data:

This dashboard shows data from 12/1/2012 to 12/31/2015, aggregated by month.

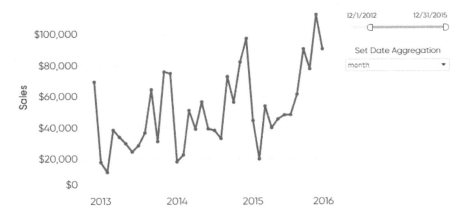

To create this alert, simply start a new worksheet and make a text-based view by adding the information you want included in the alert to the Text Marks Card. In this case, I added MAX(Order Date), MIN(Order Date), and the Date Aggregation parameter. To add the two min and max dates, I right-clicked and dragged the Order Date dimension onto the Text Marks Card, which allowed me to select the date field I wanted to display.

Once you have the information you want on the view, you can click into the Text Marks Card to format the text and written logic as you wish. At this point, your text sheet should look like this:

Finally, ensure the Order Date filter on your line graph is applied to this text sheet. This way, when an end user changes the date range, the MIN and MAX dates will change to match the filter.

For more, see Chapter 66.

Alert 2: Dynamic Labels

Wouldn't it be great if mark labels only showed up when something extra important happened? This is actually straightforward in Tableau. The trick is to build your logic for what's "extra important" in a calculated field, then use that calculated field as your label. Using the same sales-over-time example from before, here's a look at dynamic labels in action:

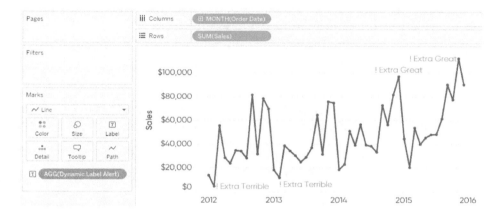

Notice that I have placed a calculated field called Dynamic Label Alert on the Label Marks Card. Here is the underlying logic for that calculated field:

This is a simple example, but you can code the logic in the calculated field to alert you when anything important to you occurs. Perhaps you want to know when a goal is met or if any marks are outside of one or two standard deviations from the mean.

Alert 3: Heat Map Dashboard with Optional Tableau Server Email

In the third dashboard alert example, we will again leverage calculated fields. Only this time, instead of adding our logic of interest to the Label Marks Card, we will add it to the Color Marks Card—creating a heat map that immediately draws attention to our best and worst performing segments.

Let's imagine a C-level executive has requested a dashboard showing the sales by region and product sub-category. They normally receive this information in a spreadsheet, but Tableau allows us to add value by immediately surfacing the most pertinent information. We decide to add value to the existing crosstab by alerting the executive in-line with the raw numbers whether the sales for a particular segment are at or below 40% of last year's sales or at or better than 160% of last year's sales. This logic looks something like this under the hood:

```
IF [YoY Sales Index] <= 40 THEN "Bad Alert"
ELSEIF [YoY Sales Index] >= 160 THEN "Good Alert"
ELSE "No Attn Needed"
END
```

Once this calculated field is created, you can add it to the Color Marks Card and change the mark type to Circle, creating a view like this:

A high-level dashboard like this can be subscribed to in Tableau Server (*http://tabsoft.co/2u1mvNx*), dropping the most current overview in your or your executive's inbox every morning or week. From here, they can decide for themselves based on the alerts if they need to click through to a more robust, interactive dashboard on Tableau Server for further analysis.

Note that this type of alert dashboard can be coded to any comparison you wish, such as performance compared to a goal, competitor, or date range. If you are comparing relative dates year over year (such as "last week"), use Week Number or an equalized date to ensure there is data in both years.

This chapter shared just three ways to add alerts to your dashboards, but the possibilities are almost limitless. Experiment with elements of these three approaches to design the alerts that make the most sense for your business and stakeholders.

CHAPTER 50

How to Add Instructions or Methodology Using Custom Shape Palettes

Instructions on a Tableau dashboard are vital to ensuring your end users can get the most out of your work whether or not you are there to explain it to them. As with most things in Tableau, there are several different approaches to adding instructions to a dashboard, and there is not necessarily one best method. Just to name a few off the top of my head, you could:

- Add a text box to your dashboard and type out the full instructions.
- Include instructions on a second tab in your workbook.
- Not include written instructions, but display color, size, and mark legends for every dashboard object.

My go-to approach for adding instructions to the corporate dashboards I create in Tableau is to leverage a custom shapes palette to display a familiar icon to my end users. When they see the icon, they know they can hover over it for more information, which is displayed to them as a tooltip.

Here is an example where I used this approach to share the methodology for one of my Tableau Public visualizations:

Methodology

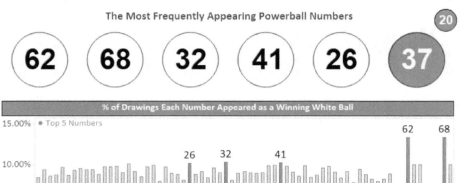

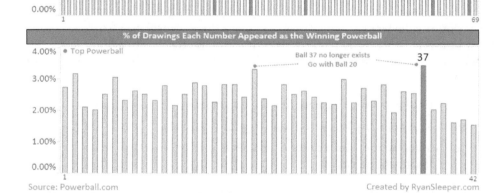

This is my favorite approach to including instructions because it ensures the end user has access to the instructions without requiring much real estate on my dashboards (I have cooler things to show, after all). My end users have learned that the gear icon is their go-to place for instructions, but they will not necessarily need to be reminded how to use the dashboard after they've used it a few times.

In this chapter, I will walk you through how to add a similar gears icon leveraging a custom shapes palette in Tableau. I will also show you how to add instructions to this custom shape using a tooltip:

1. Create a custom shapes palette with your instructions icon.

   As mentioned in Chapter 47, every machine with Tableau has a *Shapes* folder in their Tableau Repository. On a PC, it is located at *C:\Users\[User Name]\Docu-*

---

ments*My Tableau Repository\Shapes*. Every folder listed in this location is associated with a shapes palette in Tableau.

Here is how my *Shapes* folder looks on my computer:

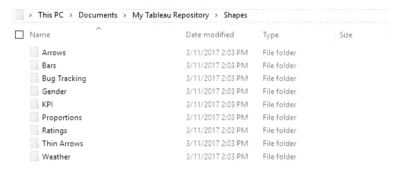

Here is how my shape palettes look in Tableau:

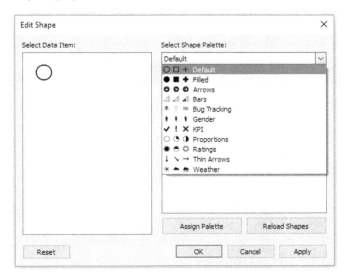

Notice every folder in my shapes directory has a corresponding palette in Tableau. By simply creating new subfolders in your shapes directory and adding images to that folder, you create custom shape palettes that can be used in Tableau.

Let's try to do this by creating a new folder called *Instructions*, and placing an instructions icon in that folder. You can use whatever image you would like, but I used the following *.png* image:

By using *.png* images with transparent backgrounds, you will have the most flexibility possible when using your custom shapes in Tableau. For example, the transparency will allow you to color the image while leaving the background white.

At this point, your custom shapes palette should look like this:

2. Create a "dummy" dimension

   Creating a "dummy" dimension will provide a field that will act as your instructions. To do this, create a calculated field that looks something like this:

3. Create a sheet with your instructions icon.

   On a new blank worksheet, change the mark type from Automatic to Shape. This will reveal a new Marks Card for Shape. Drag your Instructions dimension to the Shape Marks Card. You can now choose which shape you would like to assign to your instructions by clicking into the shapes palette. If you do not see your new custom shapes palette as an option, choose Reload Shapes in the lower-right corner of the Edit Shape dialog box.

   Map your custom instructions icon to the circle by first clicking the circle shape, then clicking your new icon. At this point, your instructions shape should look like this:

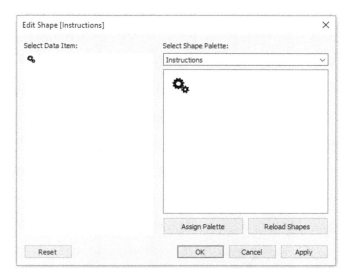

You can also change the color of your instructions icon by clicking into the Color Marks Card. I personally like to drag my dummy dimension to the Color Marks Card, which also allows me to choose from some custom colors that I have set up.

Finally, you can customize what your instructions say by clicking into the Tooltip Marks Card and typing out your instructions. This is what will show up when your end user hovers over the instructions icon. This acts as a full word processor, so you can build in different fonts, colors, and shapes to make your instructions as user-friendly as possible. Get creative and tailor your instructions for your end users.

4. Add the instructions to a dashboard.

The fourth and final step in adding instructions to your dashboard is to drag the sheet you created in step 3 to a dashboard. I typically make this dashboard object floating and set the dimensions to 50 high by 50 wide. I also clear the borders and remove any sheet legends, such as the shapes legend that will appear when you place the sheet on your dashboard.

There you have it—an elegant way to add customized instructions to your dashboards without using much valuable real estate. As a bonus to this approach, as of Tableau 9.0, tooltips are persistent. This means that end users can hover over your instructions as long as they want without the tooltip disappearing; this alleviates the one drawback to this technique before that version of Tableau was released.

CHAPTER 51

Ten Tableau Data Visualization Tips I Learned from Google Analytics

Eight years ago, I was fortunate to be introduced to Tableau, a tool for data visualization that has led to personal opportunities and contributions to my clients' businesses that I didn't imagine would be possible in such a short amount of time.

Even before that, though, I was introduced to Google Analytics.

It's no surprise then that some of my inspiration for the design, usability, and analytics of my data visualizations have been drawn from Google Analytics over the years. Sure, the Audience Overview report features an overly large pie chart for new versus returning visitors—a measure that is largely useless in an age of multiple devices, cleared cookies, and anonymous users—but Google tends to get a lot of things right.

What follows is a list of 10 Tableau data visualization best practices I use that I either consciously or subconsciously picked up from Google Analytics. In no particular order…

Use a Maximum of 12 Dashboard Objects

One of the first ideas I remember consciously thinking to myself, "Wow, that's a good idea, Google Analytics; I should use that…," was the 12 object limit Google Analytics has in place for its custom dashboards. Many data visualization specialists often remind us that "less is more," and I have encouraged designers in Chapter 89. In Google Analytics, you have no choice but to keep dashboard objects, or widgets in Google's words, to 12 or fewer. Here is what you see when trying to add a 13th widget in a Google Analytics custom dashboard:

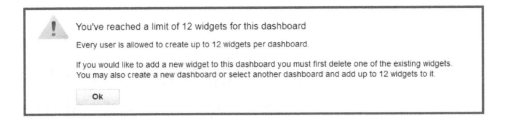

This limit forces designers to prioritize which KPIs and views are truly pertinent to the story.

Improve User Experience by Leveraging Dashboard Actions

On Google's Audience Overview report, which is my favorite report to start my analyses, seven main KPIs are shown along with sparkline trends. By clicking a sparkline, the larger line graph at the top will change to that KPI. This makes it easier to see trends and find extra detail, which is provided if you hover over data points:

Similar usability can be set up in Tableau through the use of dashboard actions. Here is a simple example using a control sheet for Segment and a sales trend over time. By adding both sheets to a dashboard and choosing to use the sheet containing the three different segments as a filter, clicking a segment will filter the trend being shown:

Sales Trend by Segment

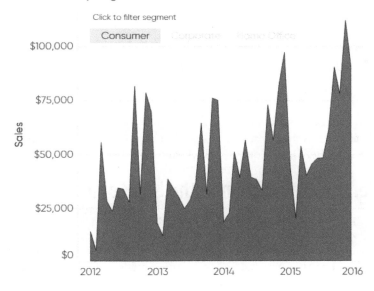

To use a sheet as a filter, click the sheet, click the down arrow that appears in the upper-right corner, and click "Use as Filter."

Allow End Users to Change the Date Aggregation of Line Graphs

Another feature I like about the Audience Overview report in Google Analytics is the ability to change the date aggregation of the trend being shown. By default, the trends are aggregated by Day, but users also have the option to change the granularity to Hourly, Week, or Month:

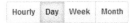

This feature can help find different stories in the data based on the date part being displayed. To learn how to replicate this in Tableau, see Chapter 66.

Keep Crosstab Widths to a Maximum of Ten Columns

Tableau allows you to make crosstab views with up to 16 columns. If you ask me, this is about 11 too many. Spreadsheets are not data visualizations and they take far too long for analysts to process. Google Analytics is at least closer, never displaying more than 10 columns including the dimension in the first column (nine measures pictured here):

Sometimes it makes sense to use crosstabs in small doses, and I am realistic that some audiences will require more detailed data in a text table. If at all possible, I would stick with this implied limit from Google Analytics of ten or fewer columns.

Use a Vertical Navigation in the Left Column

I've always appreciated the intuitive, left navigation of Google Analytics. For reports that have a lot of changeable components, such as filters, the vertical space on the left side of a dashboard is an ideal place for navigation. Placing controls here serves the dual purpose of prioritizing what changes can be made to find stories in the data and having a clear place to remind users what filters have been applied:

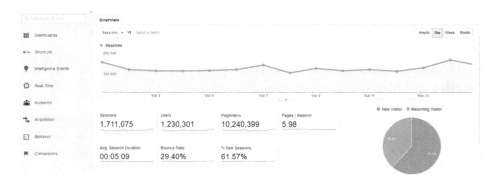

This is not a must-use tip for every situation, but makes a lot of sense for dashboards that are meant to provide self-service analytics. If you have dashboards that are not meant to be changed very often, deprioritize filters and buttons by moving them to the right navigation.

Choose Five or Fewer Colors for Your Dashboards

At times, the number of dimension members within a dimension on a view will dictate how many colors are required in a data visualization. For example, I may have a unique color for each region: North, East, South, and West. When possible, I try to limit the number of colors to five or fewer—an unspoken rule I picked up from Google Analytics' simple color choices.

Google Analytics does have a set of visuals called "Motion Charts" that contain more than five unique colors, but outside of that, it is challenging to find visuals with more than two different colors. Using five or fewer colors reduces the burden on the end users because they do not have to work as hard to look back and forth to the color legend to determine what the marks on a view represent.

If you are in a situation where more than five categories need distinct colors, consider a two-color palette—making the category of interest a color that stands out, and everything else a more muted color, such as gray. See Chapter 88 for more on getting the most from color in data visualization.

Stick Mostly to Lines and Bars

With only a few exceptions, Google Analytics' powerful analytics platform is built almost entirely on what I consider the most effective data visualizations: lines and bars. Google Analytics has treemaps in its Acquisition reports and highlight tables in its Cohort Analysis. It also uses scatter plots in the aforementioned Motion Charts and I'm sad to say, pie charts make several appearances.

Even with those other chart types, lines and bars dominate the dozens of available reports in Google Analytics, and for good reason. These simple chart types have been getting the job done for more than 200 years now, and in most cases, continue to be the best starting point for sharing trends and comparisons in data visualization.

Include Comparisons Such as Year Over Year

When I develop data visualizations, I am constantly trying to avoid the dreaded question, "So what?" If I hear this question, it means I did not do a good enough job communicating the stories in the data. One way to avoid this awkward conversation about why you've spent days developing a data visualization that doesn't tell anybody anything… is to use comparisons.

Some of my favorite approaches for showing comparisons are bar charts, small multiples, and period-over-period comparisons. The latter of which can be done very easily in Google Analytics by selecting a date range comparison when you set the date range:

Google Analytics allows you to compare your selected dates to a custom secondary range, the previous period of the same range (i.e., 15 days versus 15 days), or to that same date range versus the prior year. Similar functionality can be set up in Tableau using parameters (see Chapter 69).

Bring Your Data Visualization to Life Using Segmentation

Another way I like to provide comparisons in my data visualizations is through the use of segmentation. Segmentation is one of the most powerful tactics for adding value to your analyses, and makes it easy to quickly identify your weakest and strongest performers. Segmentation allows you to hone in on your weakest performers to figure out what characteristics to avoid, or your strongest performers to determine what you should be doing more of.

In Google Analytics, several segments including Mobile Traffic, Referral Traffic, and Returning Users (just to name a few), come ready to use "out-of-the-box." You can also set up customized advanced segments to compare users almost any way you can imagine. These standard and custom segments can be used to compare performance to each other, or the site as a whole:

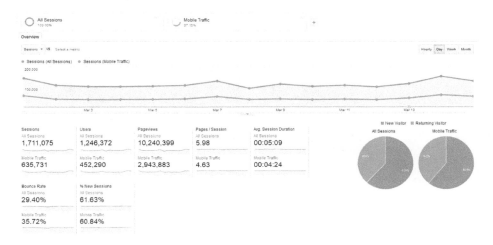

There are a couple of ways to leverage segmentation in Tableau. First, if you are using the Google Analytics connector, you can filter the data coming into Tableau on a specific segment. Note the Segment filter here in the connection setup:

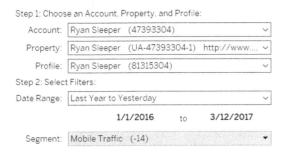

The drawback to this is you can only segment the data to one thing at a time. A much more powerful use of segmentation in Tableau is to create and compare your own segments once the data is already being used in Tableau. For more on customizing your segmentation, see Chapter 53.

Include Alerts of Exceptional or Poor Performance

Last but not least, Google Analytics taught me the power of boiling the most important stories in the data to the top. Google Analytics does this in the form of Intelligence Events, which shows any performance on a site for a particular date range that fell outside of its algorithms' expectations:

Intelligence Events are a great place to start an analysis and I love them for a couple of reasons:

- They do the heavy-lifting for you; making outliers apparent without making you dig to find them.
- They are easily understood by analysts and non-analysts alike.

In Tableau, similar alerts can be built into your dashboards to make them more user-friendly and reduce time to insight. See Chapter 49 to get you started.

Google has taught me a lot over the years and these ten data visualization best practices from Google Analytics have served me well. One of the things I like most about Tableau is the software's flexibility, and I encourage you to take the best ideas from other tools and incorporate—or even build on—them in your own dashboards.

CHAPTER 52

Three Alternative Approaches to Pie Charts in Tableau

Despite being one of the least effective means of communicating data, I often see pie charts in corporate dashboards and Tableau Public visualizations. New users likely see pie charts as an easy way to spruce up their dashboards, but they are doing themselves a disservice because pie charts *increase time to insight*—the opposite of what we are trying to achieve with data visualization.

When I share the shortcomings of pie charts, I am usually asked, "But if I can't use pie charts, then how do I show a parts of a whole relationship?" For this reason, I want to document a better approach to using pie charts in Tableau.

Why does Tableau allow pie charts in the first place?

You may be wondering, if pie charts are so bad, why does Tableau even allow you to build them with Show Me or by changing the mark type to Pie?

When pie charts were first introduced to Tableau, they were meant to be used for the specific purpose of being a secondary mark type on a filled map. You may have seen this example from Tableau where they show the sales by category by US state using a pie chart on each state:

In this example, the colors on the filled map represent the total sales per state, and the pie is used to show the make-up of total sales in each state. In this scenario, using Pie as the secondary mark type is the only way to accomplish this view.

Though its intentions were good, Tableau let the genie out of the bottle by introducing this mark type. I have actually never seen this intended use in a real dashboard, but users have instead adopted pie charts in several ways that are outside of best practices. In this chapter, I will share a couple alternatives to pie charts while building up to my recommended approach to visualizing a parts of a whole relationship.

Tableau Pie Chart Alternative #1: Bar Chart

I have two rules if you absolutely have to use pie charts in your Tableau workbooks. The first is to use five slices or fewer. More importantly, *pie charts should never be used in a time-series analysis*. For this reason, my first pie chart alternative is to simply use a bar chart, which is a great choice for comparing values at one point in time.

One thing you lose in this approach compared to the map we just looked at is the quick comparisons between states. However, you can use dashboard actions to achieve something similar by having the bar chart update when a state is clicked or hovered over. I like this approach because you gain real estate to include the actual sales numbers and/or the percent of the whole that each category is contributing:

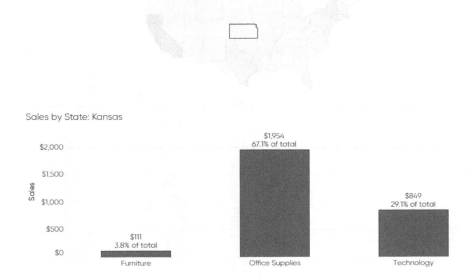

Sales by US State and Category
Click a state to filter bar chart.

Sales by State

Sales by State: Kansas

Tableau Pie Chart Alternative #2: Stacked Bars or Areas

Another Tableau pie chart alternative would be to use a stacked bar chart. I do not like this alternative as much because unless the stacked bar is on the bottom, it is very hard to compare trends of individual stacks across the view. This is still better than a pie chart. It is easy to convert a bar chart to a stacked bar in Tableau by simply moving the dimension that is creating each bar from the Rows or Columns Shelf to the Color Marks Card. With a stacked bar, the top of the highest bar represents the total, and each color below represents a contribution to that total. For example, consider the following bar chart:

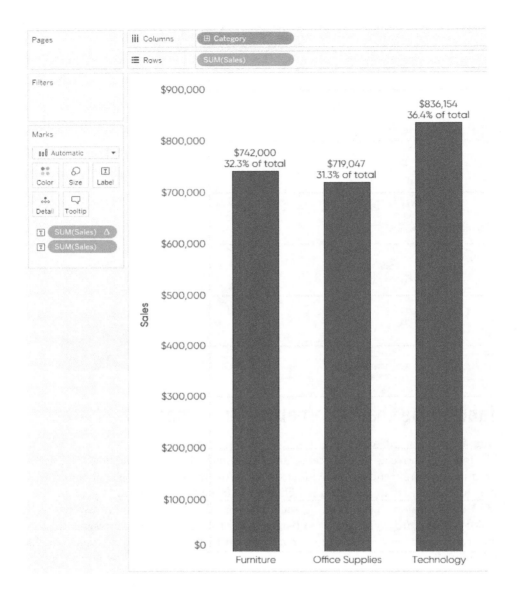

And now take a look at the same data visualized as a stacked bar chart instead:

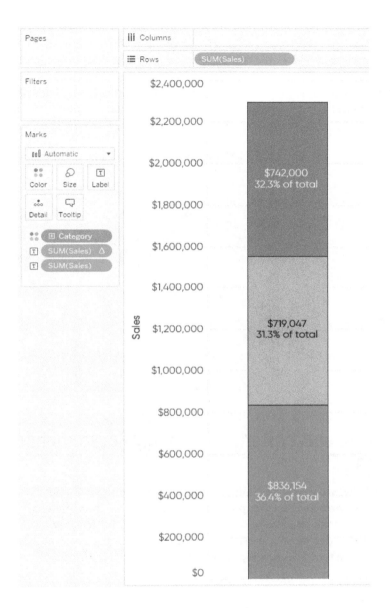

Whether you use a bar chart or a stacked bar, the values are for one point in time. For me, these chart types do not provide much value because they get stale very quickly in a corporate dashboard. For example, the bars likely will not change week to week or month to month. Even if they do, because you are always looking at one point in time, you lose the comparison to prior timeframes.

For this reason, I suggest you at least use stacked bars to show how the distribution is changing over time (i.e., have one stacked bar for each time period). To take this a step further, you can add a quick table calculation to your measure called "Percent of Total" and change "Compute using" to Table (Down). This quick table calculation will make every bar's height 100%, then each color represents a share of that 100%. For a more cohesive view, change the mark type from Bar to Area to get a result like the following:

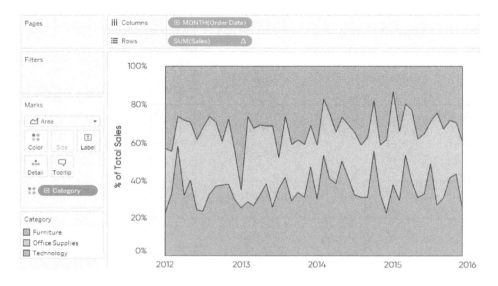

Tableau Pie Chart Alternative #3: My Recommended Approach

I mentioned that we would be building up to my recommended approach, and while the alternatives provided to this point are more effective than pie charts, they have their own limitations. Stacked areas like the one shown in the previous example can be challenging to decipher because unless the slice is on the bottom, it is difficult to precisely read the trend of each individual slice.

For this reason, the first thing I recommend for the optimal parts of a whole visualization is to change the mark type from Area to Line:

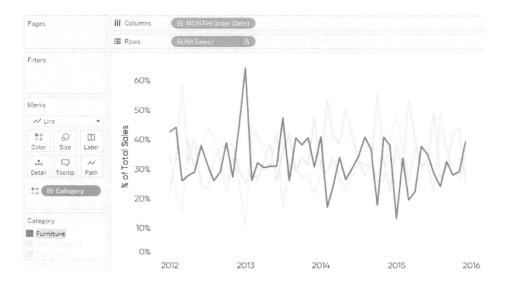

It is now easier to see the trend of each individual category. In this example from the Sample – Superstore dataset, the lines follow a similar trend so there is quite a bit of overlap. Clicking the color legend highlights each category to help illustrate each trend.

We can now see the sales contribution in percentages of each category to the total sales over time. One piece of context we lose with this approach is whether the *total* sales amount is trending up or down. So the last thing I recommend is placing the sales measure on the opposite axis, which creates a dual-axis line graph. By default, Tableau colors the total sales by Category. In this case, we only care about how the total sales amount is trending over time, so remove Category from the Color Marks Card on the SUM(Sales) Marks Shelf.

You are left with four lines instead of three, which is causing even more overlap. Total sales is a secondary insight, so I suggest changing its mark type to Area and washing it out. Finally, you can add total sales to the Tooltip Marks Card on the Percent of Total Sales Marks Shelf so that both the percent of total and total sales show up when you hover over each data point. Your finished product will look like this:

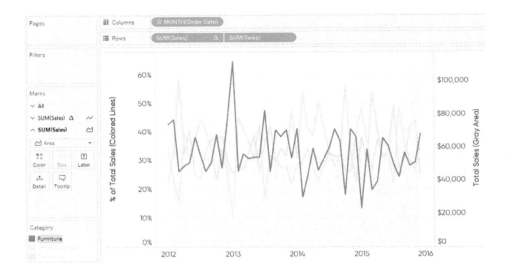

In review, in this chapter we have evolved our visualization of a parts to whole relationship from a static pie chart during one point in time, to a dual-axis combo chart showing how a distribution changes over time while not losing the context of how our total is changing.

This alternative to pie charts in Tableau will help reduce your time to insight, while also making your analysis more accurate, precise, and actionable.

CHAPTER 53

How to Create and Compare Segments

Here's the scenario: The dataset that you're working with in Tableau has several dimensions that represent different customer segments such as married versus single, new versus returning, customer score, or whatever segments are important to your business. It's good that these dimensions are available to slice and dice the data by, but it'd be *great* if you and your end users could change these on the fly, without having to drag and drop the segment of interest onto the view every time you wanted to slice the data by a different segment. It would be even more amazing if you could somehow create a segment hierarchy, allowing you to drill down to different combinations of segments (i.e., Married or Single in the first column drills down to Married or Single, plus a second column for New or Returning).

Solution: Parameters will be our solution to dynamically create and compare segments. In this case, we will create two string-based parameters that will be used to create our combinations of segments:

1. Create a parameter for segment 1.

   For demonstration purposes, I am going to use the dimensions available out of the box with Tableau's Sample - Superstore data. You will likely have segments that are more practical in your data, such as the examples mentioned in the opening sentence of this section (marital status, new versus returning, etc.).

   Create a string parameter with a list of the dimensions you want to be able to use in your segmentation:

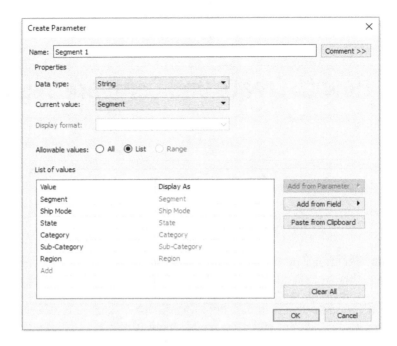

2. Create a calculated dimension for segment 1.

Remember, parameters are dependent, and do nothing on their own. In order to get this parameter to eventually work in our views, we need to create a calculated field that gives Tableau instructions on how to use the parameter. To create our first segmentation, we need to tell Tableau which dimension to display based on the selection made in the Segment 1 parameter. This turns out to be a simple mapping exercise, with the following logic:

```
CASE [Parameters].[Segment 1]
WHEN "Segment" THEN [Segment]
WHEN "Ship Mode" THEN [Ship Mode]
WHEN "State" THEN [State]
WHEN "Category" THEN [Category]
WHEN "Ship Mode" THEN [Ship Mode]
WHEN "Sub-Category" THEN [Sub-Category]
WHEN "Region" THEN [Region]
END
```

3. Create a parameter for Segment 2.

If you want to have multilevel segmentation, create a second parameter for Segment 2. This can be done by right-clicking the Segment 1 parameter and clicking Duplicate. Edit the copy and rename it Segment 2.

4. Create a calculated dimension for Segment 2.

Instead of retyping all of the logic used to create the Segment 1 calculated field, just right-click the Segment 1 dimension and choose Duplicate. The only trick here is that you not only want to rename the copy to Segment 2, but you also want to change the parameter being used in the logic. To do this, right-click the Segment 1 copy, click Edit, and replace the number "1" with "2" in the first line. At this point, your calculated field for Segment 2 should look like this:

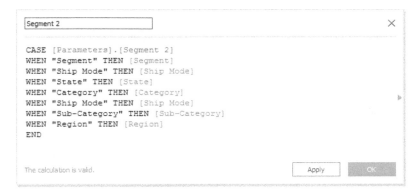

We now have the components needed to create a view that allows you and your end users to choose any combination of two segments. Here is a sparklines view with both segments:

Creating sparklines is beyond the scope of this chapter (see Chapter 24), but the key is to right-click the two parameters we created for segments and choose Show Parameter Control. This is what gives users the ability to change Segment 1 and Segment 2 on the view.

This Is Awesome; Please Tell Me Other Ways This Can Be Used!

Option 1: Create a custom hierarchy with your newly created segments

By creating a custom hierarchy using the Segment 1 and Segment 2 calculated fields, you and your end users will be able to drill down to the secondary level of segmentation and back up to the primary level of segmentation. To create a custom hierarchy, click the dimensions on the Dimensions area of the Data pane

---

that you want included in the hierarchy (Control-click on a PC to multiselect), right-click, hover over Hierarchy, and choose Create Hierarchy:

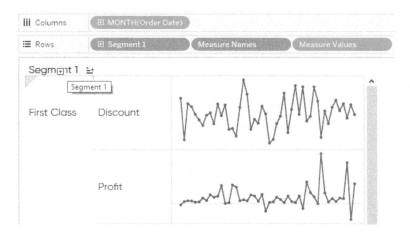

Option 2: Create additional levels of segmentation

You are not limited to two combinations of segments, though usability may become messy past three or so. If you would like to create more than two levels of segmentation, simply repeat the preceding steps three and four.

Option 3: Save a specific combination of segments for future use

If you find a combination of segments that is particularly interesting, Tableau makes it very easy to create a set straight from the view. These sets can be reused on different worksheets for deeper analysis. Let's say we want to isolate the Ship Mode: First Class → Category: Office Supplies combination for the months on our view. Simply click the axis at the deepest level of segmentation, and click the Venn Diagram icon to create a set:

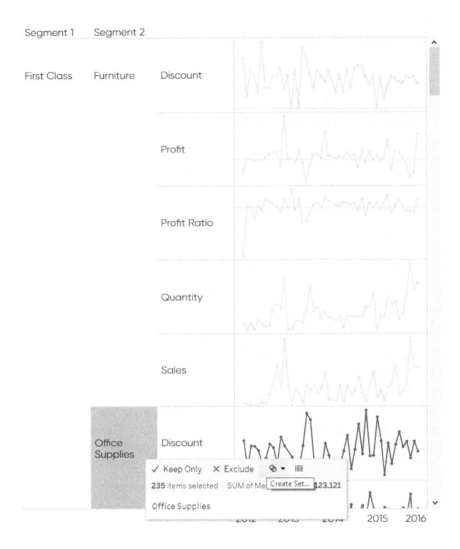

This set will appear in your left navigation and can now be used as a dimension on views, to filter, or within calculated fields:

Segmentation is one of the best ways to create comparisons that add value to your data visualization. The next time you are mining for stories in your own data, consider leveraging parameters to create custom segmentations on the fly.

CHAPTER 54

Five Design Tips for Enhancing Your Tableau Visualizations

Accurate and honest data is the core of every great data visualization. If you are able to leverage data visualization best practices to make that data easy to understand and act on, you are a huge step ahead of the game. Undoubtedly, you can't have a quality data visualization without quality data and fundamental best practices. That being said, without balancing the quality of your data with a quality design, your data visualization will never reach its full potential. Before dismissing design as an unnecessary—or worse, undoable—component of your data visualization, ask yourself why you visualize data. My answer is to *find and communicate actionable insights*. To make insights actionable, or provoke change, your data visualization needs to be seen by the most relevant and/or largest audience possible. Design is the key to reaching that audience.

I often talk about the concept of being remarkable, my favorite Seth Godin principle (*http://bit.ly/2FMOZf8*). Being remarkable means that your work is so high quality, distinctive, or compelling in some way that it moves your audience to remark about it. In today's world, that may mean sharing your work on social media. What it may also mean to you in the corporate world is that your work gets passed up the ladder—creating change, recognition, promotions … fame … and fortune! The latter may be a longshot, but it's worth a try.

To help illustrate how big of a difference design can make to a data visualization, I have stripped out most of the design elements from my most socially viral work to date, *Your Salary vs. a MLB Player's Salary* (I returned most of the fonts, colors, and formats to their default settings in Tableau, but I want to point out that I could have minimized the design even further by returning the view to its default layout and standardizing the font sizes):

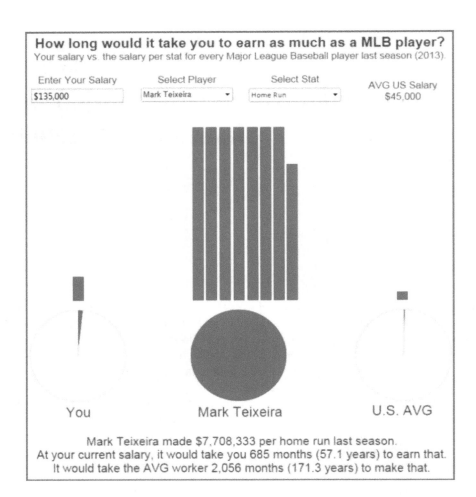

In the viz, the end users can type in their own salary and compare it to the salary of any Major League Baseball player across several different statistics. The concept and data are interesting enough—if not disheartening—to stand on their own, but I credit the "remarkability" of the dashboard to its design. Here is the exact same view with some simple design upgrades:

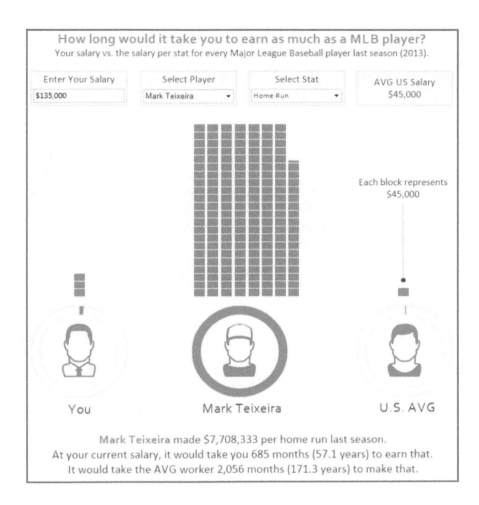

How long would it take you to earn as much as a MLB player?
Your salary vs. the salary per stat for every Major League Baseball player last season (2013).

Enter Your Salary
$135,000

Select Player
Mark Teixeira

Select Stat
Home Run

AVG US Salary
$45,000

Each block represents
$45,000

You   Mark Teixeira   U.S. AVG

Mark Teixeira made $7,708,333 per home run last season.
At your current salary, it would take you 685 months (57.1 years) to earn that.
It would take the AVG worker 2,056 months (171.3 years) to make that.

In addition to the true data purists who do not see the value in complementing data with an aesthetically pleasing design, one reason I hear people give for not trying to balance data and design is that they have no graphic design experience. If you look closely at the "after" image, you will find that the only elements in the entire view that required any Adobe Photoshop or Adobe Illustrator talent are the icons that form the center of the dashboard's donut charts. On top of that, I will let you in on the secret that those icons are from a stock photography file that I purchased from iStock. I simply recolored the icons to my liking and pasted them in the center of a circle to create the donut effect.

My point is: You can do this.

To help you get started, let's take a look at five ways you can balance data and design in Tableau without any graphic design experience.

Color

There are countless articles on color's impact on data visualization, and for good reason. The full possibilities of color are beyond the scope of this chapter, but I will share my two biggest tips for harnessing the power of color:

- Use simple color palettes with five or fewer colors. Of course, sometimes the variety of your dimension members will dictate how many colors your viz includes, but remember that every addition puts more stress on the user to efficiently decipher the story in your data (i.e., think looking back and forth at a color legend).

- Mute your colors. The technical definition of "muting" colors means that you are reducing their hue saturation. The practical definition is that you are making the colors less intense, making them more pleasing to look at. An easy way to do this is to add transparency to the colors.

If you would like to learn more about the theory and psychology of color, Chapter 55.

Typography

Tableau comes out of the box with more than 100 different fonts. If you thought that Tableau's default fonts were your only options, then this tip is for you! Fonts are a powerful way to differentiate your dashboard, and they serve the additional purpose of communicating priorities to your end user.

There is no one-size-fits-all approach to font design, but I recommend picking out one or two fonts that you think look nice, fit the message of your dashboard, and most importantly, are easy to read. Experiment with different point sizes (i.e., 8pt, 10pt, 24pt) to break up your data visualization and prioritize its elements in a subtle way.

Layout

Making thoughtful layout choices can help guide your end user through the story of your data visualization even when you aren't there to explain it. Paying special attention to the spacing of each dashboard component also helps ensure that you end up with a clean design.

One best practice regarding layout is to place the highest-priority content toward the top and left of the view, and relatively lower-priority content toward the bottom and right of the view. As mentioned in Chapter 51, I have also always followed a general rule of thumb to keep dashboard components—including titles, filters, and charts—to twelve or fewer.

For more on layout, see the most-read Tableau guest post of 2013, Kelly Martin's Dashboard Design and Layout Best Practices (*http://www.tableausoftware.com/public/blog/2013/10/dashboard-design*).

Usability

Similar to layout, implementing good usability is one way you can help end users get the most from your data visualization, even when you don't have the chance to walk them through it.

Make no mistake, usability is an important aspect of design: UX design. Add filters and dashboard actions that allow end users to find their own stories in the data. Inevitably, when users understand how to use your dashboard and find insights on their own, they are more likely to stick and be shared.

Tableau offers so many capabilities, one of the biggest challenges is communicating the interactive features available. Andy Cotgreave offers some great insight and tips on the topic in his article, "How Do You Communicate That People Can Interact with Your Designs?" (*http://bit.ly/2tTbCx4*)

Details

In this case, I saved the best for last. You've likely heard the expression, "the devil is in the details." Well, I'm here to tell you: so is the remarkability of a data visualization. Whenever I share a data visualization that doesn't have any graphic design (as in actual graphics), but the audience thinks that it looks great, I credit the meticulous attention to detail in the dashboard. Many times this type of audience can't quite put their finger on why the dashboard looks good, but I know the secret to my success is that the dashboard is more polished than other work they've seen.

Examples include reducing lines, softening gridlines, adding borders to marks, adding transparency to reveal overlapping marks, formatting filters, and potentially dozens more.

This attention to detail, combined with the four other ways mentioned to balance data and design—even without graphic design expertise—will help your data visualization achieve its full potential by reaching and engaging the most relevant and largest audience possible.

CHAPTER 55

Leveraging Color to Improve Your Data Visualization

The use of color can help a story in your data pop off the page. Color can add a level of professionalism to any project and can even elicit specific emotions in viewers. The use of color is one of the easiest ways to take your data visualization from good to great—so why do we see so many blue, orange, and green lines out there? Maybe it's that creative design is thought of as unnecessary in a corporate setting. Maybe visualization designers don't realize just how easy it is to set your dashboards apart by introducing some custom color. True, Tableau worked hard to provide standard color options that work very well together, but maybe you need to align your data visualization with your corporate identity or are just looking for a way to help your work stand out. To help you leverage color to improve your data visualization, this chapter shares an introduction to color theory and points you to a tutorial for loading custom color palettes into your own version of Tableau so you can use them every day.

The Color Wheel: Where It All Begins

The color wheel is based off of the primary colors of red, yellow, and blue, with secondary and tertiary colors between each of the three primary colors. This allows a designer to visualize the balance and harmony of colors when they are side by side. The colors on the outside ring of the color wheel shown here are at full saturation, meaning there is no black or white added. These are referred to as hues. Adding lightness (white) or darkness (black) will result in different tints and shades of each primary, secondary, and tertiary hues. These variations can be seen as you move to the center of the color wheel. Note that some color wheel illustrations you find may have the original hues represented on a middle ring, with darker shades as you move to the outside of the wheel and lighter tints as you move to the center of the wheel.

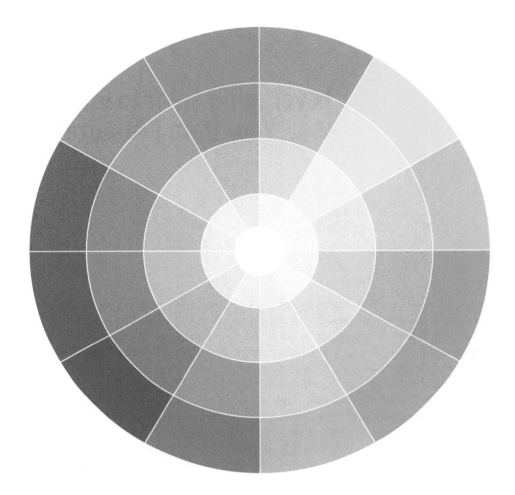

There are ten basic color schemes that can be derived from the color wheel, but for use with Tableau, I am going to recommend starting with complementary and monochromatic schemes.

A *complementary scheme* is created whenever two direct opposites on the color wheel are used. This is a great way to start a custom diverging color palette. For example, from the wheel, you could use blue-violet to represent positive values, and yellow-orange, the color on the exact opposite side of the wheel, to represent negative values. You can also use variations from the inner rings as long as the opposites are on the same ring. A complementary scheme is also a good choice when you are comparing two distinct dimension members, such as East versus West.

A *monochromatic scheme*, created with different shades of the same color, is ideal for a custom sequential palette. To create this, simply pick any column of the color wheel, then use any or all of the variations in that same column. In Tableau, this could be used to color the intensity of a measure, such as sales, with darker variations of the color representing higher sales. This type of color scheme is ideal for a heatmap. I also like to use these schemes when comparing year-over-year values, with the hue representing the current year, and lighter tints representing past years (the older the year, the lighter the tint). Many monochromatic color schemes come standard with Tableau, but maybe you would like to try a different color or control the intensities of a specific color.

The Psychology of Color

If you are looking for help with choosing a color to use in a design, consider what each color means. Thinking about color in this way will not always be necessary, but if your design is themed, using the psychology of color can help your visualization elicit emotional responses in viewers. Here is a brief psychology of each color according to the book *Color Harmony Compendium* by Terry Marks and Tina Sutton:

- Red is the most vibrant color in the spectrum. Not only does it express emotions such as excitement, power, and passion, it brings objects to the foreground. Red is a good choice if you want to illustrate a clear story in your data.

- Yellow is the most visible color and is synonymous with happiness. Yellow also has the advantage of stimulating clear thinking. Using a yellow background with dark type has been proven to aid in retention. Consider using a combination like this when you want your audience to remember one main point from your visualization.

- Orange, like red, is both a high-energy and high-visibility color. Even in small amounts, orange can help convey warning signals, which makes it a good choice for KPIs that are performing below expectations. Orange is also a favorite of children, teens, and athletes, so consider this color accordingly if you work with any of those audiences.

- Green is said to be the most physically relaxing and calming color in the spectrum. It has emerged as a global symbol for safety, so it is no wonder that green is typically associated with positive values in corporate scorecards.

- Blue is the best-liked of all colors. This color is typically perceived as positive, making it an alternative choice for positive values. Blue has the added advantage of being colorblind friendly. Use darker shades of blue to instill a sense of loyalty, trustworthiness, and integrity.

- Purple, especially darker shades of the hue, exudes luxury. Be careful with this one though—studies have shown that people get less work done around purple because it encourages daydreaming!

- Pink, no surprise, is considered the most feminine color. Pink discourages aggressiveness and has a soothing effect. This color would probably be best-served in a themed visualization, but in certain situations could also be a good choice for conveying that performance is positive, or at least in-line with expectations.

- Brown has been shown to put consumers at ease and is considered timeless. It is also closely associated with the earth, making it ideal for visualizations related to the environment.

- Gray has many similar qualities to brown, but is thought of as less warm when used alone. On the positive side, gray can represent conservative authority. Using it as a secondary color can help instill a feeling of maturity and the associated reliability.

Using Custom Color Palettes in Tableau

Now that you have some guidance on which colors to use in your designs, I will close by sharing a way to help you put the use of color into practice. In addition to the custom colors that can be entered as RGB or HSL values by clicking any color in a color legend, Tableau also makes it possible to load custom color palettes that can be saved for permanent use in your own version of Tableau. Tableau allows you to integrate three different types of custom color palettes: categorical, sequential, and diverging. If you have specific colors that you would like to have available to you while you design, start by looking up the hex values for those colors. Once you have the values, all you need to do is add a short snippet of code that includes the hex values in the *preferences.tps* file in your Tableau Repository. There is a great article in Tableau's Knowledge Base (*http://tabsoft.co/2DCM2vO*) showing you exactly what this looks like.

Use these methods for choosing and using color and your visualizations will be standing out in no time!

CHAPTER 56

Three Creative Ways to Use Dashboard Actions

Dashboard actions, filters, and parameters are three of the best tactics to use in Tableau because they provide a way to hand over control of the analysis from you to your end users. This is critical in data visualization because it helps you allow discovery for your users and makes the insights they find easier to retain. In this chapter, we will share three different ways to leverage dashboard actions to improve your user experience.

A Primer on Tableau Dashboard Actions

Before we get to the three ideas on how to use dashboard actions, here's a quick primer in case you are not familiar with this functionality. If you're comfortable with the concept of dashboard actions, feel free to jump down to the first tip, "Tableau Dashboard Action #1: Use Every Sheet as a Filter" on page 355.

Dashboard actions in Tableau allow you to add logic to dashboard components that create actions somewhere else. For example, you can add logic that says, "If a user clicks on Dashboard Sheet 1, I want something to happen on Dashboard Sheet 2." If you think about dashboard actions this way, their setup is very intuitive in Tableau. To set up a dashboard action, navigate to Dashboard → Actions in the top navigation from any dashboard view. A dialog box will appear, and when you click the button "Add Action >" in the lower-left corner, you will be presented with three options for the type of dashboard action that you want to add:

Filter
    If you click sheet 1, sheet 2 will be filtered to whatever you clicked on sheet 1.

Highlight

If you click sheet 1, sheet 2 will be highlighted by whatever you clicked on sheet 1.

URL

If you click sheet 1, open a URL (this can either be opened on a web page dashboard object or in a new browser window).

Once you choose which type of dashboard action to add, you are taken to a new screen where the logic for your dashboard action is coded:

The Source Sheets list shows you all of the sheets you have on the dashboard where you are adding the action. Any sheets selected in this list will cause the dashboard action to execute.

The Target Sheets list also shows all of the sheets in the dashboard, but these are the sheets where you want the action to take place. Pretty intuitive so far, right?

From here, there are a few options for your dashboard actions. First, you can have the action execute on three different interactions (pictured in the upper-right corner of the dialog box):

Hover

If you hover over the source sheet, the action will take place on the target sheet.

Select

    If you click the source sheet, the action will take place on the target sheet.

Menu

    If you hover over the source sheet, a menu of dashboard actions will appear in the tooltip. Clicking one of the menu items will execute the action on the target sheet.

You can also tell Tableau what you want to happen if the dashboard action is cleared (which can be done by clicking escape or clicking away from the chart):

Leave the filter

    Leaves the last dashboard action that happened in place. If you filtered sheet 2 by something clicked on sheet 1, the filter on sheet 2 will stick.

Show all values

    Reverts back to the original view as if no dashboard action took place.

Exclude all values

    Clears everything off of the target sheet, meaning the target sheet will not show unless a dashboard action is executed.

Lastly, you can refine the dashboard action to take place against certain fields using the Target Filters options at the bottom of the dashboard actions dialog box. By default, the dashboard action will run on every shared field between the source sheets and the target sheets. If you want to change the level of detail that a dashboard action runs on a target sheet, you would need to add a target filter to specify the fields—essentially telling Tableau how granular you want to be.

Tableau Dashboard Action #1: Use Every Sheet as a Filter

Any sheet in a dashboard can be used as a filter by simply hovering over the sheet, clicking the down arrow that appears in the upper-right corner, and choosing "Use as Filter." This is basic Tableau functionality, but it wasn't until I saw a presentation from Kevin Krizek of Tableau that I realized it would be good practice to allow users to use *every* sheet in a dashboard as a filter. Adding this functionality to your own dashboards gives your users flexibility in choosing how they want to look at the data.

Let's look at how this would work with the sample dashboard created in Chapter 17. Here is the original view:

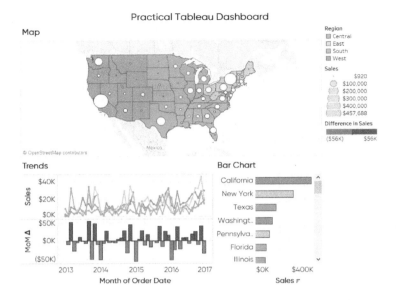

I will now choose to use every individual dashboard sheet as a filter for the entire dashboard by hovering over each sheet, clicking the down arrow that appears in the upper right, and selecting "Use as Filter":

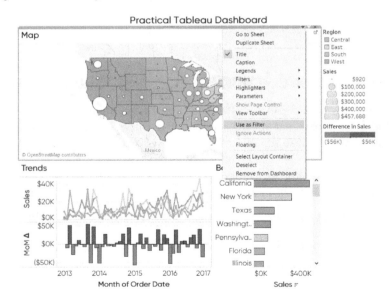

Now when I click any sheet, the other sheets are filtered to whatever I clicked. For example, if I click Washington in my map view, the trend line and bar chart sheets will be filtered to just that state:

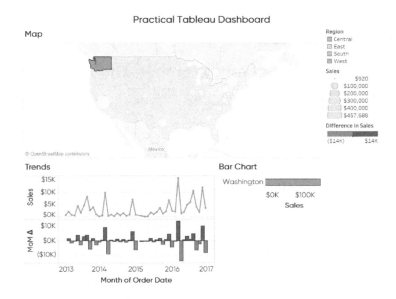

What is actually happening behind the scenes when I choose to use a dashboard sheet as a filter is that Tableau is automatically creating a dashboard action as shown in the first image in this chapter. You can confirm Tableau created dashboard actions by navigating to Dashboard → Actions:

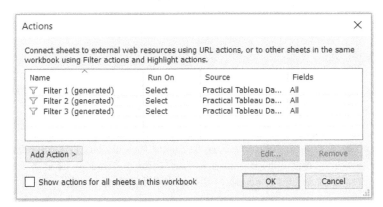

The good thing about setting up each dashboard sheet as a filter instead of sharing one dashboard action between all of the source sheets is that you can refine the actions independently of each other. For example, the bar chart doesn't add much value when it is filtered to just Washington as pictured here. Maybe it would be better if I added a target filter that filtered the bar chart to region instead of state when I click the map. On the other hand, I would like the map to show just one state on the map if I click an individual state on the bar chart. In order to have these two different levels of filter granularity, I would need two separate dashboard actions.

Tableau Dashboard Action #2: Embed YouTube Videos in a Dashboard

This is a tip I first picked up from friend and mentor, Ben Jones, at his excellent blog, DataRemixed.com (*http://dataremixed.com*). The first time I embedded a video in a Tableau dashboard was my 2013 viz, MLB Integration by Team (*http://tabsoft.co/ 2tQvXD4*). In the interactive version, clicking any hall of fame player, represented by a blue Gantt bar, will load a short biography of that player on the scoreboard:

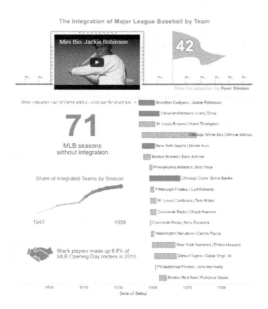

This novel effect was actually quite easy to create in Tableau. The only tricky part is finding the correct YouTube links and having the YouTube links as a field in your underlying data source. Here's a look at the underlying data for this viz:

	A	B	C	D	E	F	G	H	I	J
1	Player	Team	League	Date of First Game	Date of Last Game	Span of Career	Seasons	Debut	Integration	YouTube
2	Jackie Robinson	Brooklyn Dodgers	National	4/15/1947	9/30/1956	3456	ten	1	6.00%	https://www.youtube.com/embed/CX3tv9uKj1I
3	Larry Doby	Cleveland Indians	American	7/5/1947	7/26/1959	4404	thirteen	2	13.00%	https://www.youtube.com/embed/m6yq0BR60oY
4	Hank Thompson	St. Louis Browns	American	7/17/1947	9/30/1956	3363	ten	3	19.00%	
5	Minnie Miñoso	Chicago White Sox	American	4/19/1949	10/5/1980	11492	thirty-two	4	25.00%	
6	Monte Irvin	New York Giants	National	7/8/1949	9/30/1956	2641	eight	5	31.00%	https://www.youtube.com/embed/K6ZHOKRRl84
7	Sam Jethroe	Boston Braves	National	4/18/1950	4/15/1954	1458	five	6	38.00%	
8	Bob Trice	Philadelphia Athletics	American	9/13/1953	5/2/1955	596	three	7	44.00%	
9	Ernie Banks	Chicago Cubs	National	9/17/1953	9/26/1971	6583	nineteen	8	50.00%	https://www.youtube.com/embed/HPL-Z6cst1Q
10	Curt Roberts	Pittsburgh Pirates	National	4/13/1954	6/8/1956	787	three	9	56.00%	
11	Tom Alston	St. Louis Cardinals	National	4/13/1954	9/29/1957	1265	four	10	63.00%	
12	Nino Escalera	Cincinnati Reds	National	4/17/1954	9/25/1954	161	one	11	69.00%	
13	Chuck Harmon	Cincinnati Reds	National	4/17/1954	9/15/1957	1247	four	12	69.00%	
14	Carlos Paula	Washington Senators	American	9/6/1954	6/23/1956	656	three	13	75.00%	
15	Elston Howard	New York Yankees	American	4/14/1955	9/29/1968	4917	fourteen	14	81.00%	
16	Ozzie Virgil, Sr.	Detroit Tigers	American	9/23/1956	6/27/1969	4660	fourteen	15	88.00%	
17	John Kennedy	Philadelphia Phillies	National	4/22/1957	5/3/1957	11	one	16	94.00%	
18	Pumpsie Green	Boston Red Sox	American	7/21/1959	9/26/1963	1528	five	17	100.00%	

To find the correct link to use in your data source, follow these steps:

1. Find the video you want to embed on YouTube.

2. Click the Share icon below the video.

3. Click the Embed tab.

4. Copy the URL that appears *between* the quotation marks:

Now that you have the data, follow these steps to use dashboard actions to embed a YouTube video in your Tableau dashboard:

1. Add a Web Page dashboard object by dragging and dropping it on your view from the left navigation of a dashboard view. In my case, I used a floating Web Page object so I could make it the exact same dimensions as the scoreboard—

providing the illusion that the video is being displayed on the jumbotron. When you add the Web Page object, Tableau will ask you to enter the URL for the page you want to display; leave this blank for now because we will be using a dashboard action to provide these instructions.

2. Add a dashboard action by navigating to Dashboard → Actions → Add Action.

   The dashboard action should be a URL action. You can refine the settings to have the action run on Hover, Select, or Menu; I have chosen for the action to run on Select (which is the same as click).

3. Lastly, for the URL, click the arrow that appears next to the empty URL box. You should be shown a list of options including the URL field in your underlying data. Click the URL field so that the video associated with a particular record will start when the action is run.

   Here's how my final dashboard action looks:

Now if I click a name on the Player sheet that has a corresponding video link, the YouTube video will load in the empty Web Page object that I added. The videos can be consumed right there in line with the rest of the Tableau viz!

Tableau Dashboard Action #3: Do a Google Search or Google Image Search from a Dashboard

One of the most effective implementations of my third tip was in the winning entry of 2015 Iron Viz Championship (*http://tabsoft.co/2DDZ1gZ*) by Shine Pulikathara. In the viz, users can explore news stories or related images by following links provided within the Tableau dashboard for thousands of different data points. The first time I integrated functionality that would do a Google Image Search from a Tableau dashboard was in a viz I created for my wife to document our travels, We're Not In Kansas Anymore (*https://www.ryansleeper.com/were-not-in-kansas-anymore/*). In the interactive version, clicking any location will open a new browser with a Google Image Search for that location:

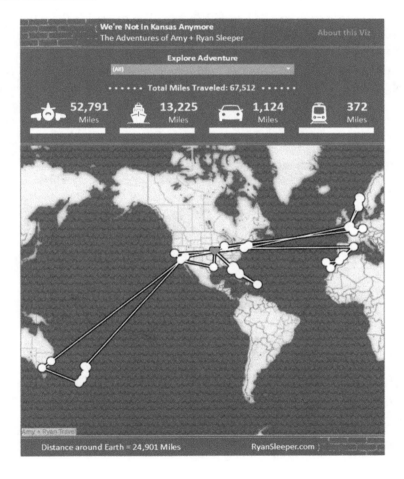

Here are the steps required to create this user experience:

1. Go to Google Images and search for one of the locations.

2. Record the URL that appears in the browser. A search for Kansas City resulted in this URL:

   https://www.google.com/search?q=kansas+city&source=lnms&tbm=isch&sa= X&ved=0ahUKEwiH6eqWhoDKAhVWz2MKHctYBJsQ_AUICSgD&biw= 1366&bih=643

   You can keep the entire link, but all that you actually need is: *https:// www.google.com/search?q=kansas+city&tbm=isch*—this URL includes the query (Kansas City) and tells Google to show results on the image tab (isch = image search)

3. Add a dashboard action by navigating to Dashboard → Actions → Add Action.

   The dashboard action should be a URL action. You can refine the settings to have the action run on Hover, Select, or Menu; I have chosen for the action to run on Select (which is the same as click).

4. Lastly, for the URL, paste the URL that you recorded from the previous search. Replace the portion of the URL for the query, which is the text immediately following the "?q=", with a field from your data. You can add a field from your data source by clicking the arrow that appears next to the empty URL box. I wanted to run a search for each city, so I used the field <City> from my data source.

Here's how my final dashboard action looks:

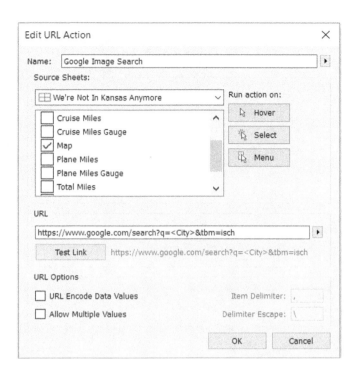

Now if I click a place on my map, a Google Image search is executed with the name of that city (from my underlying data) as the search query!

This chapter has provided an introduction to dashboard actions in Tableau, showed you how to use every sheet as a filter, how to embed a video in a Tableau dashboard, and how to do a Google search from a Tableau dashboard. All three of these dashboard action examples share a common thread of enabling discovery, one tactic for creating insights and improving retention for you and your audience.

CHAPTER 57

How to Conditionally Format Individual Rows or Columns

Almost every Tableau user has also been, or still is, a heavy Excel user. Being that we almost all learned Excel first, it is natural to approach a tool like Tableau for the first time with some preconceived notions about how we think it should work. While there is some overlap between the reporting outputs of the two software programs, it can take some time to understand how the two programs differ as well as best fit together.

While there are tremendous advantages to using both programs, I've seen firsthand how learned behavior for Excel can become a barrier to adoption of Tableau. One such example relates to conditional formatting, and the ability to modify individual rows or columns. This is very easy to do in Excel because you can modify every single individual cell exactly as you wish. While Tableau certainly has many encoding options available through the Marks Cards, it can seem a little "all or nothing." For example, if you place a measure on the Color Marks Card, then *all* marks on the view are colored.

This chapter shows you how to use the *legends per measure* feature and a trick to conditionally format in Tableau like you can in Excel.

How to Use Legends Per Measure

One of the features released with Tableau version 10.2 helps solve the limitation of "all or nothing" encoding. With legends per measure, if you build a highlight table with multiple measures, then color the marks by the Measure Values field, you can create a color legend for each measure on the view.

The first step to use legends per measure in Tableau is to set up a table that uses the Measure Names field. Next, place the Measure Values field on the Color Marks Card. In the past, this would result in one color legend for the measure values, with the same colors being applied across the entire table of different measure names. With legends per measure, simply clicking the Measure Values field on the Color Marks Card and choosing Use Separate Legends will result in independent legends for each measure in the table:

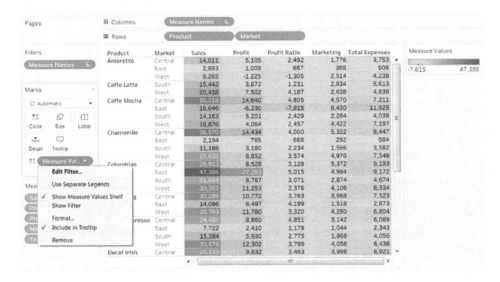

Here is how the highlight table looks with legends per measure applied:

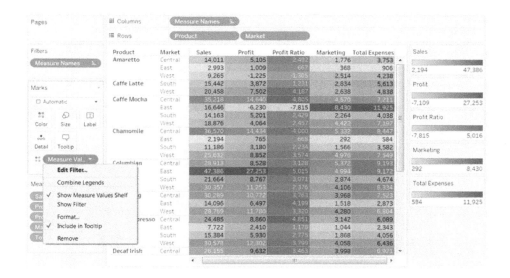

Note you can also recombine the legends by clicking the Measure Values field on the Color Marks Card again and choosing Combine Legends.

How to Conditionally Format in Tableau Like Excel

Legends per measure is a nice step toward providing flexible formatting for highlight tables, but it still doesn't allow you to *conditionally* format the individual columns for measure names. For example, what if you wanted to color the cells for each measure name based on whether a condition was met for each respective measure? Fortunately, there is a trick that leverages a placeholder field to allow you this level of Excel-like conditional formatting in Tableau.

To illustrate the need for this trick and provide a tutorial on how it's used, we will be using this Tableau dashboard that is used to evaluate results for A-B split tests on a company's website:

Testing Dashboard: Test #206

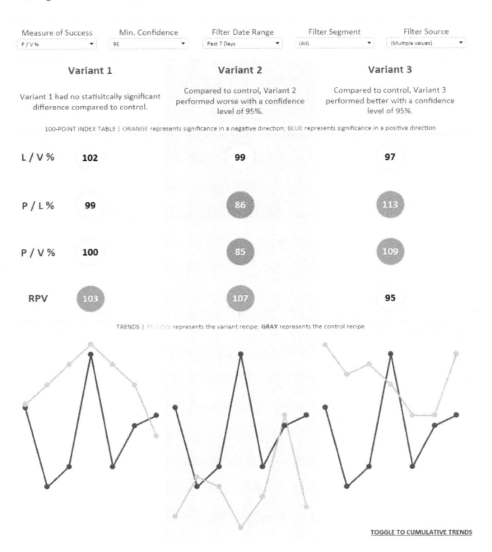

	Measure of Success	Min. Confidence	Filter Date Range	Filter Segment	Filter Source
	P / V % ▼	95 ▼	Past 7 Days ▼	(All) ▼	(Multiple values) ▼

Variant 1

Variant 1 had no statlsitcally significant difference compared to control.

Variant 2

Compared to control, Variant 2 performed worse with a confidence level of 95%.

Variant 3

Compared to control, Variant 3 performed better with a confidence level of 95%.

100-POINT INDEX TABLE | ORANGE represents significance in a negative direction; BLUE represents significance in a positive direction

	Variant 1	Variant 2	Variant 3
L / V %	102	99	97
P / L %	99	86	113
P / V %	100	85	109
RPV	103	107	95

TRENDS | YELLOW represents the variant recipe; GRAY represents the control recipe

TOGGLE TO CUMULATIVE TRENDS

We will be focusing on the 100-point index table in the middle. The table has a column for each variant recipe in a split test and rows for common web KPIs such as Leads/Visits Rate, Purchases/Leads Rate, Purchases/Visits Rate, and Revenue Per Visit. The label on each circle is a 100-point index score with a score of 100 indicating the variant performed the same as the control recipe; scores above 100 indicate higher performance; scores below 100 indicate lower performance.

The special aspect of this table is that the circles are colored by whether or not the variant recipes performed differently than the control recipe with statistical significance. There is a parameter at the top that allows the end users to choose their minimum confidence level, then statistical significance is calculated for each recipe and each KPI.

Normally to create a table with different measures, you would use the generated fields for Measure Names and Measure Values. Here's how this table might normally be constructed (control recipe is filtered out for consistency):

So far so good, but the issue presents itself when I go to conditionally color the circles for statistical significance. With this default setup, I can only color the circles by one field at a time. Further, every row will be colored by that same field. So which one do I pick? Here's what the table looks like if I color the table by statistical significance for P/L % (Purchases/Leads Rate):

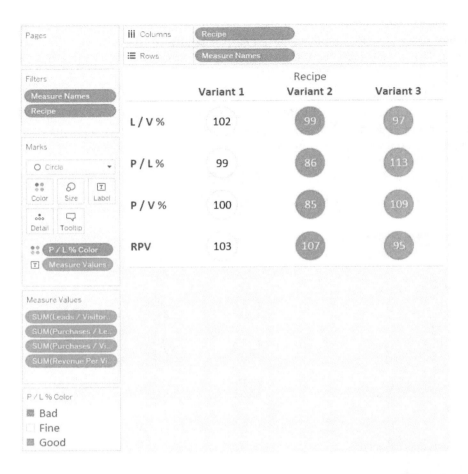

The color is correct for the P/L% row, but because the Color Marks Card is coloring every mark on the view by the same thing, all four KPI rows receive the same color treatment. What I really want is to conditionally format the KPI rows independently of each other so that the color indicators are applied only to their respective KPI.

The Solution: A Calculated "Placeholder" Field

The trick for conditionally formatting the rows independently of each other is to create separate Marks Shelves for each row. This is achieved through a simple calculated field that looks like this:

MIN(0)

Now if the table is built with a Placeholder for each of the four rows instead of the Measure Names field, the rows can be modified independently of each other. Here's how my final table looks under the hood:

Notice that there are now four different sets of Marks Cards, one for each Placeholder field, or in this case, each KPI. Since there are independent Marks Cards, you can independently modify each row. This way, the P/L% row can be colored by the statistical significance for P/L%, while the row for L/V% can be colored by the statistical significance for L/V%, and so on!

Note that this example modified rows, but the same exact approach can be used for columns.

The one big drawback to this approach is that you lose the row headers, but it is fairly easy to add text boxes for each row on the dashboard as pictured here.

This is just one example of applying conditional formatting in Tableau like you can in Excel, but you can format the rows with any of the options available to you on the Marks Cards. For example, one row could be just text, while the other rows could be circles. Some rows can have different shapes. You could have different sized marks to highlight a key finding. The list goes on and on…

CHAPTER 58

Five Tips for Creating Efficient Workbooks

One of the most common questions I receive from new Tableau users is, "How much data can Tableau handle?" Further, I commonly undertake Tableau engagements with the exclusive goal of making workbooks run more efficiently. Tableau is capable of handling extremely large datasets, and the software only becomes more powerful with each new release.

That being said, providing an answer on how much data Tableau can handle is a tricky question, and that's because "big data" is a relative term. Whenever a new field is placed on a view, Tableau queries the underlying data to visualize the answer. This works much like when a database query language like SQL is used to ask questions of a database. For this reason, the efficiency can depend on many factors, including not only the number of records, but the processing power of the hardware, the complexity of calculations, the type of data, and so on.

I won't go deep into technical details and optimizations in this chapter, but give five tips anyone can use to make Tableau workbooks run more efficiently. While Tableau likely won't crash on you when dealing with a large dataset, the time it takes your visualization to load should be considered as a measure of good user experience.

Credit: It's hard to pick just five Tableau efficiency tips, but the following was prioritized in part because of this great Tableau post: "6 Tips to Make Your Dashboards More Performant" (*http://tabsoft.co/2DEgJAN*) by Nicholas Hara.

Five Tips for Creating Efficient Workbooks in Tableau

Tip #1: Think Strategically About the Data You Absolutely Need

By far the most powerful efficiency gains that I've witnessed were when the size of the dataset was reduced by removing irrelevant data from the file. This may seem obvious, but I can't tell you how many times I've seen authors attempting to visualize more data than they need. For example, if the company-wide standard for your analyses is year over year, don't even bring in the data from three years ago. In this scenario, you immediately remove at least one-third of the data before you've even started!

Another piece of low-hanging fruit I often see is the aggregation of dates. For example, your company may be collecting data at the timestamp level, but if your analyses do not require hour/minute/second level views, you can aggregate the dates by day. This will significantly reduce the number of records.

These are just two common examples, but bringing in only the data you need is the first step to creating efficient workbooks in Tableau.

Prepare data before it gets to Tableau

In Chapter 79, I mention that I prefer to prepare my data before it gets to Tableau. While Tableau has many powerful data preparation features, they are not the primary value of the software, and there are better tools for this specific job. I recommend using a tool outside of Tableau to prepare the dataset, so that once you start using it in Tableau, Tableau can do what it's best at.

Use context filters

I've combined the "first" tip into three parts because preparing and limiting the size of the data are that critical to the efficiency of your Tableau workbooks. Another way to limit the data that Tableau is visualizing is to leverage "context filters." *Context filters are processed before anything else and can be thought of as temporary tables for your view.* When a context filter is used, Tableau creates a subset of the dataset limited to the filter selection; then all subsequent filters hit only the subset of the data. Any dimension filter can be used as a context filter by right-clicking the filter from the Filters Shelf and choosing "Add to context."

Tip #2: Limit Filters; Use the "Apply" Button

When you think about filters as queries on the data, it makes logical sense that each incremental filter on a view will add processing time. While I don't have a hard-and-fast rule for how many filters are acceptable, prioritizing which fields should be available as a filter can dramatically improve the efficiency of your views. If fields should be filtered more permanently, consider tip #1 and either filter the data before it gets to Tableau or add the filter to context to speed up processing.

One way to reduce filters on a dashboard is to use dashboard actions instead. Using a sheet as a filter or adding a filter dashboard action that runs on hover or select provides a more efficient means for filtering the rest of the dashboard.

If you *are* using filters, a handy feature of Tableau is that dimension filters that are being shown to end users on the view can be set to process only after all changes to the filter have been selected. For example, if you are showing a dimension filter that includes 10 dimension members, then by default, Tableau will apply the filter every time a dimension member is checked or unchecked on the filter. So if you uncheck one dimension member, the view is reprocessed; uncheck a second dimension member and the view is reprocessed again. If you would prefer that the view only process after both dimension members have been unchecked in this scenario, click the drop-down arrow on the filter, hover over Customize, and select "Show Apply button." Now the filters will be processed only after the end user has made her filter selections and then clicked the Apply button.

Tip #3: Reduce the Number of Marks

When you think of each data point, or mark, as a record that needs to be processed on a view, this tip also makes logical sense: the more marks that need to be processed, the longer it may take for the visualization to appear. The efficiency tips to this point should have a big impact on the number of marks you are left to work with, but this is still good to keep in mind. Depending on your analysis requirements, it may not always be possible to reduce the number of marks on a view, but sometimes there is an opportunity to change the level of detail to improve efficiency. Consider ways you can aggregate data points into hierarchies and/or make the analysis less granular.

Tip #4: Boolean ☒Integer ☒Float ☒Date ☒Date Time ☒String

One of the most valuable features of Tableau is its ability to execute custom calculations on the fly. This allows for "discovery" analytics, where you can quickly pivot through different analyses without even necessarily knowing exactly what you are looking for. While the calculations are very powerful, they can come with a cost to the efficiency of the workbook. To help get the most out of the calculated fields functionality and keep your workbooks running smoothly, think about the data types in your calculations. Not all data types are created equal in terms of efficiency; here is a list of data types going in order from most efficient to least efficient, with a short definition:

Boolean
    A true or false binary result

Integer
    Whole numbers

Float
    Any number including decimals

Date
    Date aggregated at the day level

Date Time
    Date including the timestamp level

String
    Text

When possible, use more-efficient data types. Rather than a column with two possible text outcomes, convert it to a Boolean that has the outcomes of True or False. If you have a large dataset of numbers, consider whether it's possible to throw out decimals and deal only with whole numbers as integers. If you have dates with timestamps, consider aggregating them at the date level and leave out the timestamps.

Tip #5: Reduce Sheets, Dashboards, and Data Sources

This tip not only helps with efficiency, it will help you keep your sanity and improve the end user experience. In general, the more sheets, dashboards, and data sources you have in a workbook, the more potential there is for the workbook to run slowly. This is especially true when you are combining many different sheets on a dashboard with views that are blending data from multiple data sources.

As with database architecture, your Tableau workbooks will run more efficiently if you put some thought into how workbooks can be broken down into smaller, individual files. Not only will this help with efficiency, it will be easier for you to manage and help your end users. This is even easier and more efficient if you have Tableau Server or Tableau Online because several smaller workbooks can share the same data source saved to the cloud.

In the case that I truly have several dashboards that are connected, I like to create a navigation dashboard that helps the end user locate the most relevant views for their specific business questions. If you have Tableau Server or Tableau Online, the navigation links can be set up to open new dashboards by simply adding URL dashboard actions with links to the dashboard locations online. This same technique can be used from within specific dashboards (i.e., add a URL action to run on Menu that links the end user to another dashboard/additional information).

While this isn't a comprehensive list of Tableau efficiency tips, I have found that implementing these tactics follows (at least) the 80/20 rule, in that these five tips alone should help capture at least 80 percent of the possible efficiency gains in your workbooks.

CHAPTER 59

Using Level of Detail Expressions to Create Benchmarks

One of the most powerful features that shipped with Tableau 9.0 was "Level of Detail" (LOD) functionality, which provides a syntax for explicitly assigning a different level of detail, or granularity, to a measure. This unlocks many valuable analysis opportunities, with just a few outlined in Tableau's post, Top 15 LOD Expressions (*http://www.tableau.com/LOD-expressions*). I admit that I've probably leaned on this functionality *too* much since its release because it is such a handy way to get the exact results I am looking for.

This chapter shares one of my favorite uses for LOD expressions: the ability to create a constant measure that can be used as a benchmark. For example, sometimes you want to compare the performance of a KPI now versus a KPI last year. Another example is in split testing, where it is common to need to compare the performance of a variant recipe to the performance of a control recipe. In the past, table calculations were the easiest way to create these comparisons, but the simple LOD calculation I'm about to share makes the analysis slightly more foolproof because you do not need to worry about the scope or direction of a table calculation.

This chapter shares a specific use case for using LOD expressions, but is not a comprehensive training on what LOD expressions are and how they work. If you need more information, I encourage you to read the Tableau whitepaper, "Understanding Level of Detail (LOD) Expressions" (*http://tabsoft.co/2DDSm6q*).

How to Use Tableau Level of Detail (LOD) Expressions to Create Benchmarks

There are several analyses where a fixed comparison measure would be valuable. To name just a few: the performance during a specific year, a goal, a competitor, or the performance of a control recipe. For the purposes of this illustration, I'm going to use the Sample - Superstore data to compare the sales each year to the sales in the year 2012.

Here's a simple table showing sum of sales by year:

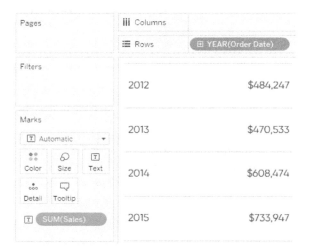

As you can see, we have four years of sales data. Let's pretend that because 2012 is the oldest year in our company's dataset, management wants to use 2012 as a benchmark for the lowest acceptable sales number. So we will create a comparison metric that isolates the sales in 2012. I realize this isn't the best example of a true business scenario, but work with me momentarily—I'm showing how you can isolate a comparison metric without using table calculations.

In order to isolate 2012 sales, your first instinct may be to create a calculated field that looks like this:

```
SUM(IF YEAR([Order Date]) = 2012 THEN SALES END)
```

I'm going to go ahead and make a calculated field with this formula and add it as a second column in the view:

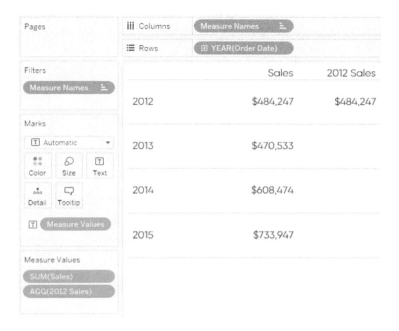

Our calculated field worked, but you can see that only the row for 2012 is populated with the 2012 Sales amount. That's because Tableau is looking at each row and running our IF/THEN logic. It looks at the first row and sees that the year of 2012 matches the year in the calculated field, so it shows a result. It then looks at the second row, which is for 2013, sees that YEAR([Order Date]) does not equal 2012, so it does not display the sales amount. The same is true for 2014 and 2015, so there are nulls for 2012 Sales in the cells for every year other than 2012. This doesn't provide any value for our analysis because we can't, for example, divide 2013's sales amount by 2012's sales amount. In order to create that type of growth calculation, 2013 Sales and 2012 Sales would need to be on the same row.

This is where a LOD expression is handy in creating a fixed comparison measure for 2012 sales.

There are three types of LOD expressions: EXCLUDE, INCLUDE, and FIXED. To create my benchmark for 2012 Sales, I am going to leverage the EXCLUDE expression, which basically means Tableau is going to ignore whichever dimension I put in the expression.

My calculated field using LOD expressions for 2012 Sales is:

```
{EXCLUDE [Order Date]: SUM(IF YEAR([Order Date]) = 2012 THEN Sales END)}
```

This calculation says, "Regardless of the Order Date dimension, which is currently being used to display one year per row, always show the sum of sales from 2012."

Note that because I am wanting to ignore the date dimension in this specific example, Order Date is the dimension following the EXCLUDE function. If you are creating a benchmark for something else such as a product category, manager, or test recipe, substitute Order Date with the appropriate dimension for your use case.

Now my table looks like this:

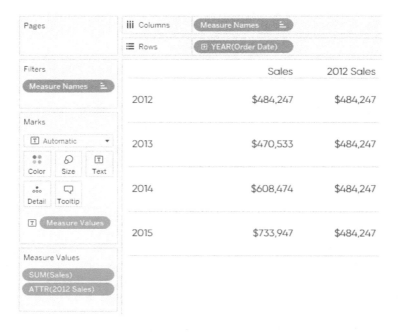

Now every year displays the 2012 Sales amount in the 2012 Sales column. Now that the sales for each respective year and the sales for 2012 are on the same row, they can be used for calculations, such as percent growth.

As just one example, I'll create a calculated field to show percent difference from 2012 Sales and place it on the view as a third column. The formula is:

```
SUM(Sales) / SUM(2012 Sales)-1
```

Here's the final view:

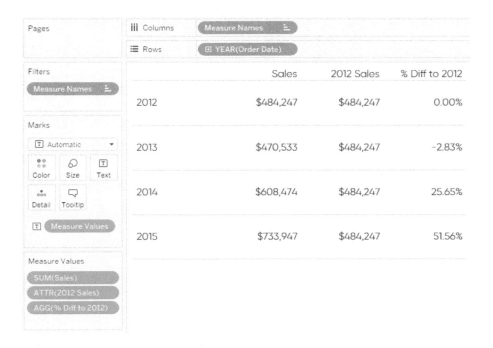

	Sales	2012 Sales	% Diff to 2012
2012	$484,247	$484,247	0.00%
2013	$470,533	$484,247	-2.83%
2014	$608,474	$484,247	25.65%
2015	$733,947	$484,247	51.56%

The percent difference from 2012 Sales is just one example, but now that this benchmark measure is available, it can be used in a variety of calculated fields. I have personally used it to calculate t-statistics in test results and to create more reliable 100-point index scores in Tableau (discussed in Chapter 61). You can even create a parameter to dynamically change the benchmark measure. For example, in my formula for 2012 Sales, I could replace "2012" with an integer parameter that allows you to toggle between any of the four years on the view. This would allow the end user to change the benchmark metric on the fly. I have found this approach to be a simple alternative to table calculations that provides a more consistent, user-friendly, and foolproof result.

CHAPTER 60

Designing Device-Specific Dashboards

One of the most common questions I receive while conducting Tableau training is "What dashboard dimensions should I use?"

As is the case with many aspects of analytics, the answer is largely dependent on the audience. Or more specifically, the answer in this case comes down to how the audience will be consuming the dashboard.

For example, will the dashboard be consumed by people at work on large desktop monitors? Or even larger conference room monitors?

Do you expect the end users to consume the dashboard on their laptops outside of working hours? What about their mobile devices outside of working hours?

As you know, there are many different devices that your dashboard can be consumed on, all with their own unique dimensions. So which one should you design for? Sure, you can use automatic sizing, but the results are unpredictable and not always ideal.

If I wasn't positive on this answer in the past, my default dashboard size of choice was 850 pixels wide by 1100 pixels tall. These dimensions are the same as an 8½- by 11-inch piece of paper, so at the very least, I knew the dashboard would look great if it was printed out or saved as a PDF and attached to an email.

Fortunately, I no longer have to pick just one dashboard size, thanks to a new feature in Tableau 10: *Device-Specific Dashboards*, or DSD. The DSD feature allows the Tableau dashboard author to lay the same dashboard out with different dimensions, then Tableau will automatically detect the screen size the dashboard is being consumed on and display the appropriate version.

Before Tableau 10, it was possible to display a dashboard with different dimensions based on the end user's screen size, but it required a separate file to be built for each dashboard as well as technical understanding of CSS code. While not truly "responsive," DSD makes it possible to deliver a much better user experience that is tailored to the end user's environment.

To illustrate how to design device-specific dashboards in Tableau 10, we will look at my dashboard, NFL Concussions by Collision Source (*https://www.ryansleeper.com/ what-collisions-cause-the-most-concussions-in-the-nfl/*). This dashboard was featured in the online version of *U.S. News & World Report*. Since *U.S. News & World Report* receives a large amount of traffic across several different devices, they asked me to create two different versions of the dashboard. Their web development team would then add some code within the article to display the most-appropriate version of the dashboard based on the viewer's screen size. For this reason, you can see two separate workbooks in my Tableau Public profile for the same analysis:

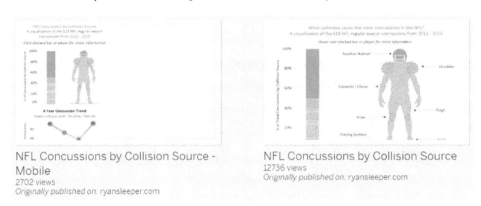

NFL Concussions by Collision Source - Mobile
2702 views
Originally published on: ryansleeper.com

NFL Concussions by Collision Source
12736 views
Originally published on: ryansleeper.com

With the DSD feature in Tableau 10, I'm able to combine the different versions into one file and have the best one displayed automatically. I also don't need any technical web design knowledge to make it happen.

I will start this tutorial by downloading the original version of the NFL Concussions by Collision Source visualization from my Tableau Public profile page and opening it in Tableau 10:

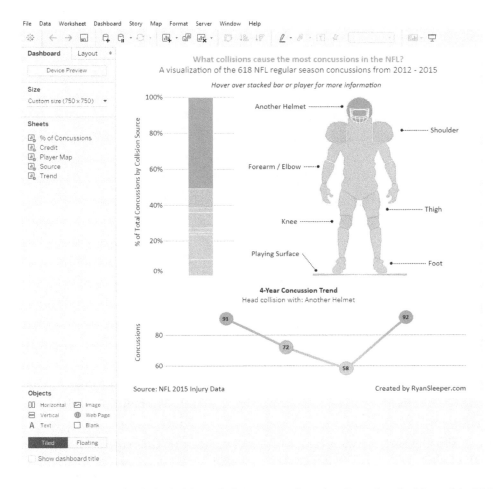

As you can see in the left dashboard design panel under Size, the dashboard is 750 pixels wide by 750 pixels high. What's new is that I now have the ability to click Device Preview see how this 750 by 750 dashboard will look on different devices. If I were to click the Device Preview button, Tableau draws a border around the dashboard to show you the dimensions of common devices. By default, the first preview is for a tablet in landscape (or horizontal) layout:

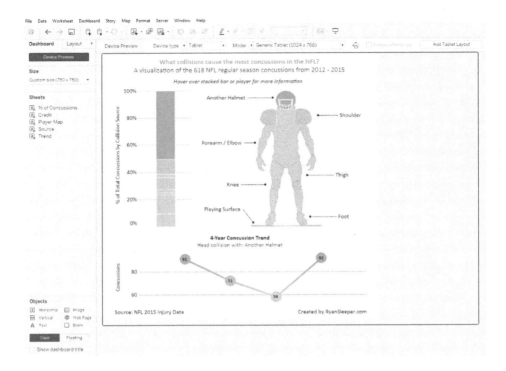

The Generic Tablet dimensions are 1024 wide by 768 high. I designed the visualization to be 750 by 750 so there is some blank space on the right and 18 pixels of blank space along the bottom.

I can also flip through the device previews by choosing different device types and even models at the top. For this real-life example, I wanted to create one 750 by 750 dashboard that would be the original full-size version, but also one additional version suitable for a phone. To create a separate layout for phone, navigate to the Phone device type from within the device preview, choose a model, and click Add Phone Layout. I have chosen the Generic Phone dimensions:

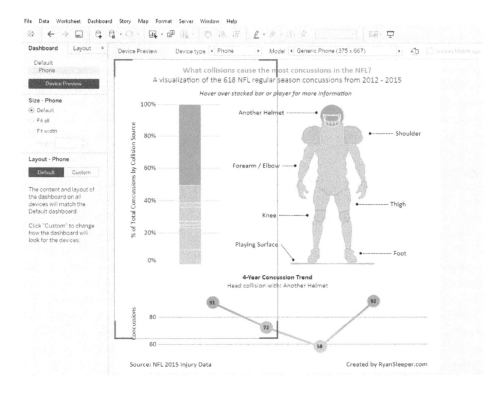

As with the tablet preview before, you can now see how my full-size dashboard would fit when being consumed on a phone. Since I clicked Add Phone Layout, you also see this version show up in the upper-left corner. To get a head start on resizing the dashboard within these generic phone dimensions, choose "Fit all" from the options on the left. After making this selection, my dashboard looks like this:

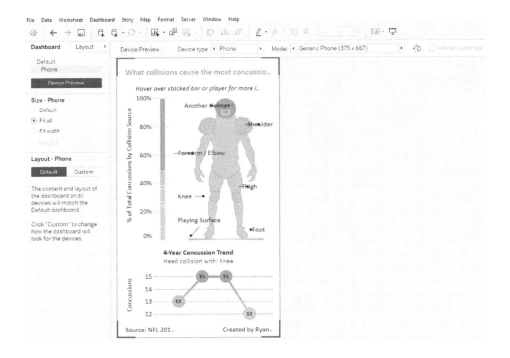

You can see many different problems with this view. What's scary is this is close to how my dashboard would look on a phone if I chose automatic sizing! For this version, I will resize each dashboard component to make it look better when viewed on a phone. To show the full functionality of DSD, I will even delete an entire dashboard component so you can see how much you can customize device-specific dashboards. Here's how my phone-specific layout looks:

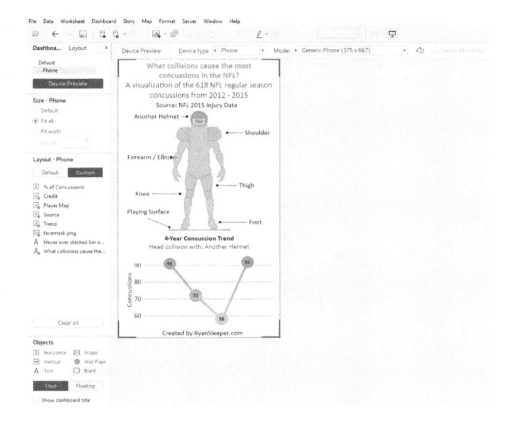

Notice that on the phone-sized version, I opted to delete the stacked bar chart in the upper-left corner of the dashboard. Even though I deleted it from the phone-sized version, this chart still exists on the original version. I can compare the two versions by toggling back and forth between Default and Phone in the upper-left corner of the dashboard authoring interface.

Now when I publish this, Tableau will identify the screen size for me and automatically display the most appropriate version!

CHAPTER 61

How to Make a Stoplight 100-Point Index

As an analyst, the stoplight 100-point index is a reporting mechanism that I cannot live without. If you are not familiar, the 100-point index is a simple way to know whether a measure is outperforming or underperforming a comparison measure, with the comparison measure typically being a goal or the performance during a prior period. An index score of 100 means that the measure in question matches the comparison measure; a score greater than 100 indicates the measure is outperforming the comparison; a score less than 100 indicates the measure is underperforming the comparison.

This chapter shares three ways for getting the most out of 100-point index scores in Tableau: how to set up a 100-point index, how to make a custom color palette to be used in a stoplight 100-point index highlight table, and a trick for how to handle reverse 100-point index scores (when outperforming the comparison means a negative impact on the business).

What Is a Stoplight Index?

A stoplight index enhances the traditional 100-point index score by encoding the scores by color for faster processing. This is essentially a highlight table with 100-point index scores for different measures. Outperform the comparison (i.e., a score >= 100) and the indicator is green; come close but fall just short (i.e., the score is between 90 and 99) and the indicator is yellow; underperform goal or prior period (i.e., a score < 90) and the indicator is red.

Here is an example showing a year-over-year index. For the purposes of illustration, this is the Sample – Superstore data with filters for year (keeping only 2014 and 2013) and Sub-Category (keeping only Chairs):

	2013	2014	Index
Discount	15.94%	17.88%	112
Profit	$6,228	$5,763	93
Profit Ratio	8.68%	6.87%	79
Quantity	528	614	116
Sales	$71,735	$83,919	117

Note that Discount, Quantity, and Sales were all up year over year, so they are colored green. Profit was down year over year, but still within 10%, so it is colored yellow. Profit ratio is down more than 10% year over year, so it is colored red.

Why Do I Have to Use the Fancy Approach You're About to Share?

If you're used to working in Tableau, your first instinct to get the desired color encoding shown and described here would be to make a calculated field, similar to this:

```
IF [Measure 100-Point Index] >= 100 THEN "Green"
ELSEIF [Measure 100-Point Index] < 100 AND [Measure 100-Point Index] >= 90
THEN "Yellow"
ELSE "Red"
END
```

You would then place this calculated field on the Color Marks Card to encode the values.

This approach would work for each individual measure, but as discussed in Chapter 57, not if you are wanting to show more than one KPI at a time. It's also a relatively manual approach because you would have to re-create these color instructions for every single measure. This approach would be much easier if you were able to use the Measure Values field in calculated fields, but that functionality is not currently available.

How to Set Up a 100-Point Index

There are always multiple ways to accomplish the same objective in Tableau, and each approach tends to have its own pros and cons. I am going to demonstrate how to set up 100-point index scores using table calculations, which have a major pro of being one of the fastest ways to set up calculated fields, but can be tricky to work with if you lose track of the direction that the table calculation is being calculated. Note that this is an alternative to the approach covered in Chapter 59.

Here is how my table of year-over-year KPIs is set up in Tableau:

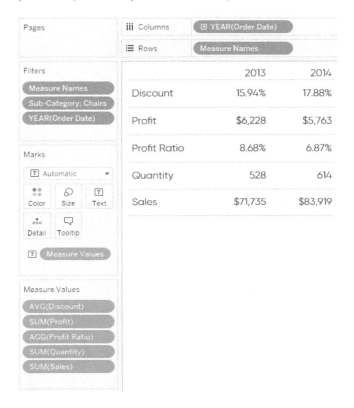

The formula for a 100-point year-over-year index is: (This Year's Performance / Last Year's Performance) * 100

Note you could use a different comparison point than last year's performance by just substituting "Last Year's Performance" with something else, such as a goal.

To create this calculated field in Tableau, you could manually create a calculated field and type out the logic, but I am going to lean on table calculations for a headstart. First, right-click a measure on the Measure Values Shelf and choose Quick Table Calculation. The Difference table calculation is the closest to my index formula so I am going to choose that:

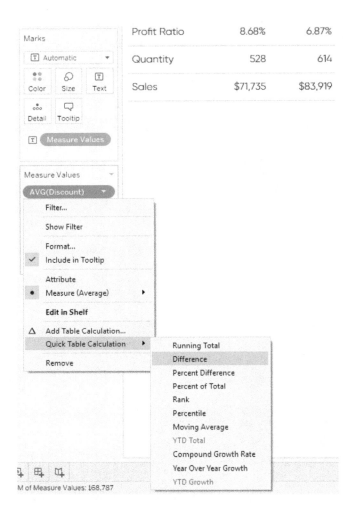

After adding the table calculation for difference, the formula looks like this:

```
ZN(AVG([Discount])) - LOOKUP(ZN(AVG([Discount])), -1)
```

In English, this is just saying if there is a value for Discount in the right column, take that value and subtract the value from one column prior.

There are just two small changes that need to be made to this calculation to convert it into a 100-point index score. These changes can be made by simply double-clicking the measure that you just added the table calculation to on the Measure Values Shelf.

First, change the minus sign to a division sign ("/"). Then add "*100" to the end. The formula for a 100-point index score looking at the Discount measure is:

```
ZN(AVG([Discount])) / LOOKUP(ZN(AVG([Discount])), -1)*100
```

If your measure had any predefined number formatting, you will want to change the formatting to number custom with no decimal places. This can be accomplished by right-clicking the measure, choosing Format, then changing the number format. For example, my discount measure is normally displayed as a percentage, so I need to change the number format for my index score so that it is not displayed as a percentage or multiplied by 100 again.

At this point, my view looks like this:

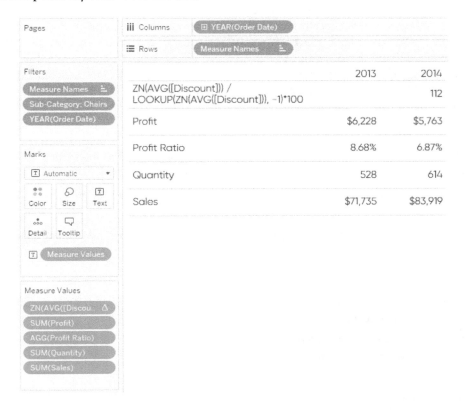

If you want to give the calculation a better name and have it available for future use, drag the newly created measure from the Measure Values Shelf to the Measures area of the Data pane where the rest of your measures reside. You will then be able to give it a name and Tableau will save the calculation as a calculated field in your workbook.

Repeat this process for the rest of your measures on the view and you have a nice table of 100-point index scores.

Adding Color to a 100-Point Index Table

The view we have created at this point is providing a lot of value because the user can very quickly determine at what scale the KPIs are underperforming or outperforming the comparison point. However, the view can be processed even faster by converting the crosstab of index scores into a highlight table. For more on highlight tables, see Chapter 19.

I mentioned earlier that Measure Values cannot currently be used in calculated fields, which prevents us from creating one calculated field to provide logic on how Tableau should color each index score. Fortunately, Measure Values *can* be used on the Color Marks Card. Now that all of our scores are normalized on a 100-point scale, they can share the same color scale. If you drag the Measure Values field onto the Color Marks Card, the higher index scores will be colored darker green, and the lower index scores will be colored lighter green.

Now here's the cool part.

You can use a custom ordered-sequential color palette, combined with specific step-sizes and ranges, to get the index scores colored as you would like.

Creating custom color palettes is beyond the scope of this chapter, but if you would like to learn more about color, see Chapter 55.

In the meantime, follow these steps and you can use the custom color palette shown next:

1. On your computer, navigate to Documents → My Tableau Repository.

2. Right-click the file called Preferences and open it with Notepad or TextEdit (or your favorite text editor).

3. Paste this code over everything in the file (assuming you don't have other custom colors), then save the file:

```
<?xml version='1.0'?>
<workbook>
<preferences>
<color-palette name="Stoplight 100-Point Index (1 Scale)"
    type="ordered-sequential" >
<color>#db5656</color>
<color>#db5656</color>
<color>#db5656</color>
<color>#db5656</color>
<color>#db5656</color>
<color>#db5656</color>
<color>#db5656</color>
<color>#db5656</color>
<color>#db5656</color>
<color>#edc64c</color>
```

```
<color>#42af9b</color>
<color>#42af9b</color>
<color>#42af9b</color>
<color>#42af9b</color>
<color>#42af9b</color>
<color>#42af9b</color>
<color>#42af9b</color>
<color>#42af9b</color>
<color>#42af9b</color>
<color>#42af9b</color>
</color-palette>
</preferences>
</workbook>
```

In order for new custom colors to be available, you have to close and re-open Tableau.

Now that you have this color palette available, you can choose this palette and apply some additional settings so that every score above 100 is colored green, every score between 90 and 99 is colored yellow, and every color below 90 is colored red. To change the color palette and edit the settings, click the color legend for Measure Values.

My color palette has 20 colors in it that go in sequential order. The first nine colors are red, which covers scores 0–90; the tenth slot is yellow, which covers scores between 90–100; the rest of the slots are green and cover scores 100 and up. With this in mind, the color settings are the result of some basic mathematical problem solving. I'll make the scale go from 0–200 and set the step size to 20 so that I know that each color on my sequential palette will represent 10 points or 5% of the spectrum.

Here's how my view looks with my color settings:

After saving the color settings, convert the view to a highlight table by changing the mark type from Automatic to Square. My final index score view looks like this:

From here, I could hide the 2013 column or even float this view next to the original table of numbers on a dashboard as pictured at the beginning of this chapter.

What If Outperforming the Comparison Is Bad?

Sometimes an index score greater than 100 is bad. For example, we probably don't want to increase the discounts we are handing out to customers each year, but the index table we just made shows discount as green because it increased 12 points year over year.

To alleviate this, I've come up with a little trick for creating stoplight 100-point index tables, even when an index greater than 100 can mean something positive or negative. First, I've extended my custom sequential color palette to include 40 steps. The first 20 steps cover scores that would be bad if the index is greater than 100; the next 20 steps cover our existing index scores, when a score above 100 is positive. Here is the palette if you want to add it to your custom colors as outlined before:

```
<color-palette name="Stoplight 100-Point Index (2 Scales)"
    type="ordered-sequential" >
<color>#db5656</color>
<color>#db5656</color>
<color>#db5656</color>
<color>#db5656</color>
<color>#db5656</color>
<color>#db5656</color>
<color>#db5656</color>
<color>#db5656</color>
<color>#db5656</color>
<color>#edc64c</color>
<color>#42af9b</color>
<color>#42af9b</color>
<color>#42af9b</color>
<color>#42af9b</color>
<color>#42af9b</color>
<color>#42af9b</color>
<color>#42af9b</color>
<color>#42af9b</color>
<color>#42af9b</color>
<color>#42af9b</color>
<color>#db5656</color>
<color>#db5656</color>
<color>#db5656</color>
<color>#db5656</color>
<color>#db5656</color>
<color>#db5656</color>
<color>#db5656</color>
<color>#db5656</color>
<color>#db5656</color>
<color>#edc64c</color>
<color>#42af9b</color>
<color>#42af9b</color>
<color>#42af9b</color>
<color>#42af9b</color>
<color>#42af9b</color>
<color>#42af9b</color>
<color>#42af9b</color>
<color>#42af9b</color>
<color>#42af9b</color>
<color>#42af9b</color>
</color-palette>
```

Once you have saved the new colors and closed/reopened Tableau, there are just two steps to get the desired effect:

1. Using the new custom color palette, change the steps to 40 and the range from −200 to 200.

2. For any measure that you don't want to outperform the comparison, multiply it by −1.

In the Sample - Superstore example that we are working with, I will multiply Discount by −1 by double-clicking the Discount Index field on the Measure Values Shelf and adding "-" to the beginning. Adding a negative sign to the beginning is the same thing as multiplying the calculation by −1.

My view now looks like this:

Now the index score for discount will be green only if it's less than 100. If it's within 10% higher, it will be colored yellow, and if it's more than 10% higher it will be colored red.

You'll see that a negative sign was added to the score. You can edit the format of negative numbers, but cannot get rid of the extra distinction. I personally like to have a visual indicator that some metrics are on a different scale than the others. Here is how my final view looks with the KPI table and index highlight table on two scales:

	2013	2014	Index
Discount	15.94%	17.88%	(112)
Profit	$6,228	$5,763	93
Profit Ratio	8.68%	6.87%	79
Quantity	528	614	116
Sales	$71,735	$83,919	117

Finally, I would be remiss if I didn't mention that the stoplight color palette is not the best choice for the colorblind. Not to mention that (in my humble opinion) red and green is one of the ugliest color pairings. I provided the stoplight example because those are the most common colors requested, and the stoplight concept, as well as the meaning of the stoplight's traditional colors, are (for better or worse) ingrained in the human psyche.

That being said, I encourage you to substitute the hex color values for green, yellow, and red with your own alternatives. Try blue for good, white for OK, and orange for bad. Or maybe there's a way to put the stoplight index into your own brand's colors. I assure you it will be fine if you try something other than red and green!

CHAPTER 62

The Case for One-Dimensional Unit Charts

This year I have found myself gravitating toward stacked bar charts as a way to show comparisons. The chart type is featured prominently in both my NBA Records by Player (*https://www.ryansleeper.com/nba-records-by-player/*) and 50 Years of AFC vs. NFC Matchups (*https://www.ryansleeper.com/50-years-of-afc-vs-nfc-matchups/*) visualizations. I even used a stacked bar chart as the primary visualization to share how much progress I was making while writing *Practical Tableau*.

Something is different about these stacked bars though. I'm generally not a fan of stacked bars because if the stacks are different sizes, and if the stacks do not sit on the baseline, it can be challenging to compare and contrast the different pieces of the bars.

In all three cases I just mentioned, the stacks have equal units. This removes the challenges I have with traditional stacked bars, so I do not think the name gives these charts justice. So that got me wondering if these should be called unit charts.

If you're not familiar with unit charts, here is a well-done example (*http://bit.ly/ 2DEdR6Q*) from one of my data viz heroes, Andy Cotgreave. My issue with the multiple columns and multiple rows approach to most unit charts—especially when they are showing a part to whole relationship—is that these are pie charts in disguise. Very sneaky. Andy always does an amazing job of eliciting dialogue around data visualization in the community so I assume he had a reason behind his chart type selection. Even if he didn't, I'm not mad at him; we all have guilty pleasures. I once made a donut chart (*http://tabsoft.co/2DDYUSc*)… and I enjoyed it.

Pie charts are different though. Pie charts are terrible. I could not have one of my new favorite chart types associated with a pie chart. So I kept searching.

"What are these charts called?!" I screamed (or Googled, actually).

The best I could come up with was a paper authored by another one of my Data Viz Heroes, Stephen Few.*" In classic Few fashion, the paper is unapologetically called, "Unit Charts Are For Kids" (*http://bit.ly/2DEYgnC*).

 Stephen Few has a reputation of being critical, demeaning, and perhaps unkind. I had the privilege of having dinner with him in 2016, and found him to be exceptionally kind and humble. He introduces himself as Stephen, asks questions about you, and intently listens. Even in the cases where the first sentence in this paragraph is true, I have tremendous respect for his passion about the data visualization discipline and his tireless efforts to educate on the topic.

He even opens up the comments on his own popular site to take on debates from anyone. And I do mean anyone. The person that made this chart (*http://bit.ly/2DEdsRV*) could go onto Few's site and tell him why he doesn't know anything about data visualization. I find that admirable.

In the paper, Few walks through why you shouldn't use unit charts. But what really stood out to me is the image of the chart type I was searching for… and a name!

One-Dimensional Unit Charts

Even better, Few *almost* gives this visualization type praise:

The simplest form of a unit chart displays a single row or column of units, rather than a matrix of both as we saw in the previous example. As you can see, a one-dimensional unit chart is simpler to read than a two-dimensional version.

However, he goes on to say:

Given improved ease of use, are one-dimensional unit charts worthwhile? We can read them much as we read bar graphs, with one minor difference—the segmentation of values into units inclines us to slow down and count, as opposed to the simpler, faster task of comparing their overall heights and then decoding their values in relation to a quantitative scale, which is missing. Not a big problem, some might argue, but significant enough to discourage their use when better means are available.

As promised in the title of this chapter, here's my case for one-dimensional unit charts.

By the way, if I were to make a unit chart about the portion of this chapter so far showing how many seconds you've spent reading while not learning the case for one-dimensional unit charts versus the seconds you've spent learning the case for one-dimensional unit charts, it would look something like this:

So let's get to it.

I agree with Few that at the highest level, bar charts communicate data faster than one-dimensional unit charts. He makes a great point that this chart type inclines people to slow down and count the individual units.

But what if the units each mean something unique? The values are equal, but each unit has its own story to tell. That is the case with all of the examples that I've mentioned from my portfolio.

Here is the NBA Records by Player viz:

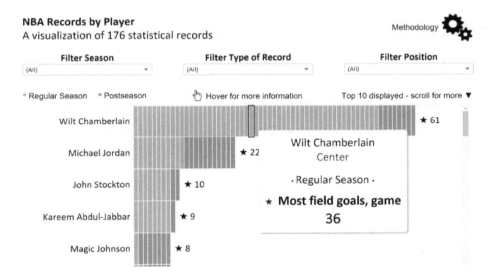

In the interactive version, if you hover over each unit, you are presented with additional information such as which record was achieved, what type of record was achieved, and whether or not the record is shared with any other player. In tools like Tableau, you can take this a step further by linking to additional context. This is the case with my *Practical Tableau* progress to completion unit chart:

This moves the bar chart from a high-level *descriptive* visualization, to a *prescriptive* visualization, which helps add context to why something is the way that it is. Descriptive bar charts certainly have their place with certain audiences, but generally a prescriptive view is always going to be more valuable.

Not only that, in my personal opinion, the units help add context to the scale, even when the final view will be a flat, descriptive chart.

How to Make One-Dimensional Unit Charts in Tableau

One-dimensional unit charts are easy to make in Tableau as long as you remember one thing, and that is that each unit needs some type of unique identifier in the data. In the case of the NBA Records by Player viz, the unique ID was NBA record.

From here, you build a bar chart just like you always do in Tableau, then drag the unique ID to the Detail Marks Card. Here's a look at the NBA Records by Player viz under the hood:

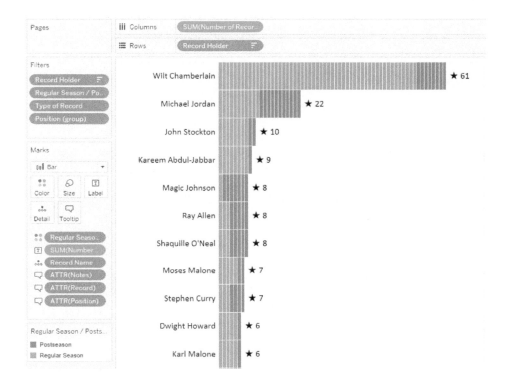

If you don't have a unique ID and are purely going for the unit chart look (sorry Stephen Few!), you can simply add reference lines that will draw a line across the equal units you want to display. This is a manual approach, but has the advantage of allowing you to format the reference lines to your liking.

Finally, people always ask how to add totals to stacked bars (like you see here with the star and total number of NBA records per player). I considered doing a chapter to cover this topic by itself because it is a valuable capability, but it has been covered regularly and is just plain easy. All you have to do is add a reference line by right-clicking the axis of the measure in question, set the scope to cell, change the label to value, and set the formatting of the line to none.

CHAPTER 63

How to Highlight a Dimension

In my US Income by Age and Marital Status viz (which we'll look at momentarily), I wanted my end users to be able to choose their personal combination of age, marital status, and income—then have the chart not only filter down to their demographic information, but highlight their income in context of their other selections. This is another example of driving engagement by making the end user part of the story.

I thought this would be as easy as right-clicking the axis for income, a field that is a bin dimension in my viz (i.e., used to make a histogram), and choosing "add reference line." I would then make a reference band to get the nice yellow highlight effect you see pictured.

This is when I found out you can only add reference lines to measures or date dimensions.

This chapter shares a workaround for adding a "reference line" to a dimension.

How to Add a Reference Line to a Dimension

Let's start by taking a look at the visualization. In the interactive version, plugging in your own combination of age, marital status, and income filters and highlights the viz:

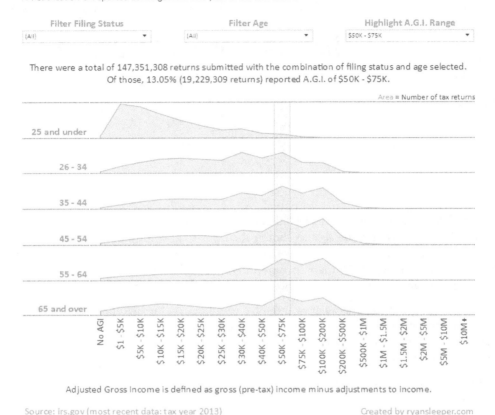

Distribution of Adjusted Gross Income by Age and Marital Status in the U.S.
A visualization of reported earnings from one year of IRS tax returns

Filter Filing Status   Filter Age   Highlight A.G.I. Range
(All)   (All) $50K - $75K

There were a total of 147,351,308 returns submitted with the combination of filing status and age selected.
Of those, 13.05% (19,229,309 returns) reported A.G.I. of $50K - $75K.

Area = Number of tax returns

25 and under

26 - 34

35 - 44

45 - 54

55 - 64

65 and over

No AGI / $1 - $5K / $5K - $10K / $10K - $15K / $15K - $20K / $20K - $25K / $25K - $30K / $30K - $40K / $40K - $50K / $50K - $75K / $75K - $100K / $100K - $200K / $200K - $500K / $500K - $1M / $1M - $1.5M / $1.5M - $2M / $2M - $5M / $5M - $10M / $10M+

Adjusted Gross Income is defined as gross (pre-tax) income minus adjustments to income.

Source: irs.gov (most recent data: tax year 2013)   Created by ryansleeper.com

The first two filters, filing status and age, are simply filters that filter the entire viz to the end user's selection. The viz also works when the end user does not change these filters, in the case that he wants to see how his income compares across the entire population of tax returns.

The trick comes in with the income filter, which is actually a parameter. This parameter, combined with a calculated field on a dual-axis combination chart, is what produces the highlight effect. Here's how it's done.

1. Create a parameter for the dimension you want to highlight.

    Create a parameter with a data type of String and allowable values of List. Parameters are very sensitive in that the values have to match the underlying data exactly, including casing, to work how you want. As a shortcut, you can add the members of your dimension to the allowable values list by choosing "Add from Field" when creating your parameter. Here is how my income parameter looks:

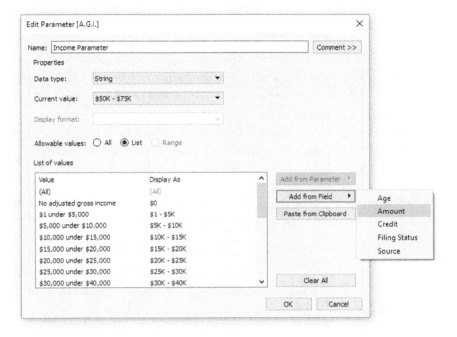

2. Create a calculated field with your dimension parameter.

The second step is to create a calculated field that will eventually be used as the measure on a dual-axis combination chart. The formula is:

```
IF [Dimension I Want to Highlight] = [Dimension Parameter] THEN 1.5 ELSE
NULL END
```

This calculated field is simply saying, "If the dimension member equals the current value selected in the parameter, then show the number 1.5; otherwise don't show anything." The 1.5 is kind of arbitrary because this approach will work as long as the axis for this new measure is fixed to be a smaller number than the number in your calculated field.

3. Create a dual-axis combination chart.

   Assuming you've created a chart that you want to add this highlight to, put the newly created calculated field on the opposite axis to create a dual-axis chart.

   In my case, the original chart was a histogram with a mark type of Area. When I put the new calculated field on the opposite axis, it inherits the same mark type as the original chart by default. Here is how my view looks at this point:

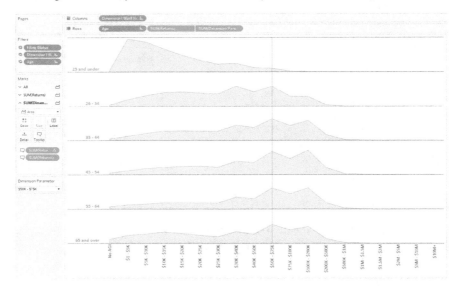

4. From here, there is just a little cleanup to make a nice highlight/reference band effect:

   a. Fix the axis of the right axis by right-clicking the axis and choosing Edit Axis. For the best results, fix the axis at a number smaller than the number in your newly created calculated field (mine is fixed at 1, which is less than 1.5).

   b. Change the mark type of the second axis to Bar, which will create the band look.

   c. Change the format of the bars to the size and color that you want. I recommend adding borders and transparency.

d. Hide the headers for your second axis by right-clicking the axis and unchecking Show Header.

My final product looks like this:

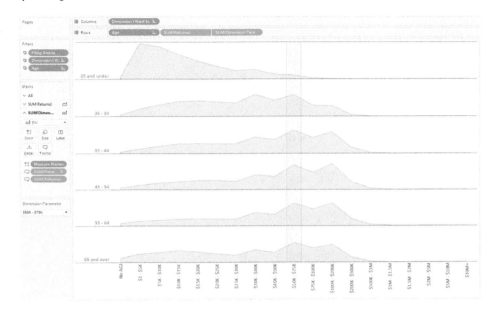

Now if the name of the dimension member matches the parameter selection, you will see a nice highlight of that choice on the x-axis—a reference band on a dimension in just three steps!

CHAPTER 64

Allow Users to Choose Measures and Dimensions

This book has often discussed how powerful parameters are in Tableau because outside of filters and dashboard actions, they're one of the only methods for putting control into the hands of your end users. In other chapters, I show you how to create and compare segments (Chapter 53), how to change the date aggregation on a line graph (Chapter 66), and how to create a what-if analysis in Tableau—all using the power of parameters (Chapter 48).

This chapter will walk you through how to leverage this same functionality to allow you and your dashboards' end users to decide which dimensions or measures are displayed on your views. This is a great approach for keeping analyses focused as well as saving real estate on your dashboard by displaying only one dimension and measure at a time.

How to Use Parameters to Select a Measure in Tableau

In this example, let's assume we have a continuous line trend showing the measure that we care about by month. We want to set up the view so that we (and our end users) have the ability to change which trend is being displayed between Sales, Profit, Quantity, and Discount.

1. Create a parameter for your four measure choices.

   The most intuitive way to create a parameter is to right-click somewhere in the Parameters area of the Data pane in the lower-left corner of an individual sheet, and clicking Create Parameter. You are presented six data type options for your parameter. To allow users to select which measure is displayed on a view, we are going to be using a data type of *String*. You will also want to change the allowable values to *List* so that you can specifically define which options the users will have. Once you choose List you will see a new menu that allows you to input the values for each of the choices. Type in the names of each measure, give the parameter a name, and your parameter should end up looking like this:

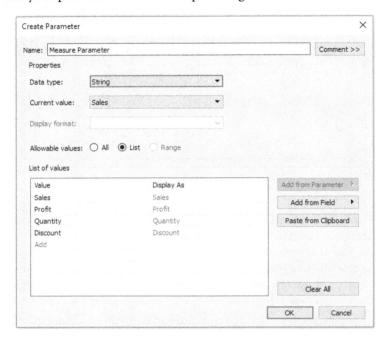

2. Create calculated measure.

Parameters are dependent in that they don't do much on their own. In order to make them work, you also have to provide Tableau with instructions on what each of the parameter inputs should do. This can be accomplished through a calculated field. Since we are starting with a way to allow users to choose between one of four *measures*, we will create a calculated measure that will tell Tableau which measure to display based on the parameter value selected. In case you are not familiar with the syntax, the definitions will look like this in the calculated field:

```
CASE [Measure Parameter]
WHEN "Sales" THEN SUM([Sales])
WHEN "Profit" THEN SUM([Profit])
WHEN "Quantity" THEN SUM([Quantity])
WHEN "Discount" THEN AVG([Discount])
END
```

Note that I gave every measure an aggregation. If I didn't assign the aggregations here, all four measures would share the same aggregation. It doesn't make sense for us to sum up the discounts, so I assigned that measure an aggregation of average using AVG. My final calculated field looks like this:

3. Create the view.

At this point, we are ready to create our continuous line graph with our newly created calculated measure. I know this is meant to be a continuous monthly trend over time, so I start by putting my date dimension on the Columns Shelf with an aggregation of continuous month. To create the line graph, I put my newly created "Measure Selected" measure onto the Rows Shelf. At this point, we see a monthly trend for whatever measure is the current value in the parameter that we created. By default, the current value will be the first value (Sales) in the parameter. The view currently looks like this:

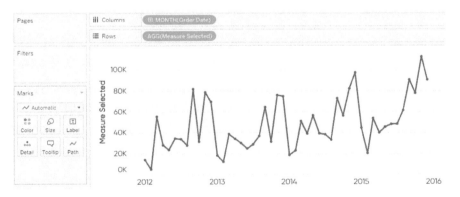

4. Add parameter control to view.

There is just one last step to allow your end users to choose between the four options you have created. Right-click the parameter that was created on the Parameters area of the Data pane and select Show Parameter Control. You will see a new menu appear in the upper-right corner that will allow you and your end users to choose between the four different measures. Changing the selection will change the measure being displayed on the line graph.

How to Use Parameters to Select a Dimension in Tableau

If you want to allow users to select a dimension instead of or in addition to a measure, follow the same four steps just outlined with your dimension options instead of your measure options. The only difference is that the dimensions in your calculated field will not need an aggregation. For example, let's say that in addition to allowing our users to choose between the measures of Sales, Profit, Quantity, and Discount, we also want them to be able to slice and dice those measures by the dimensions of Segment, Category, and Region.

We would follow the preceding steps and create a new string parameter with an entry for each of our dimensions. We would then create a calculated field that looks like this:

This newly created calculated field can now be placed on the Rows Shelf of our line graph to allow users to view the trends of not only four different measures, but also by three different dimensions. The final product looks like this:

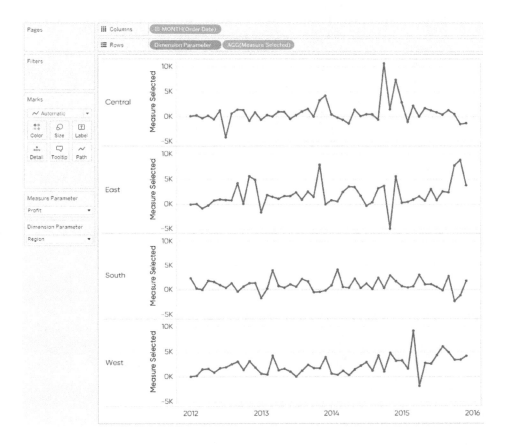

With three different dimension and four different measure choices, we have provided users with *twelve* different view options—all of which they are able to control without any Tableau development experience needed!

CHAPTER 65

How to Dynamically Format Numbers

One of my favorite tricks in Tableau is to provide the ability for myself and my end users to choose which dimension or measure is displayed on a view (see Chapter 64). This user experience is provided by setting up a parameter with the options and then creating a calculated field that tells Tableau what to display when each option is selected. The parameter approach to dimension and measure display has two huge benefits: (a) it puts the power of the analysis into the hands of end users (which allows discovery), and (b) it saves valuable real estate on a dashboard by displaying only what is selected.

However, there is one big drawback to dynamically displaying measures: number formats. To produce the user experience described, a calculated measure must be created, and calculated measures can only have one default number format. This is problematic if you are allowing your end users to choose between measures that have varying number formats such as integer, percent, and/or currency. Having one shared number format across all of the measure options is usually not a deal breaker, but wouldn't it be great if you could pick a different number format for each number?

This chapter shares how to dynamically format measures in Tableau. We will be using the Sample – Superstore dataset to dynamically format the Quantity, Discount, and Sales measures into integer, percent, and currency formats, respectively.

How to Dynamically Format Numbers in Tableau

This is the most flexible approach possible to dynamically formatting numbers in Tableau. It allows you to customize both the prefix and suffix for any measure and works whether the values are negative or positive. To begin, set up a string parameter with the three measure options:

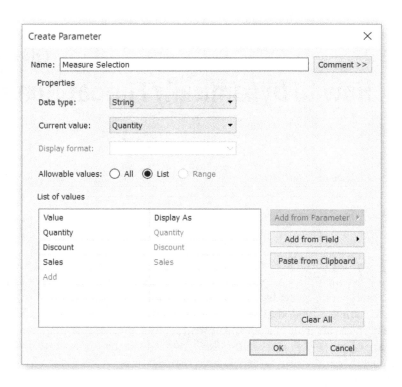

Next, you have to create a calculated field that tells Tableau how to handle each parameter selection:

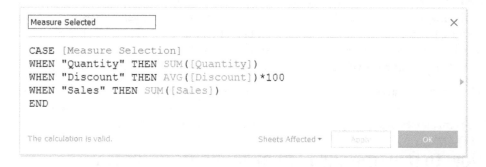

Note that in this case, I handled the Discount measure differently from Quantity and Sales. I've forced the aggregation to be average and multiplied it by 100 so the decimal moves over two spots to the right (making it easier to read the percentages).

Now whenever this Measure Selected KPI is used in combination with the Measure Selection parameter control—which appears by just right-clicking it and choosing

Show Parameter Control—the end user will have the ability to choose between the three measures. This is a great user experience, but look what happens when the Sales measure is selected, for example:

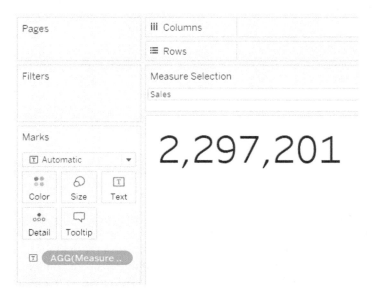

Sales should be in currency format, but there is no dollar sign. That's because all three measures in our Measure Selected calculated field have to share the same format and, by default, the format is set to Automatic. We could change the format to currency, but then a dollar sign would be shown for the Quantity and Discount measures. This same problem happens when the Discount measure is selected because it is the only measure of these three that should display a percent sign.

My solution involves setting up two additional calculated fields that are based on the parameter; one for the Measure Selected Prefix, and one for the Measure Selected Suffix. For these three measures, my prefix calculated field would look like this:

This formula is telling Tableau that if the Sales measure is selected, display a dollar sign; otherwise don't display anything. Since the Discount measure needs a percent sign added to the end of the number when it is chosen, I will also set up a calculated field for the number suffix:

Now I will add both the prefix and suffix calculated fields to the Text Marks Card. After all of the fields needed are on the view, click into the Text Marks Card to edit the order that the fields are displayed. To get the measure selected to display properly with its respective format prefix and suffix, place the prefix calculated field in front of the measure selected field, and the suffix calculated field behind the measure selected field:

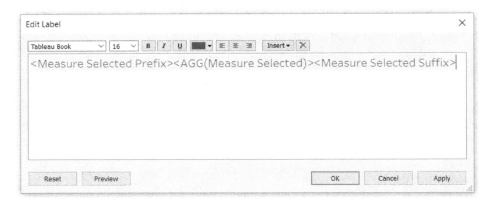

Now when the Sales measure is selected, a dollar sign is shown as the prefix:

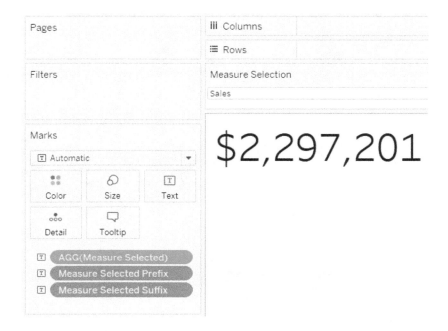

When the Discount measure is selected, the dollar sign goes away and a percent sign is shown as the suffix:

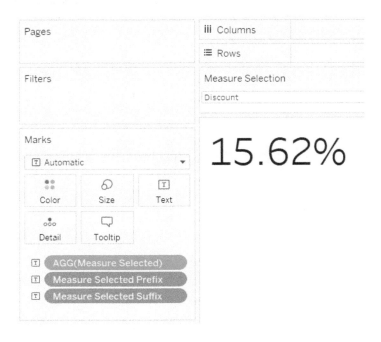

When the Quantity measure is selected, no prefix or suffix is displayed:

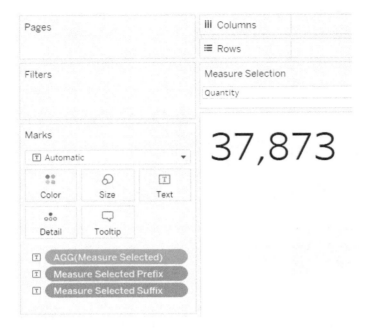

We were using a basic view for the purpose of illustration, but this approach works in larger crosstabs, with mark labels, and tooltips.

CHAPTER 66

How to Change Date Aggregation Using Parameters

Problem: Tableau makes selecting and changing the aggregation of a date dimension very easy while you are building a view. However, unless an end user is viewing an individual sheet in Tableau Desktop, she can't easily pivot the date part between day, week, month, quarter, and/or year on her own.

Solution: Create a parameter that includes each date granularity option you want your end users to have access to (i.e., Day, Week, etc.), and create a calculated field that will act as your aggregation-changeable date.

In many cases, it makes sense to change the granularity of a line graph over time. The Sample – Superstore dataset, for example, includes four years of daily data. If you are trying to view your sales over time and you set the date aggregation to year, you are provided a 10,000-foot view of your sales trend, but no seasonal insight. On the other hand, set the date granularity to continuous day, and while outliers stand out, it is nearly impossible to differentiate between individual days because you are looking at more than a thousand marks at the same time.

As you can see, viewing your sales over time at different levels of date granularity will tell very different stories. Why permanently choose the date aggregation of your view when you can allow your end users to choose for themselves?

How to Change Date Aggregation Using Parameters

In order to provide you and your end users with the ability to change the date part on the fly, follow these steps:

1. Create a string-based parameter with each level of date aggregation, as follows:

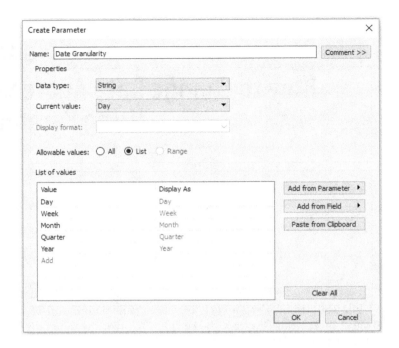

Note that the values have to be lowercase for this to work properly.

2. Create a calculated field, leveraging the DATETRUNC function to change the date aggregation to the appropriate level based on which parameter option is selected. Here is the logic:

```
DATETRUNC([Date Granularity parameter from step 1],[Order Date])
```

3. Instead of Order Date, use your newly created Date Granularity field. For best results, add the date field to the Columns Shelf by right-clicking and dragging; then choose the first option (Continuous).

4. Ensure you right-click the Date Granularity parameter and choose Show Parameter Control so your end users can choose their level of date aggregation. Your final product will look like this:

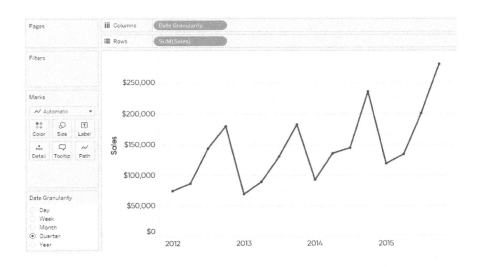

CHAPTER 67

How to Equalize Year-Over-Year Dates

Comparing an exact date in the current year to the same date in prior years—at least on the *same* date axis—is tricky in Tableau. The challenge comes from the lack of a "Month/Day" date part option when using dates in Tableau. If I were to right-click and drag the Order Date dimension from the Sample - Superstore dataset in Tableau to the Columns Shelf, I am presented with these options:

```
Order Date (Continuous)
Order Date (Discrete)
YEAR(Order Date)
QUARTER(Order Date)
MONTH(Order Date)
DAY(Order Date)
WEEK(Order Date)
WEEKDAY(Order Date)
MY(Order Date)
MDY(Order Date)
CNT(Order Date)
CNTD(Order Date)
MIN(Order Date)
MAX(Order Date)
YEAR(Order Date)
QUARTER(Order Date)
MONTH(Order Date)
WEEK(Order Date)
DAY(Order Date)
ATTR(Order Date)
```

The only choices that include the most-granular, day-level aggregation that I want to use, also include year. This prevents me from having the lines for each year in my analysis overlap for easy year-over-year comparison. It also makes it impossible to choose a date range such as 2/1/2018–3/30/2018, and still be able to see a line for all of the years in my data (this range would filter the data to just the year 2018). To illus-

trate, if I looked at the Sales measure in the Sample – Superstore data by the continuous DAY(Order Date), then colored the lines by YEAR(Order Date), the view would
look like this:

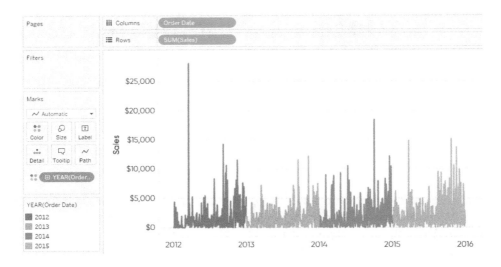

And if I wanted to choose a smaller range such as 2/1–3/30 for each year:

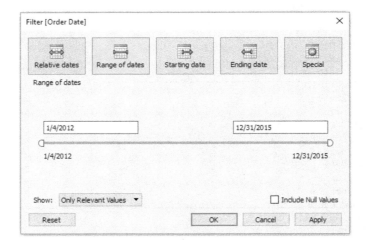

No luck because I have to choose the month, day, *and* year.

How to Equalize Year-Over-Year Dates in Tableau

One way to equalize year-over-year dates in Tableau is create a calculated field that adds the appropriate number of years to prior years, so that all of the dates end up on the current year's axis. For example, if the year is 2018, you would equalize the year-over-year dates so that everything would be on an axis for the year 2018. If you were wanting to equalize three years of data, the formula would be:

```
IF YEAR([Order Date]) = 2018 THEN [Order Date]
ELSEIF YEAR([Order Date]) = 2017 THEN [Order Date]+365
ELSEIF YEAR([Order Date]) = 2016 THEN [Order Date]+365+365
ELSE NULL
END
```

This formula is saying that if the Order Date is in the current year, then show the Order Date; if the Order Date is sometime last year, show the Order Date from that year, but add 365 days to it to get the dates on the current year's axis; if the Order Date is from two years ago, then add two years' worth of dates; if the Order Date isn't in the last three years, don't show anything.

This solution works, but is a bit manual to set up and dealing with leap years is a confusing topic.

A second, and more effective approach, is to create a calculated field that provides the "Month/Day" date aggregation that was mentioned in the chapter introduction. The formula for this calculation is:

```
DATE(STR(MONTH([Order Date]))+"/"+STR(DAY([Order Date]))+"/2018")
```

This calculation is telling Tableau to take the individual month and day from each Order Date, but make the year for all of them the current year.

Now if I look at Sales by this Month/Day/Current Year calculated date, I can look at all of the years in my data on the same date axis:

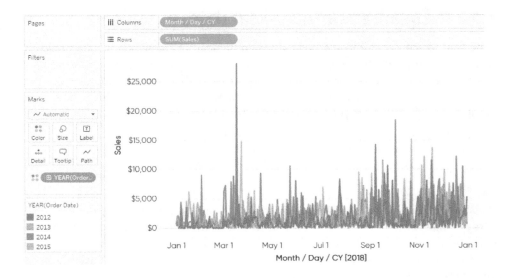

Note that if the year you are using for the date axis does not contain Leap Day (February 29th), but one or more of the lines in the graph do, that line that contains Leap Day will add the result from February 29th to March 1st together into one date (March 1st). Conversely, if the year you are using for the date axis does contain Leap Day, February 29th will be skipped for years that do not have Leap Day.

I can also use the newly created Month/Day/Current Year calculated field to filter the equalized date range. Changing the date range to 2/1/2018–3/30/2018 makes it much easier to compare individual, year-over-year dates, on the same date axis!

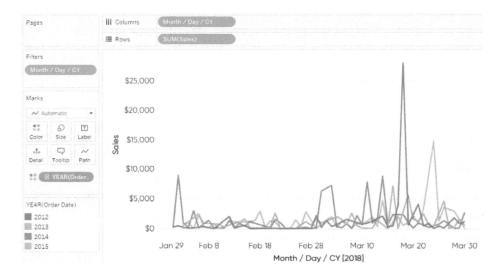

As a final note, now that you have the dates equalized on the current year axis at the most granular level, you can also change the aggregation to something less granular such as month or year and the dates will still line up.

CHAPTER 68

How to Filter Out Partial Time Periods

One of the most panic-inducing visuals in data visualization is a line graph that has a sudden, and steep, decline. When there is truly an issue with the business that needs to be addressed, it is important to share the illustrated insight with stakeholders that can take action.

However, an apparent steep drop on a line graph can also be caused when time periods are not the same number of days, as is the case when a week, month, or year starts over (i.e., one day in the current week versus seven days in the prior week).

When the latter scenario happens, it can lead to misinterpreted findings and unnecessary panic; both of which you want to avoid in data visualization. Misinterpretations can lead to the wrong actions and unnecessary panic is a distraction from finding the real stories in the data.

This chapter shares a technique for filtering out partial time periods in an analysis.

How to Filter Out Partial Time Periods in Tableau

To illustrate when it helps to filter out partial time periods in Tableau, let's first take a look at a view that often shows up in real life. Using the Sample – Superstore dataset, we'll say we're looking at an annual report for the year 2015 with data through December 6th:

By the looks of this graph, after a brief downturn in February, the business recovered and has been steadily trending upward. That is, until December, when we see sales plummet again to near the low-point for the year. There is nothing on this graph that indicates that December's data is not yet complete. If we are looking at this graph on December 7th, we likely will understand why December is not complete, but there are other reasons that may cause the December view to not be ready to share. The data may take time to collect, process, and update, for example.

If you are in a similar situation and want to filter incomplete time periods out of the view, build a calculated field with this formula (use your own date dimension in place of Order Date):

```
DATETRUNC('month',[Order Date]) <> DATETRUNC('month',TODAY())
```

This calculation is telling Tableau whether or not the first day of the Order Date's time period matches the first day of today's time period. Today will always be part of an incomplete time period, so if we want to filter out partial time periods, we would keep only the Order Dates that don't match today's time period. This is a Boolean formula meaning it's either true or false; in this case, we want to keep only the "True" results.

To show how this works using the Sample – Superstore dataset, I have replaced TODAY() with the hardcoded date 2015-12-06:

Once I have this calculated field, I will drag it to the Filters Shelf and choose True:

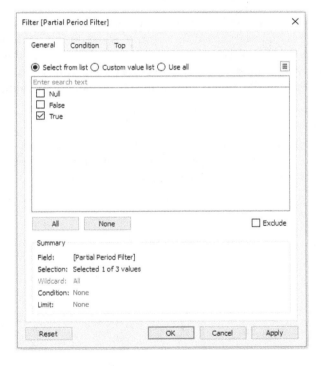

And after applying the filter—the partial time period disappears from the view, and holiday-happiness and visions of year-end bonuses are restored!

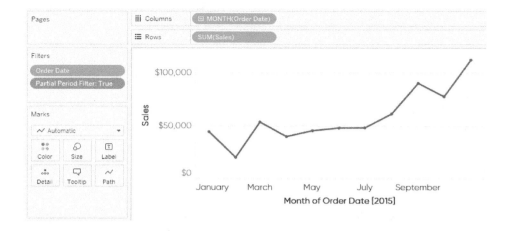

This technique can be combined with the trick for changing the date granularity of a line graph so that the partial period filter works whether you are looking at weeks, months, quarters, or years. If you are using a parameter to change the date granularity from day, to week, to quarter, etc., just replace the "month" granularity in the preceding formula with the parameter. The formula would look something like this:

```
DATETRUNC([Date Granularity Parameter],[Order Date]) <>
DATETRUNC([Date Granularity Parameter],TODAY())
```

As long as the values in the parameter are lowercase, the partial period filter will dynamically filter out the incomplete period as you choose different aggregations, whether it be the most-recent incomplete week, quarter, month, or year.

CHAPTER 69

How to Compare Two Date Ranges on One Axis

In Chapter 51, I shared that before I started using Tableau, I began my career in digital analytics using Google Analytics. One of the features I utilize most in my analysis work in Google Analytics is the ability to compare the performance during any date range to the performance during an equal date range immediately preceding it. For example, if I choose a date range of 10 days, I would like to see the performance of those 10 days as well as the 10 days that preceded my selected range. In Google Analytics, this is the first option if you choose a comparison date range, but it is tricky in Tableau.

I have seen a solution to this that uses an axis of number of days, but this solution leverages a date equalizer calculation to compare any date range to the equivalent prior period on the same *date* axis—a much friendlier user experience! There's an example of this experience in my Tableau Public visualization, Super Sample Superstore (*https://www.ryansleeper.com/super-sample-superstore/*).

How to Compare Any Date Range to the Previous Date Range on the Same Axis in Tableau

If you ever need to equalize dates to compare two ranges on the same axis, follow these steps:

1. Create parameters for date range.

   Build two separate parameters with a data type of "Date"; one will be the minimum end of your range, and the other will be for the maximum end of your range. Once these are created, right-click each one and choose Show Parameter

Control. If you would like to follow along using Sample – Superstore, the view looks like this at this point:

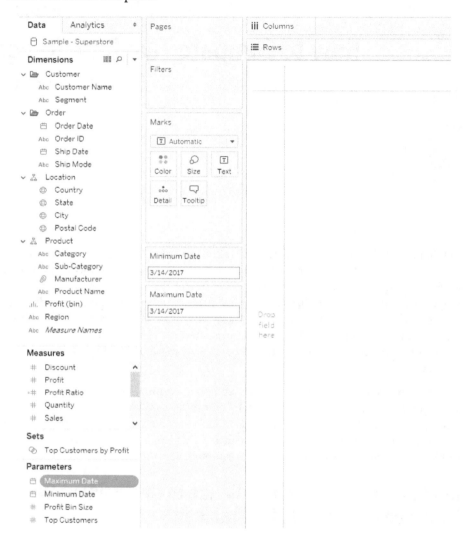

2. Create a calculated field for days in range.

Create a calculated field that uses the DATEDIFF function to calculate the number of days in the selected range. In this tutorial, we are using a date part of day, so we will want to include a "+1" to ensure we capture the current day. The calculated field looks like this:

```
DATEDIFF('day',[Parameters].[Minimum Date],[Parameters].[Maximum Date])+1
```

Days in Range   ×

DATEDIFF('day',[Parameters].[Minimum Date],[Parameters].[Maximum Date])+1

The calculation is valid.   Apply   OK

Note that if you want to spot check that your formula is working correctly and calculating the correct answer, add this calculated field to your view with an aggregation of average. By default, the aggregation will be sum so the calculated field will take the number of days multiplied by the number of records (which is not what we want).

Also note that the Minimum Date parameter is first in our calculation. If you do this backwards, you will get the wrong result.

3. Create boolean calculated fields for current period and prior period.

The final step in the setup process is to create two calculated fields—one which will limit the dates to the current period, and one which will limit the date to the period immediately preceding the range selected in the parameters from step 1:

```
[Order Date] >= [Parameters].[Minimum Date] AND [Order Date] <=
[Parameters].[Maximum Date]
```

Date Filter CP   ×

[Order Date] >= [Parameters].[Minimum Date] AND [Order Date] <= [Parameters].[Maximum Date]

The calculation is valid.   Apply   OK

```
[Order Date] >= [Parameters].[Minimum Date] - [Days in Range]
AND [Order Date] <= [Parameters].[Maximum Date] - [Days in Range]
```

The date logic used to create these boolean calculations could have instead been nested within the calculations in the following steps but I prefer to leave them as their own fields in my data.

4. Create a date equalizer.

The date equalizer is a calculated field that will put both the date range selected and the date range immediately preceding the selection on a single axis! The formula is:

```
IF [Date Filter CP] = True THEN [Order Date]
ELSEIF [Date Filter PP] = True THEN [Order Date] + [Days in Range]
ELSE NULL
END
```

5. Create calculated fields for your measure.

We are now ready to use the special date fields we set up before to create the measures that will be used on our view. For this to work, you will need to set up a calculated measure that shows the performance for the current period, and a second calculated measure that shows the performance for the prior period. I am going to use Sales as my measure, but this same approach works for any measure without having to replicate the first four steps. Here are my two calculated measures for Sales:

```
SUM(IF [Date Filter CP] = True THEN [Sales] END)
```

SUM(IF [Date Filter PP] = True THEN [Sales] END)

6. Create the view.

   If you are wanting to create a continuous line graph comparing the performance of a measure to the selected date range and the date range immediately preceding it on the same axis:

   a. Place the newly created Date Equalizer dimension onto the Columns Shelf with an aggregation of continuous day.

   b. Place the newly created Current Period Sales measure on the Rows Shelf.

   c. Drag the newly created Prior Period Sales measure onto the same axis as Current Period Sales—you could also create a dual-axis with one measure on each, but this would require you to synchronize the axes; a step that is unnecessary since these two measures should be an apples-to-apples comparison on the same y-axis.

   In my example, I have chosen the final 10 days of November 2015. The blue line represents the performance during my selected range, and the red line represents the performance during the 10 days prior to my selected range (11/11/2015–11/20/2015):

You can now select any date range you want and have Tableau show the performance during the current period to the prior period immediately preceding it—on the same date axis!

Once you've got the foundation down, try using parameters to change which metric is being graphed (Chapter 64) or change the date part (Chapter 66) of the date equalizer.

CHAPTER 70

How to Compare Unequal Date Ranges on One Axis

In the previous chapter, I shared a technique for comparing any date range in Tableau to the equal date range that immediately preceded the selection. But what do you do if you want to pick both ranges, even if they aren't right next to each other on the calendar? What if one range has a different number of days than the other?

This chapter shows how to compare the performance during any two date ranges on one axis, even if the selected date ranges have unequal durations.

First, create four separate parameters with a data type of Date:

- Range 1 Minimum Date
- Range 1 Maximum Date
- Range 2 Minimum Date
- Range 2 Maximum Date

To start the view, show all four parameter controls by right-clicking on them and choosing "Show parameter control." This allows the end user to choose the two date ranges. For the purposes of this illustration, I will compare 10/1/2015–10/11/2015 to 9/8/2015–9/27/2015. Notice that not only are these date ranges disconnected (there are three days skipped between them), but the first range is 11 days while the comparison range is 20 days:

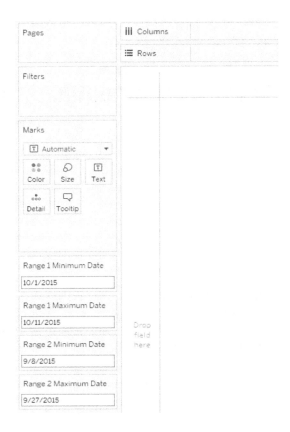

Next, set up a calculated field that classifies whether the date falls into Range 1 or Range 2. If you are following along using the Sample – Superstore dataset, the formula looks like this when using Order Date as the date dimension:

```
IF [Order Date] >= [Range 1 Minimum Date] AND [Order Date] <=
    [Range 1 Maximum Date] THEN "Range 1"
ELSEIF [Order Date] >= [Range 2 Minimum Date] AND [Order Date] <=
    [Range 2 Maximum Date] THEN "Range 2"
END
```

The last component needed to compare any two date ranges on one axis is a calculated field with a level of detail expression that computes the "age" of each date range and normalizes the two ranges by a relative date. This is where the magic happens. Hat tip to Tableau Zen Master, Joshua Milligan, who provided the foundation for this calculation in his blog post, "Tweaking Data Stories in Tableau" (*http://bit.ly/2DEDULo*).

The formula is:

```
MIN(DATEDIFF('day', {FIXED [Date Range 1 / Date Range 2] :
    MIN([Order Date])}, [Order Date]))
```

Once you have the four date range parameters, a calculated field that classifies dates as Range 1 or Range 2, and a calculated field that calculates the date range age, you are ready to build the view.

Start a line graph by adding the measure you want to visualize across the two date ranges onto the Rows Shelf and the Date Range Age measure onto the Columns Shelf. Here's how the view looks so far using Sales as the KPI:

This view is showing a single mark because we need to include the Order Date dimension for Tableau to calculate the age of the date range. This can be accomplished by dragging the Order Date field (discrete at the M/D/Y level) to the Detail Marks Card:

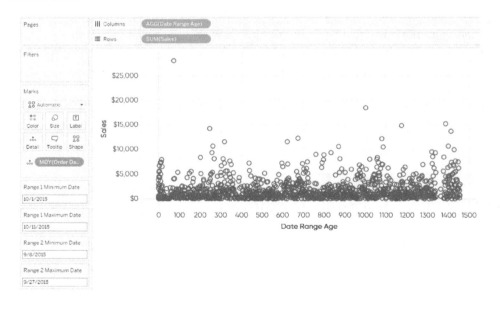

Tableau is now able to do the calculation, but we've now got 1,237 marks—one for every date in the Sample – Superstore dataset. To filter the view to use only the relevant dates for this analysis, drag the Date Range 1/Date Range 2 calculated field to the Filters Shelf and keep only the dates classified as Date Range 1 or Date Range 2:

After applying the filter, we are left with only the 31 marks for the date ranges we have selected using the parameter controls:

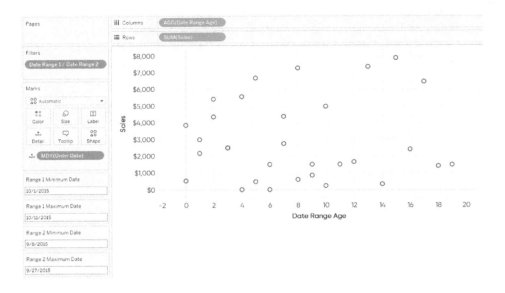

To change this to a line graph, change the mark type from Automatic, which is currently Shape, to Line. This creates one continuous line graph:

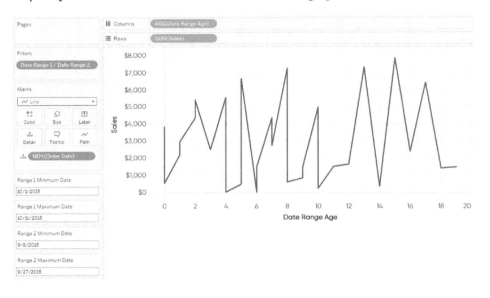

The final step to compare the performance between the two date ranges is to drag the Date Range 1/Date Range 2 dimension to the Color Marks Card. Here is how my final view looks after coloring the lines by date range and polishing the formatting:

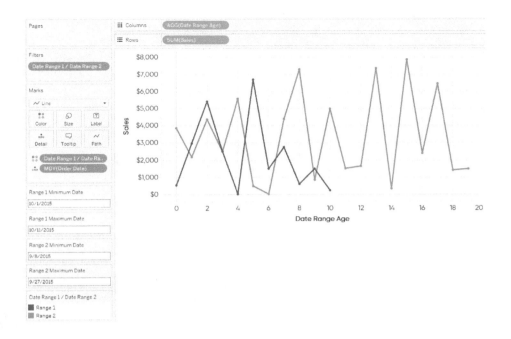

We are now able to choose *any* two date ranges and compare them to each other on the same relative date axis!

CHAPTER 71

How to Make a Cluster Analysis

Clustering is a powerful feature released with Tableau 10 that allows you to easily group similar dimension members. This type of clustering helps you create statistically based segments that provide insight into how different groups are similar as well as how they are performing compared to each other. I've always leaned on segmentation as a tactic for making my analyses with Tableau more powerful, and Chapter 22 in Tableau, shares how to make a simple quadrant-based segmentation. Clustering takes this a step further by statistically grouping the objects on a view using the variables on the view.

This chapter shows you how to use the cluster feature in Tableau and how to make the generated clusters more permanent for segmentation analyses.

To demonstrate, I will first re-create the scatter plot just mentioned, which looks at sales and profit ratio by the Product Name dimension in the Sample – Superstore dataset:

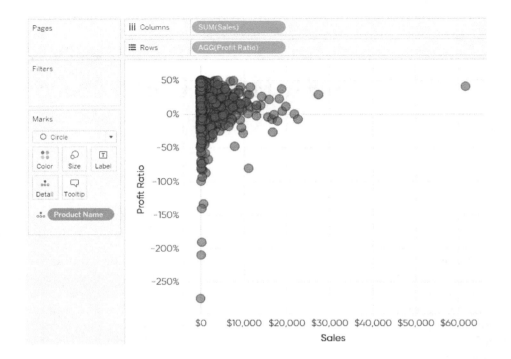

To create quadrant-based segments, at this point I would add a reference line for average on each axis. Now with Tableau 10, we can make this segmentation much more scientific by using the Cluster feature. Cluster lives on the Analytics pane in Tableau, so to create a cluster analysis, simply navigate to the Analytics pane (toward the upper-left corner of the authoring interface) and drag "Cluster" onto the view:

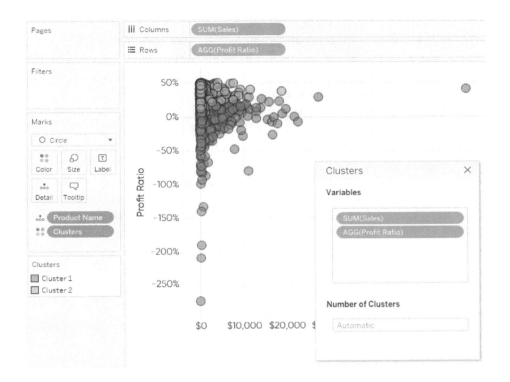

A few things to point out here:

- By default, Tableau created the clusters from the variables on the view (Sales and Profit Ratio). You can add or take away variables to customize the clusters.

- "Clusters" was added to the Color Marks Card, which colored each circle by its respective cluster segment. Remember that you can only color marks by one thing at a time in Tableau.

- Tableau automatically identified two similar groups of marks. This number may go up or down based on the variables in the cluster analysis. You can also manually set the number of clusters by entering a number in the box that says Automatic.

After you're done creating the clusters, click the X in the upper-right corner of the Clusters dialog box to remove it from the view. You can always edit the clusters again by right-clicking the Clusters dimension on the Color Marks Card and choosing Edit clusters.

Creating a cluster analysis is that easy, but here are a few more ways this feature can be used:

- If your resident data scientist is scoffing at your work because they don't know how the segments were generated, you can right-click the Clusters dimension on the Color Marks Card and choose "Describe clusters." This will provide all of the summary statistics and modeling you can handle!

- You can filter the view to look at only certain clusters at a given time. Dragging Cluster from the Analytics pane onto the view does not create a permanent dimension on the Dimensions area of the Data pane, but you can still filter on the field by right-clicking it from the Color Marks Card and choosing Show Filter.

- If you would like to create a permanent segment from a cluster for future analyses, filter the view to the cluster of interest, use Ctrl-A to select all of the marks (or left-click and draw a box around all of the marks), right-click one of the highlighted marks and choose Create Set.

For more on filters, review Chapter 11.

For more on sets, review Chapter 15.

CHAPTER 72

Five Tips for Making Your Tableau Public Viz Go Viral

To this day, I am grateful when even a single person checks out one of my data visualizations. I often think back fondly about my very first Tableau Public visualization, a simple view showing NFL interconference records over time. The viz is not my best work—if anything, it's my worst work—but I was so excited to discover that I can share interactive data stories for free through Tableau Public (so awesome!).

The viz now has over 25,000 views.

What I like most about this viz is that it's a constant reminder of how much you can improve if you stick with something, and it's also a testament that any viz has a chance to be a popular success. Among a few other vizzes with at least 25,000 views, I now have five others with at least 50,000 views, one that recently cracked the six-figure milestone, and even one with over a quarter-million views (shown later in this chapter)! My work has been featured by *The Guardian*, *U.S. News & World Report*, and *Grantland*—all with zero marketing budget and no established journalism platform on which to share my work. This chapter shares the five tactics that made it possible.

 While I certainly do not believe that a visualization's value should be judged exclusively by how many views it has, I do believe that part of a data visualization's success should be judged on whether or not it made an impact. And sometimes you need a larger audience to see a viz in order for it to make an impact. I have seen incredible work on Tableau Public with fewer than 100 views. In fact, that's why I wanted to write this chapter—to help as many Tableau Public authors as possible have their deserving work discovered by a larger audience.

Tip #1: Create "Remarkable" Content

For your viz to have any chance of going viral, it is critical that it is remarkable in some way. When I say remarkable, I am talking about Seth Godin's literal definition of remarkable, meaning your work is interesting enough in some way that it makes people remark about it. In today's social media age, remarking about your work often means sharing it on social media with new audiences—one of the biggest contributors to viral success.

Tableau Public visualizations can be remarkable in different ways. Perhaps you have found a compelling story to share or a unique approach to sharing that story in Tableau. Or maybe you have done a phenomenal job using the next tip to your advantage: balance data and design.

Tip #2: Balance Data and Design

It seems there are two camps in data visualization: the data purists who feel aesthetics are unnecessary or even counterproductive, and those that believe design is a worthy component to data visualization. I am firmly in the second camp. My stance stems from how I define the purpose of data visualization: to find and share actionable stories that are based in quantitative evidence.

To make your insights actionable, this means sharing them with the most relevant, and many times, largest audience possible. If you don't provide your data stories in a well-packaged design, you drastically minimize the chances of your work spreading, and thus, it is consumed and acted on by fewer people.

The good news is that anybody can improve the design of their Tableau Public visualizations. See Chapter 54 for some inspiration.

Tip #3: Leverage Search Engine Optimization (SEO)

I mentioned in the introduction that even my first and most basic Tableau Public visualization has hit the 25,000 views milestone. Here's a Google search result for the term "NFL Interconference Records":

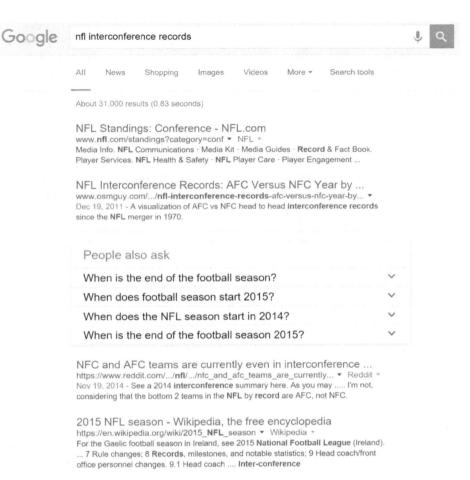

Among the 31,000 results, there's a link to my (possibly worst) Tableau Public viz in the second position, right behind the NFL itself and ahead of popular websites Reddit and Wikipedia. I attribute this search result directly to search engine optimization, or SEO.

SEO can feel like a mysterious marketing strategy, and in some ways, it is. After all, nobody knows Google's search algorithm and we have no control over it. However, there are some basic SEO tactics that will dramatically improve the chances of your viz going viral by being discovered by the right person in search.

These tips are assuming that you have the ability to embed your visualizations on a platform that you control. If you don't have your own blog, I encourage you to work through the "A-Z Miniguide on Setting Up a Data Blog" (*http://tabsoft.co/2DCb2TP*).

Most importantly, try to get in the heads of your audience and think about the terms they might use to talk about your viz. People go to Google to ask questions, and if you can integrate the words people are using to ask those questions into your work, there will be a better chance that Google will believe your viz is the best answer to their question.

Create a descriptive page title using the terms people are searching for. It is tempting to try to be cute with your page titles, but descriptive titles do better in search. For example, I could have named my Odds of Going Pro in Sports viz and chapter "You won't believe how hard it is to do this in sports." Like a bad clickbait ad with a strange picture on it, this title may do a good job of getting clicks when it's shared on social media, but it's not what people are searching for in Google. So after the initial social push, it would be difficult for this to be found again. Instead, people are searching for "What are the odds of going pro in sports?" and this viz continues to be found regularly today, years after it was originally published.

Provide some thoughts around your viz in your post. Google's algorithms are designed explicitly to understand textual content that's written for people—and they're getting better and better at it every day. Unfortunately, there is very little metadata for Google to find in a Tableau Public visualization itself. For this reason, it's important to write at least 250–500 words about your viz to describe what it's showing and what key insights it provides. This will give Google more information about what your viz is about so that it knows if your viz can help answer a searcher's question.

Tip #4: Network

Everyone knows that if you want a visualization to be publicly consumed, one of the first places to share it is on social media networks such as Facebook, Twitter, LinkedIn, Pinterest, and so on. To take this a step further, I note whenever I have a breakthrough. That's when a popular account shares my work or a journalist picks it up for his or her own content. I will then reach out to them directly the next time I have new material that is relevant to them. This tactic takes time to cultivate, but the snowball effect can be extremely impactful.

There is a fine line between building relationships and spamming, so beware. I am not suggesting you send an email to everybody in your audience who has ever looked at your work, but I may pick two to three people to share each new viz with directly, and only occasionally when I genuinely think the work is relevant to them. This tactic has led directly to second shares on *U.S. News & World Report* as well as the popular social sharing site Digg. Be sure to pay back these members of your network by supporting their work as well. And also be sensitive to not spamming them if you are getting hints that your work may not be as relevant as you may think it is for them anymore.

Tip #5: Use Reddit

The reddit.com/r/dataisbeautiful (*http://bit.ly/2q2UnnP*) subreddit has an enormous and relevant audience for Tableau Public authors. Using Reddit provided the majority of views on my most popular viz to date, The Cost of Attending the Baseball Championship Series (*http://tabsoft.co/2FWpknH*), and provided a spring board for the most viral viz I've ever seen, Tableau Zen Master Adam McCann's Analysis of the Beatles. With such a huge potential audience, it is exciting to jump right in and think you'll instantly gain fame and fortune. However, it took me several years to have a breakthrough on Reddit, and here's what I learned along the way.

You have to genuinely immerse yourself in the community there. You cannot get away with only posting your own content. Support others by upvoting and commenting on their work or by sharing content from others.

When you share your own content, make sure a thumbnail preview image is picked up with your post. The easiest way to guarantee this is to embed your Tableau Public visualizations on your own site, with a prominent feature image somewhere in the post. Studies have shown that email campaigns with images earn a 42 percent higher clickthrough rate (*http://bit.ly/2DHZTBe*), and the same principle applies to the dataisbeautiful subreddit.

Reddit says that original content (OC), or content submitted directly by the content's creator, performs better on its platform compared to non-OC content. This may be true after you have been using Reddit for a long time and built a strong reputation in the community, but this has not been my personal experience. My work has always performed better when somebody else submitted it. I don't have the science to back this up, but I think people are less likely to view and share work if they think there is even a chance that the person posting the content is self-promoting or sharing the content for the wrong reasons. I encourage you to experiment with both OC and non-OC content. If you don't have a colleague handy to submit your content, I'd be happy to take a look and share relevant visualizations myself (just let me know @ryanvizzes on Twitter).

Ultimately, we don't have full control over how popular a Tableau Public visualization will be, but don't let that discourage you. Not every single one of my Tableau Public visualizations have been a hit, but there is always something positive that comes out of every one. I've either discovered a new approach to visualizing certain types of data or created a new example that I can use in training. At a minimum, I get a chance to practice and learn something new for next time.

I also know that if the five tips mentioned here are taken to heart, the viz can be discovered and go viral at any time. If you adopt these tactics as part of your process and stick with it, I'm confident you will see a noticeable lift in your Tableau Public visualization views.

CHAPTER 73

Three Ways to Make Beautiful Bar Charts in Tableau

When it comes to data visualization, bar charts are still king. With all due respect to my other favorite fundamental chart types such as line graphs and scatter plots, nothing has the flexibility, ease of use, and ease of understanding, as the classic bar chart. Used to compare values of categorical data, bar charts work well because they take advantage of a basic preattentive attribute: length. Our ability to process the length of bars with extreme efficiency and accuracy makes the bar chart arguably the most powerful data visualization choice available to us.

The invention of the bar chart is credited to William Playfair, with his *Exports and Imports of Scotland to and from different parts for one Year from Christmas 1780 to Christmas 1781* being the first appearance. Extraordinarily long and descriptive titles aside, bar charts have been making an impact for a long time. In fact, I hypothesize that the fact bar charts have been around for so long is one of the reasons some attempt to find a "more engaging" chart type to tell their data story.

This chapter attempts to add some love for bar charts by sharing three ways to make them more engaging in Tableau.

Approach #1: Use Formatting Available in Tableau

My first tip for making beautiful bar charts is to use the formatting options you already have available in Tableau. Consider the following Sales by Category bar chart that shows all of the default Tableau settings:

This bar chart gets the job done, as you can immediately decipher that Technology leads the way with over $800,000 in sales, Furniture contributes the second most, and Office Supplies contribute the least. However, there are several opportunities to make this bar chart more engaging and effective. The most obvious of which is to widen the columns so the categories can be read:

Making the columns wider makes the bars themselves wider. In my opinion, these bars are now too heavy relative to the rest of the visual. The next step I'll take is to reduce the size of the bars by clicking the Size Marks Card and dragging the slider to the notch in the middle:

The next tip is arguable, but I'm not as descriptive as William Playfair was with his 110-character chart name. In my experience, the context of the chart is provided in surrounding text and/or dashboard titles, so I am going to hide the sheet name by right-clicking the title and choosing Hide Title. I am also going to right-click the bar chart header, Category, and click "Hide Field Labels for Columns." If this is a standalone visualization, I recommend keeping the title:

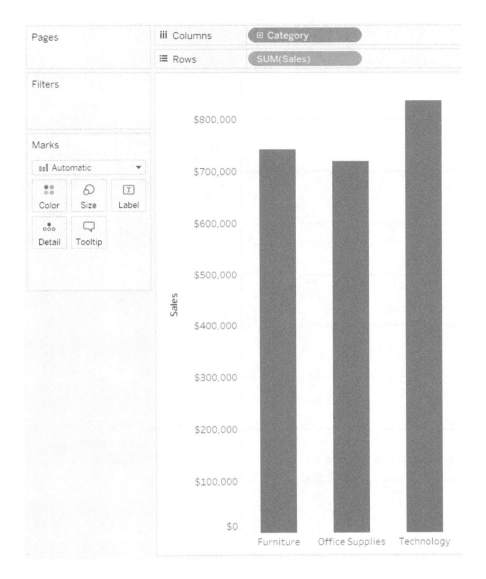

The bars in this chart are unnecessarily tall because there is not much variance between the categories in this analysis. Here's how the bar chart looks after I reduce the height by about 40%:

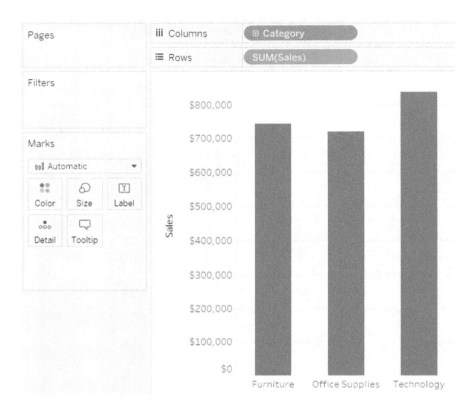

Take this next step on a case-by-case basis, but another side effect of having limited variance between the three bars is that there are too many gridlines and axis marks. This is negatively impacting the data-ink ratio, and can be cleaned up. To reduce the number of axis ticks, right-click the axis, click Edit Axis, and navigate to the Tick Marks tab:

Here's how the bar chart looks after fixing the tick marks at 200,000:

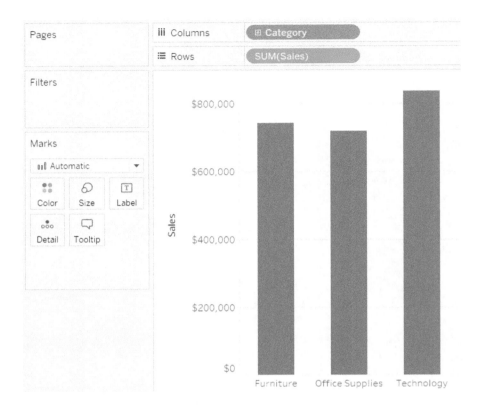

Last, but not least, color. I have written quite a bit about color, including Chapter 55, and in Chapter 75 and storytelling tip #3 in Chapter 88. There is so much to be said about color, but for the purposes of this chapter, I will offer just three thoughts on coloring your bar charts:

- Avoid double encoding. The bars in our chart are already separated by category. Adding category again to the Color Marks Card to color each bar with a unique color is unnecessary and potentially confusing. The one exception to this is if the colors are being used to provide a link between multiple visuals on a dashboard.

- Reduce the opacity from 100% to 80%–90% by clicking the Color Marks Card and moving the opacity slider to the left. This is a very subtle technique for reducing the saturation of the color and making the visual a little easier on the eyes.

- Use this as an easy opportunity to brand your data visualization. If you can't decide on a color, consider using a primary or secondary color from you or your end users' brand.

Here's how my final bar chart looks after choosing a secondary color from my personal brand and reducing the opacity of the bars to 90%. Note that I also added a very subtle border to the bars, which can be found in the options on the Color Marks Card:

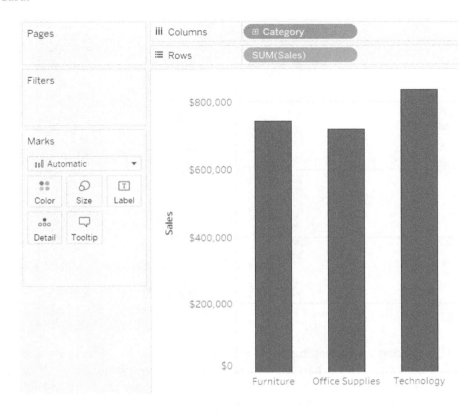

Approach #2: Use Axis Rulers to Add a Baseline

In the last tip, I mentioned the data-ink ratio. This a concept introduced by Edward Tufte that essentially says you should dedicate as much "ink" on a data visualization to the data as possible. One way I sometimes achieve this is by hiding the axis altogether and adding labels to the bars:

To add to the first tip, formatting, I also made the font larger and in brand. I like this look, but don't like how the bars appear to be floating. What I would like to do is add a solid foundation for the bars to sit on; this provides a practical purpose and also enhances the design. The easiest way to add a baseline is to modify the formatting of the view's axis rulers. By default, axis rulers are set to be a very light, thin gray line. To make the line heavier and match the color of the bar chart you are creating, right-click the view and click Format:

This will open the Format pane on the left. Navigate to the Format Lines tab and modify the formatting for the Axis Rulers for Rows and Columns. To clean up the view, I'm going to set the Axis Rulers for Rows at None, which removes the thin gray vertical line on the left side of the bar chart. I'm then going to format the Axis Rulers for Columns to be a solid, thick line that matches the color of the bars' borders:

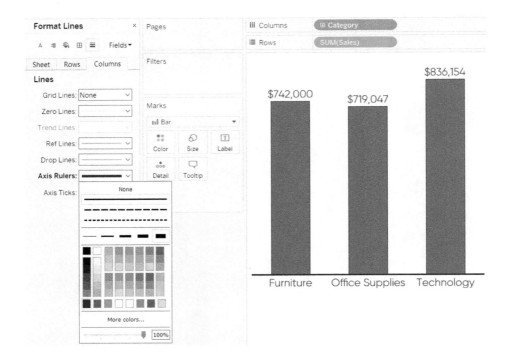

Here's how my final bar chart looks after removing all of the other lines except for the baseline. Compare this to the default Tableau bar chart in the first image!

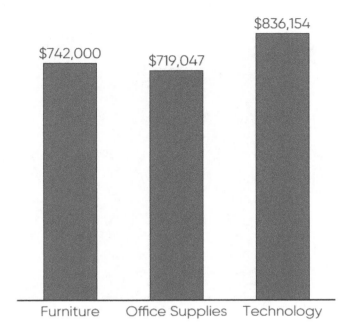

Approach #3: Add Caps to Bars

As I explained in my blog post, "Tableuprint 2: My Tableau Public Viz Views" (*http://bit.ly/2DCGIZq*), capped bar charts have two benefits: (a) they enhance the design of a bar chart, and (b) add value by potentially doubling as a secondary comparison point. For example, the size of the cap can represent the value of a goal or be colored by a different measure (i.e., length of the bars represent sales; color of caps represent profitability). While I like the style of capped bars and the subtle way they can provide additional information, beware they can easily be confused with stacked bar charts, and should be used with caution. Here's what a capped bar chart looks like when added to our previous example:

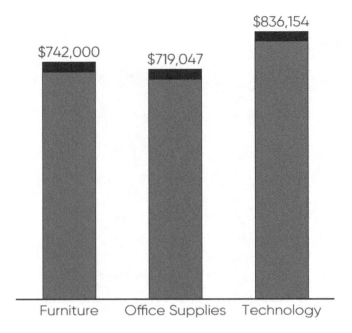

To create a capped bar chart in Tableau, start by adding a dual axis to the original bar chart. This can be accomplished by dragging the measure onto the Rows Shelf a second time, clicking the second occurrence of the pill, and choosing Dual Axis:

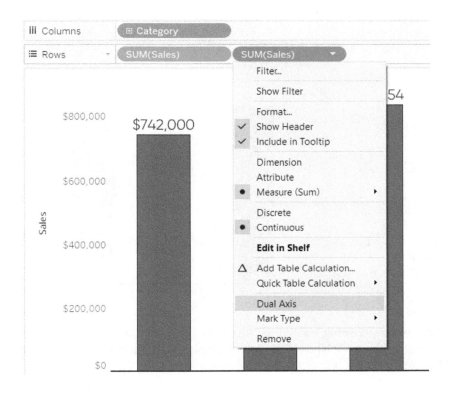

Once you've created the dual-axis chart, change the mark type of the first measure back to Bar and the mark type for the second measure to Gantt Bar. Also ensure the axes are synchronized by right-clicking the right axis and choosing Synchronize Axis. At this point, my view looks like this:

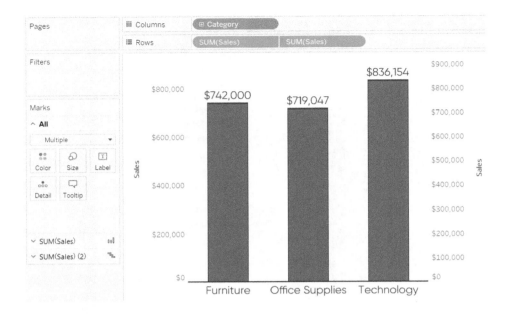

The next step to creating capped bar charts in Tableau is to create a calculated field for the size of the caps. The calculation is simply -MIN([insert size]). It is critical to add the negative sign before the bar size to ensure the caps go the correct direction. Here's how my calculated field looks when setting the cap size at 30,000:

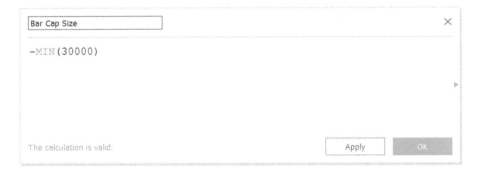

Lastly, drag this newly created Bar Cap Size calculated field to the Size Marks Card on the Marks Shelf for the measure you set as a Gantt Bar:

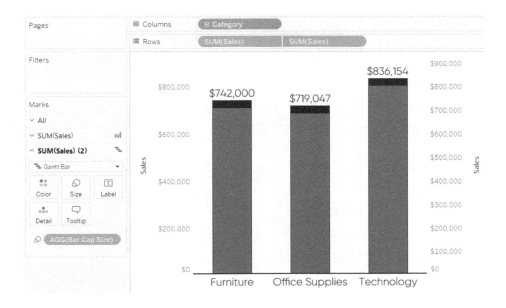

To finalize my capped bar chart, I colored the caps to match the bar borders and hid both axes.

CHAPTER 74

Three Ways to Make Lovely Line Graphs in Tableau

Line graphs are a close second to bar charts as my favorite fundamental visualization type and are the obvious choice for evaluating trends over time.. Like bar charts, the invention of line graphs is generally credited to William Playfair at the end of the 18th century Also like bar charts, I blame their age and people's familiarity with line graphs as the reason some data visualization enthusiasts look for "more engaging" choices. Line graphs have stood the test of time and their effectiveness cannot be denied. I'm hoping that these three approaches help cement line graphs as a top choice for your Tableau data visualizations.

Approach #1: Use Formatting Available in Tableau

My first tip for making line graphs more engaging is to use the formatting options available to you in Tableau. Consider the following sales by segment line graph with all of the default Tableau format settings. Note that I've used the Month([Order Date]) field as continuous and filtered the data to the year 2016:

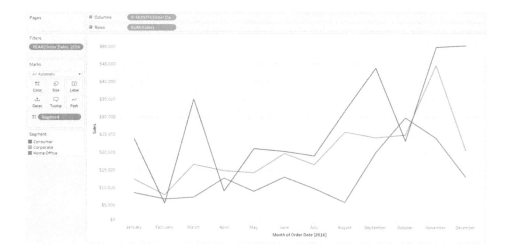

A great deal of thought went into Tableau's default formatting including the fonts, colors, and mark sizing. So as can be expected from my data visualization tool of choice, this graph is already getting the job done and providing good insights. That being said, if one of your objectives is to make the graph as engaging as possible, there are several opportunities to add value to this view.

First, I've never personally liked the axis title that is used to designate the date part when you are using a date field continuously. While I appreciate the clarity the axis title provides, this information is typically already implied in the graph itself and usually stated in surrounding context (i.e., "This is a graph about Sales by Month last year"). I almost always get rid of this axis title. Unfortunately, if you right-click the axis and deselect Show Header, both the axis title and month names disappear. To get rid of only the axis title but keep the month names, right-click the axis, and choose Edit Axis. This will open a dialog box where you can change the axis title. The trick is to simply delete all of the text on this line; then click the OK button:

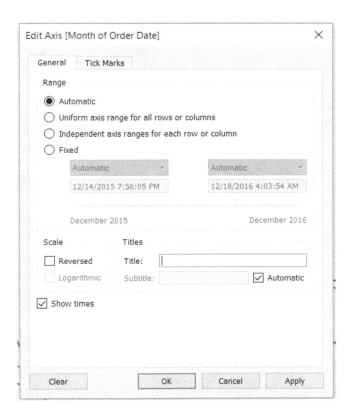

Next, if this is a standalone visualization, the weight of the lines is too light. To change the weight of the lines, click the Size Marks Card and drag the slider left or right until the lines are weighted as desired. I normally find that the second "notch" on the Size Marks Card is a good option for lines:

Take this on a case-by-case basis because sometimes heavier lines won't look good when used in a tighter space (such as one of several objects on a dashboard).

The next formatting tip addresses one of the most common questions I am asked while speaking about Tableau (*https://www.ryansleeper.com/speaking/*): Markers. Markers are the small circles that are sometimes seen on data points of a line graph. Markers serve the practical purpose of telling the end user where there is data in a subtle way, and they also are an easy way to enhance a line graph. To add markers, click the Color Marks Card and select the second Markers option:

The next tip is optional, but many times I like to make the line or insight that I care about "pop" on the view. This can be accomplished in several ways; the easiest of which is to click a dimension member on the color legend:

This approach also allows the end users to make the selection that they care about. Another way to highlight a dimension member would be to show a highlighter for the Segment dimension. This is accomplished by right-clicking the Segment dimension (currently on the Color Marks Card) and choosing Show Highlighter.

There are other times that you want to make the highlight more permanent. Maybe I am the manager of the corporate segment, so I always want it highlighted throughout all views. Or maybe I'm not allowed to see the performance of the other dimension members, but my boss wanted me to see my segment's performance in context of the others. There is a way to do this with parameters that is beyond the scope of this chapter, but it can also be accomplished easily by changing the colors of the dimension members. Here's how my line graph looks after "graying out" two out of three dimension members by clicking the color legend and remapping the colors. To finalize the view, I've also put the colors and fonts in brand:

Approach #2: Maximize the Data-Ink Ratio

As mentioned in the last chapter, the next tip should be considered for any visualization you create: Maximize the Data-Ink Ratio. The Data-Ink Ratio is a concept introduced by Edward Tufte, who says you should dedicate as much "ink" on a view to the data as possible. This means getting rid of unnecessary lines, effects, and anything else that detracts from the data itself.

There are a couple of opportunities to make our line graph even more minimalistic than it already is. First, the axis ticks on the Sales axis can be reduced by at least half. The axis ticks for Sales on this line graph are the multiples of $5,000 going up the y-axis. By default, these are often too granular for my taste, and cause too many extra lines and too much ink. To fix the axis ticks, right-click the y-axis, click Edit Axis, and navigate to the Tick Marks tab. You should beware that this option truly does fix the axis tick marks, so if you filter the view later, this setting will stick:

Here's how my line graph looks after fixing the tick marks at 15,000 units:

This same approach can be taken on the x-axis with months if you are using a continuous axis. This is not always an appropriate choice, but often the range of the axis is enough to communicate what the visualization is about. I often show only the starting point and end point of the x-axis of a line graph, especially when using sparklines. Here's how my line graph looks after fixing the axis ticks at eleven months with an origin of January 1st:

To finalize the view, I will hide the axis rulers and change the gridlines to dotted. Both of these options are found in the formatting pane, which you can reach by right-clicking the graph and choosing Format:

Compare this to the default line graph at the beginning of the chapter!

Approach #3: Leverage the Dual-Axis

There are at least two ways the second axis on a line graph can be used to enhance the visualization. Let's say that we really like the markers from the formatting tip, but would like to make them more pronounced. To do this, start by putting the Sales measure on the Rows Shelf a second time, right-click it, and choose Dual Axis:

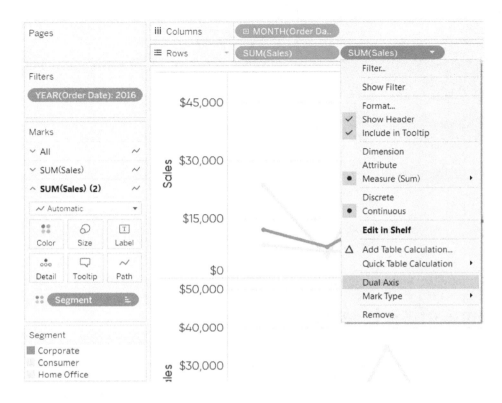

Ensure the axes line up by right-clicking the right axis and choosing Synchronize Axis.

Now that you've got two measures on the Rows Shelf, you've also got two sets of Marks Cards for the SUM(Sales) measure. These can be edited independently, which means you can keep the mark type for the first occurrence of Sales as Line, but change the mark type for the second occurrence of Sales to Circle. After sizing the circles, which are your new markers, hide the right-axis by clicking it and choosing Show Header:

The last tip for using the dual-axis to enhance a line graph is a design inspired by Google Analytics. When showing only one measure and dimension member at a time, Google Analytics shows a dual-axis line graph/area graph combination. To show you this approach, I am going to filter the view to only the segment that I care about—Corporate:

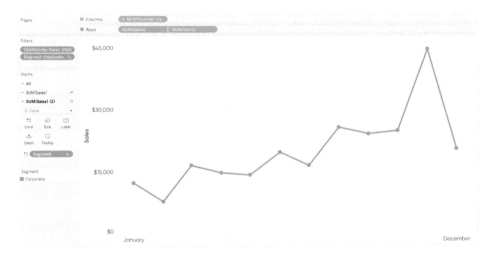

Now that we've isolated a single dimension member, change the mark type on the second occurrence of Sales to Area. Lastly, reduce the opacity of the area to something very light, such as 10%. Here is how my final view looks:

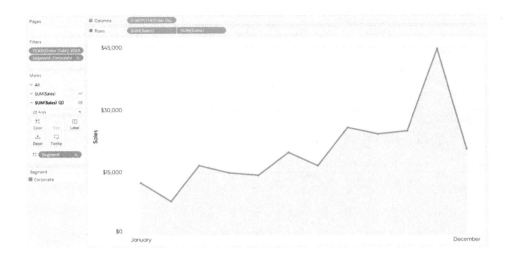

CHAPTER 75

Three Ways Psychological Schemas Can Improve Your Data Visualization

Whether you are aware of it or not, you are constantly recognizing and processing patterns in your everyday life. Think about when you go to dinner at a sit-down restaurant that you've never been to before. Even though you're trying the restaurant for the first time, you will have some expectation about the order of events, which usually looks like this:

1. You walk in and are greeted by a host or hostess who shows you to a table.

2. The waiter comes by to introduce himself and takes your drink order.

3. After returning with your drinks, the waiter takes your dinner order.

4. Throughout the meal, the waiter may stop by every once in a while to make sure you're doing OK and refill your drinks.

5. After the meal, the waiter will make a bad joke about "saving room for dessert."

6. After declining, he will either produce your bill from his pocket or run over to the register to get it for you.

7. You pay and go on your way.

This is one of many examples of a *psychological* schema (not to be confused with a *database* schema) in your everyday life. These patterns help society align diverse audiences and help us process varying situations very efficiently. These schemas are so powerful and ingrained that a disruption to the pattern can be confusing and challenging to overcome. As one extreme example, imagine showing up to a restaurant and having the waiter bring you a check before you've sat down.

The restaurant pattern goes in an intuitive order so it is unlikely to vary much, but you also create schemas that are personal to you based on your own life experiences and worldview. These expectations help you avoid "reinventing the wheel" because you've experienced the same or similar situation before and know how to handle it.

Schemas play an important role in data visualization because they have the ability to make or break the two biggest benefits of visualizing data: reducing time to insight and improving the accuracy of insights. Tap into your audience's schemas and you improve their experience; disrupt their schemas and you run the risk of leading your audience in the wrong direction.

This chapter shares three ways to leverage schemas to improve your data visualization.

Schema #1: Spatial Context

Maps help us process data because in addition to the data point, they provide spatial context that help our analyses. Consider the following bar chart showing the lowest cost per section to attend the 50th American Football Championship:

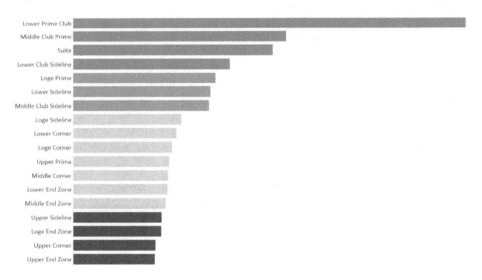

This a good data visualization within best practices, and there are definitely insights to be found in this chart. However, adding spatial context immediately helps the analysis make sense, even if you are not familiar with the stadium where this game was played:

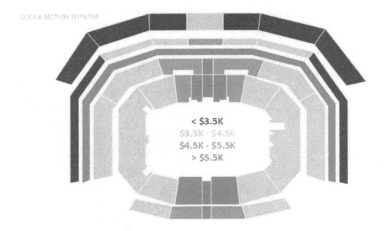

< $3.5K
$3.5K - $4.5K
$4.5K - $5.5K
> $5.5K

I can use the schema I've constructed in my mind from my experiences buying tickets to many sporting events over my lifetime to know that the lower and closer to midfield you are, the more expensive the ticket will be. This will help reduce my time to insight because it's much faster for me to determine if the numbers on the bar chart make sense to me intuitively or if there is a disruption to my schema, which in this case would also lead to insight (i.e., if lower bowl tickets are going for less money than the upper deck). Depending on what story you are trying to tell, it may make sense to display a map like this in addition to, or even instead of, the bar chart. For my *Cost of Attending the 50th American Football Championship* visualization, I chose to show the stadium map and a line graph.

Schema #2: Icons/Shapes/Symbols

A picture tells a thousand words. The second schema that can improve your data visualization is the use of icons, shapes, and/or symbols. There's a thin line between graphics that enhance a data visualization and chartjunk (discussed in Chapter 98), but when done tastefully, graphics have the ability to provide much more information than words alone.

At the most basic level, think about how much value a "+" or "–" sign adds when it precedes a number on a dashboard. When used to show if there was a positive or negative change in a KPI, just one character reduces the time to insight and increases the accuracy of insights. Arrows or triangles pointing up or down work the same way.

That's a basic example, but many graphics work in this way because we have preconceived notions about what they mean. Take a look at the navigation I used on my visualization, *The Odds of Going Pro in Sports*:

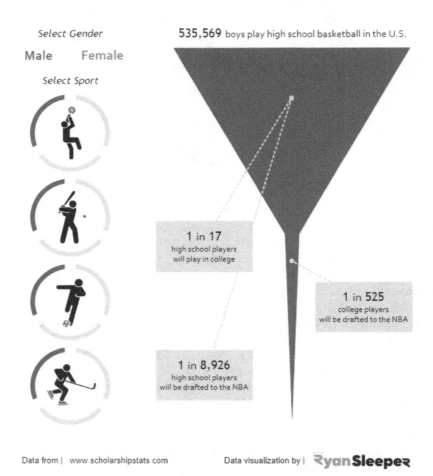

WHAT ARE THE ODDS OF GOING PRO IN SPORTS?

An analysis of high school, college, and pro sports in the United States by gender.

Select Gender

Male   Female

Select Sport

535,569 boys play high school basketball in the U.S.

1 in 17
high school players
will play in college

1 in 525
college players
will be drafted to the NBA

1 in 8,926
high school players
will be drafted to the NBA

Data from | www.scholarshipstats.com   Data visualization by | **Ryan Sleeper**

I used icons instead of words to display the different sport options. In my opinion, this makes the view more engaging, but icons also provide the advantage of reducing, and often eliminating, language barriers.

In another example, I used a polygon map of a football player to help illustrate what body parts cause the most collisions in the NFL:

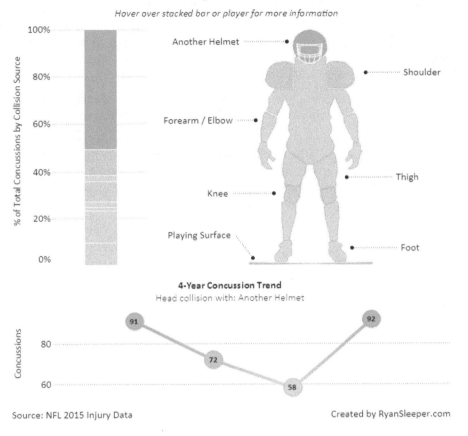

What collisions cause the most concussions in the NFL?
A visualization of the 618 NFL regular season concussions from 2012 - 2015

Hover over stacked bar or player for more information

Another Helmet

Shoulder

Forearm / Elbow

Thigh

Knee

Playing Surface

Foot

% of Total Concussions by Collision Source

4-Year Concussion Trend
Head collision with: Another Helmet

Concussions

91

72

58

92

Source: NFL 2015 Injury Data

Created by RyanSleeper.com

I could have simply made a bar chart by collision source, which would be a fine approach, but by overlaying the heat map onto the player's shape, the viewers can tap into their existing schemas to process the view and discover insights.

Schema #3: Color

For better or worse, I bet you associate green with good and red with bad. I'm not exactly sure where that preconception was born, but it seems to be with us to stay. It is a schema. You don't have to teach your audience what red and green mean; they know (or think they know, so be careful!).

I don't recommend this color combination for both scientific (color blindness) and personal reasons (I believe it's ugly), but this is an example of a schema you can leverage to help your audience make sense of your data visualizations.

Being aware of your audience's existing associations can help you help them decrease their time to insight and improve the accuracy of their insights. It works both ways though, so be careful not to completely disrupt their schemas. If you're making a visualization about fruit, don't color oranges purple and grapes orange.

If you're using color outside of the common green/red or blue/orange color palettes, be consistent so your audience becomes conditioned to understand your use of color.

Leveraging these three schemas in a thoughtful way can go a long way toward maximizing the two biggest benefits of data visualization: decreasing the time to insight and improving the accuracy of insights. At the very least, be aware that your audience has their own preconceptions, and disrupting them can make it more challenging for your audience to find value in your data visualization.

PART IV

Framework

CHAPTER 76

Introducing the INSIGHT Framework for Data Visualization

To this point in *Practical Tableau*, we've introduced the basics, provided how-to tutorials for dozens of chart types, and covered some of my favorite tips and tricks. All of this will help you on your journey to becoming a Tableau expert, but it is not enough. It doesn't matter how good you are at the technical aspects of Tableau if you don't consider some intangibles that will help tie it all together. The information in Part IV is the missing link to help bring your data visualization from good to great.

Over the past eight years, I have personally designed and constructed hundreds of data visualizations. To this day, I have yet to build a dashboard that *every* viewer thought was perfect. Data visualization is an art, and its value is in the eye of the beholder. There are limitless possibilities and variables involved in creating a data visualization, too; no wonder that many people, when confronted with a data visualization issue, stick to an inoffensive template that does … OK. But you can do better! With a structured approach to the task of data visualization, you can maximize the chances that your work will be well received—and communicate the valuable information inside the data.

The strategic framework I've developed—the INSIGHT framework—has saved me hundreds if not thousands of hours of iteration, increased value for stakeholders, and led to countless business insights—and now I'm sharing it with you!

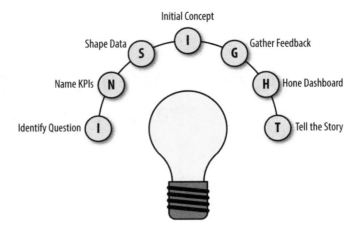

Identify the business question

One of the most common pitfalls in data visualization is trying to answer too many questions in one view. By prioritizing what the data visualization will answer, you are able to keep the view simple and make it clear to the end users what stories they should be looking for in the dashboard.

Name the KPIs

These key performance indicators (KPIs) should all help answer the business question that the data visualization is trying to answer.

Shape the data

In order to work with the data in a data visualization software, data should be prepared in tabular form in advance. For the most flexibility, each column header should represent a unique field, with subsequent rows representing every entry for each of those fields.

Initial concept

Get an idea documented, even if it is simply a sketch of the direction you are planning to take. By not committing too much time to the initial concept, you will have the flexibility to pivot based on stakeholder input.

Gather feedback

Ask end users what they think of your initial concept and if they believe it will meet their needs. This step helps instill some stakeholder ownership during the design process so they are more likely to support the final product.

Hone the dashboard

This is your opportunity to incorporate stakeholder feedback and finalize the data visualization.

Tell the story

Finally, you are ready to distribute the dashboard and allow the stories in the data to begin making an impact.

The following chapters will take you through each step of the process.

CHAPTER 77

Identify the Business Question

The first—and most critical step in the INSIGHT framework for data visualization—is to identify why you are making the data visualization to begin with! As a data visualization practitioner in a corporate environment, I call this step "Identify the Business Question," but the concept can be applied to any question you are attempting to answer through visualizing data, whether that's a business question or just something you're curious about. For example:

- What is contributing to our business growth?
- Where is the best place to get a cup of coffee in Seattle?
- What are the odds of becoming a professional athlete?

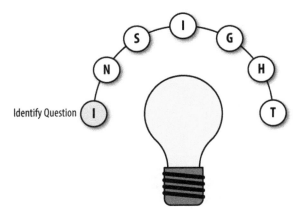

It's incredible to see how often this fundamental step is overlooked in the real world. My theory as for why is that it is becoming increasingly easy to access data and it can be tempting to look at too much at one time. While it may sound convenient to put every number you care about on a single dashboard, this approach typically does more harm than good.

By having a single business question in mind going into a data visualization design, you set yourself and your end users up for success by providing a clear purpose for the dashboard. Furthermore, most times it's appropriate to literally state the question to open a dashboard. This not only provides a purpose, but gives you an opportunity to frame what end users will be looking for in your dashboard even when you're not there to explain it to them.

Notice that this step is called Identify the Business *Question*, and I can tell you that the singularity of the word "question" is not coincidental. Some of the best data visualizations I've seen as well as some of my own most popular dashboards state a single question at the top. From there, the rest of the dashboard attempts to answer that single question. Sure, additional insights/context /"rabbit holes" are likely to emerge, but by going into a data visualization design with one question in mind, you improve the chances of your work providing value. This is because when you identify a single question, you're almost guaranteed that your dashboard will serve at least one purpose: answering the question.

Throughout the chapters about the INSIGHT framework for data visualization, I will use my dashboard, *Do Old Movies Get Better with Age?*, to illustrate how the framework can be applied in a real-life scenario. This was the winning entry in Tableau's 2013 Iron Viz Championship, a popular data visualization contest held live at the Tableau Conference each year. I'm using this as my example to show both that I practice what I preach, and that you can have success adopting this framework.

Here is a screenshot of the viz:

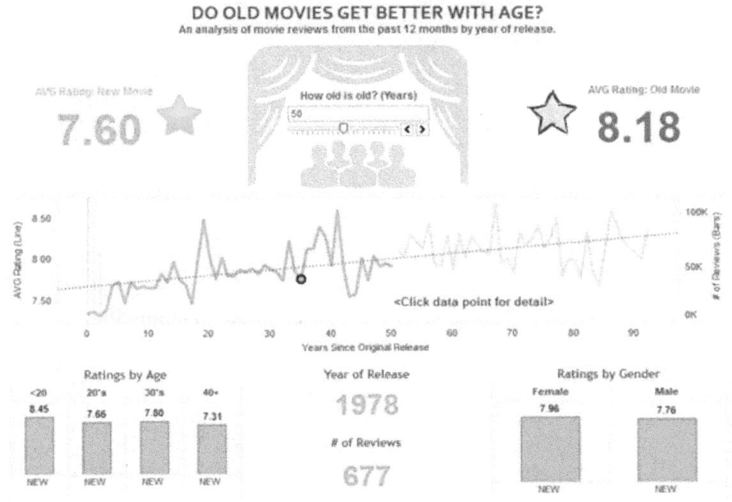

DO OLD MOVIES GET BETTER WITH AGE?

An analysis of movie reviews from the past 12 months by year of release.

AVG Rating: New Movie

7.60 ⭐

How old is old? (Years)
50

☆ AVG Rating: Old Movie

8.18

<Click data point for detail>

Years Since Original Release

Ratings by Age				Year of Release	Ratings by Gender	
<20	20's	30's	40+	**1978**	Female	Male
8.45	7.65	7.80	7.31		7.96	7.76
				# of Reviews		
NEW	NEW	NEW	NEW	**677**	NEW	NEW

Notice that the dashboard asks a single question in the title, which makes it clear what the audience should be looking for throughout the rest of the dashboard. The next chapter will share how you help answer the business question.

CHAPTER 78

Name KPIs

The second step in the INSIGHT framework for data visualization is to name the key performance indicators, or KPIs, that will help answer the business question identified as the focus for the dashboard. More specifically, the KPIs should be documented, which serves three key purposes:

- Aligning stakeholders on the data they agree about will help answer the business question that is important to the organization. It is much easier to debate the merit of each KPI and make modifications to the list at this point rather than waiting until you have a data visualization developed.

- Informing the dashboard design. Once a consensus is reached on the KPIs that should be included in a data visualization, you basically have a blueprint in terms of what should be included in the final product.

- Providing a historical record so you can review how requirements change over time. It is common for a business environment to change to the point where new KPIs or ways of looking at the data emerge. You may discover a customer segment you want to focus on or realize that a KPI is no longer helping answer the business question. Allowing some room for change is OK, but it helps to maintain a record of the dashboard evolution:

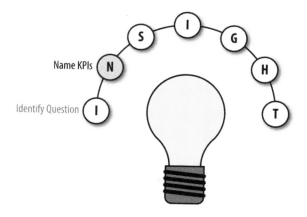

The KPI-naming exercise is not a one-size-fits-all task. It's possible that a single KPI can answer the question at hand. Other times, several more KPIs will be required. I personally try to limit my dashboards to twelve total components, including KPIs. They are called *key* performance indicators for a reason. If you are finding you have more than five or six key metrics, you likely need to put some thought into what is really moving the needle for your business and differentiate between key and secondary indicators. The secondary indicators may be better served in a drilldown type of view, or you may run the risk of them muddying up the primary focus.

So How Do You Name the KPIs?

I find the best KPIs come from one of two places, or a combination of both:

Measurement planning
> Putting some thought into how success should be measured and what information is required to answer a business question is half the battle when it comes to building valuable data visualizations for your organization. Many times, this step alone provides enough to inform a dashboard's requirements.

Discovery analytics
> If you're attempting to answer a new business question, it is not always known what KPIs are most equipped to help answer that question. By using data visualization tools such as Tableau, there is an opportunity to quickly pivot through many metrics to get a better feel for which may be most helpful.

Let's take another look at my data visualization, *Do Old Movies Get Better with Age?*; this time to see how the KPIs ladder up to answering the identified question:

DO OLD MOVIES GET BETTER WITH AGE?
An analysis of movie reviews from the past 12 months by year of release.

In the case of this question, "Do old movies get better with age?", there is at least one metric that should obviously be required to help answer the question: age. From here, there was a choice on how success should be measured, or what constitutes a movie being "better." Should the measurement of success be the amount of money the film grossed? Oscar nominations? Times it made me laugh? All potential choices (assuming the data is available), but I chose to focus on the average IMDb movie rating. I also included a third metric for number of reviews because I thought an important component of the analysis was that older movies tended to have a smaller sample size of reviews. But that's it—three "KPIs."

The rest of the dashboard looks at those three KPIs in different ways in an attempt to answer the question. The first and second parts of the dashboard are descriptive in nature, providing the answer and a trend right off the bat. The final third is more prescriptive in that it slices and dices average rating by demographics, which helps answer the "why" behind the results.

The next chapter will share how to prepare the KPI dataset so that it's usable in your data visualization.

CHAPTER 79

Shape the Data

The first two steps in the INSIGHT framework for data visualization—identify the Business Question and nme KPIs—will inform what should be included in the third step: Shape the Data. In Chapter 4, I discussed the ideal way to shape data for use with Tableau, but this step is also about accessing the required data, doing any preparation such as joins or aggregations, and making sure the dataset is laid out for your data visualization requirements:

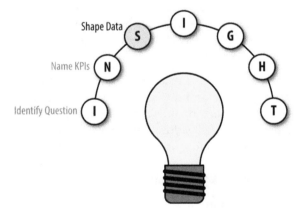

Mastering this step is truly half the battle when it comes to data visualization, and this chapter will touch on different tactics for ensuring your analyses are set up for success.

Shaping Data for Use with Tableau

As mentioned in the introduction to this chapter, we have already covered the ideal way to shape data for use with Tableau, but it's worth repeating some of this critical concept. In general, it is easier to work with "vertical" tables than with "horizontal" tables. In most cases, each column should represent one field with the field name in the column header, and each subsequent row should be an entry under that column header.

One common type of data that usually requires reshaping is survey data. In survey data, each column corresponds to a different question, such as "on a scale of 1 to 5 indicate the degree to which you agree or disagree with the following statement," and each row represents the answers to every question from a single respondent. This is a recipe for disaster as the data is wide. It may be easy for analysts to look at but Tableau won't like it and you will be fighting to glean any insights. Now, if you reshape, or what Tableau calls "pivot," the data so that there are only a few columns with lots of rows, you may not like looking at the data in a spreadsheet but Tableau will be much happier.

Joining and Aggregating Data

As your analyses become more sophisticated, it is not uncommon to require access to data across multiple sources—and when possible, it is often best to consolidate the data into one centralized data connection. Further, as the size of your data grows, you will need to start thinking strategically about how to aggregate your data so it continues to be manageable to work with.

One of the most common questions I receive is if it's better do this type of data preparation *in* Tableau or *before* you connect to the data with Tableau. Tableau comes with some useful data preparation functionality, including the ability to do joins, blending, interpretation, reshaping, and aggregation. My general recommendation is to prepare the data as much as possible before it gets to Tableau, but these capabilities are extremely handy for trying new things on the fly before making them more permanent in the underlying data source or stream.

One big exception to pre-Tableau preparation that I would be remiss if I didn't mention, is with calculated measures. One of the most powerful features of Tableau is its ability to do quantitative calculations on the fly across any dimension you throw on a view. If you are aggregating your dataset before it gets to Tableau to the point where every number is predetermined, you are basically working with an OLAP, or cube, data source. This takes away a lot of the exploratory value of Tableau. I suggest having the raw calculated measure inputs in the dataset before connecting with Tableau, but creating calculated measures themselves within Tableau.

Laying Out Data for Specific Analyses

Certain chart types, such as Sankey Diagrams and Funnel Charts (pictured in Chapter 40), are much easier to create if there is some thought put into how the underlying dataset is laid out. Situations like this are a case-by-case basis, but I do want to point out again that the dataset itself can actually help you create data visualizations more efficiently. If you come across a situation like this where a certain chart type requires a unique data format, I advise keeping a master data connection for the rest of your workbook, but creating a second data connection for these unique requirements. The second dataset may have the exact same data, but it can be laid out in a way that makes it easier to accomplish the special use case.

Shaping Data for the Iron Viz Example

Sticking with the *Do Old Movies Get Better with Age?* dashboard example, let's take a look at how the "Shape the Data" step was applied.

In the case of the Iron Viz competition, all three contestants were provided with a clean and easy-to-work-with dataset. After all, this contest is meant to be a data visualization contest, and not a data preparation contest. So I admit, this dataset was a lot easier to work with compared to many of the datasets I come across in my day job. That also means that I did not literally need to transpose or reshape the dataset in order to use it. That being said, there was one notable hole in the underlying data: age. As mentioned in the previous chapter, age was my number one KPI for my analysis, and I simply could not create the visualization I had envisioned without this field.

Rather than move on to a different concept, I evaluated the existing fields that I had to work with. Fortunately, I found that the titles of each movie included the year it was released in the text. If I could strip out the year of release from each title, I would have a numeric field. From there, I could subtract the year of release from the current year, creating my field for Age.

So I created a calculated field to isolate year of release that looked like this:

```
Year of Release = int(mid([Main Movie Title],find([Main Movie Title],"(")+1,4))
```

This calculated field tells Tableau to look at each dimension member in the Main Movie Title dimension and find the "(" character. The number four in the calculation tells Tableau to return the four characters following the "(" character.

After isolating the year of release, I created another calculated field for Age:

```
Age = Current Year - Year of Release
```

I was then able to use these fields as part of my analysis. This is a perfect example of creating something on the fly in Tableau by getting creative with the existing data. If this were a situation in my day job, upon proving the value of this field, I would try to make Year of Release and Age permanent fields in my underlying dataset before it gets to Tableau.

In the next chapter, we will finally start to visualize data!

CHAPTER 80

Initial Concept

Are you ready to finally start visualizing data? I feel like Mr. Miyagi in *The Karate Kid* —making us spend months "waxing on" and "waxing off" before getting to the reason we came here. The truth of the matter is the Identify Business Question, Name KPIs, and Shape Data steps in the INSIGHT framework for data visualization are the foundation required to make your visualizations as effective as possible:

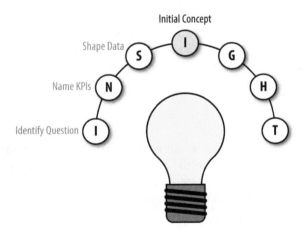

They also make the visualization component itself more efficient, and dare I say *fun*, because the preceding steps help reduce frustration and potential pitfalls. The strategic thinking put in during the I and N steps inform what should be included in the dashboard and the S step makes working with the data more seamless.

After this groundwork has been laid, you're ready to create an initial concept for your data visualization.

Creating an Initial Concept

There is no single best way to create a data visualization. There are seemingly endless factors that can influence a dashboard concept, which was actually my motivation behind creating this framework to begin with. If I had to choose the two largest factors though, I would say they are the data visualization's (a) audience and (b) purpose. These two factors should at least provide a starting point for what your data visualization will look like. When creating an initial concept, think about these questions:

Who is my audience?
- If the audience is fellow analysts, you may be able to provide more advanced chart types (i.e., box-and-whisker plots, Pareto charts, etc.).

- If the visualization is meant for a mass audience, consider simplifying the concept both in terms of layout and chart selections to make your story clearer.

- If the visualization is being created specifically for a C-level audience, more weight should probably be put on boiling explicit insights to the top before diving into any in-depth prescriptive analyses.

  See Chapter 86 for more on this topic.

What is the purpose of the data visualization?
  We have covered this in the Identify Business Question step, as well as put some thought into answering the question in the Name the KPIs step. During the initial concept phase, you have a chance to prioritize the KPIs in order to communicate the answer in a way that is intuitive to the end users.

With the answers to these two questions in mind, I create an initial concept in one of two ways:

A hand-drawn sketch
  That's right—I will literally draw out a concept. In fact, this has become my preferred method of creating an initial concept because it is extremely efficient, and since I am not investing much time building an idea out, I do not get frustrated when I inevitably have to make a change.

  I cannot draw, but that is OK! The outline, prioritization, and chart selections will come through and it will make it much easier to pivot if and when I receive feedback. Here's a real-life example from a project with one of my data visualization partners:

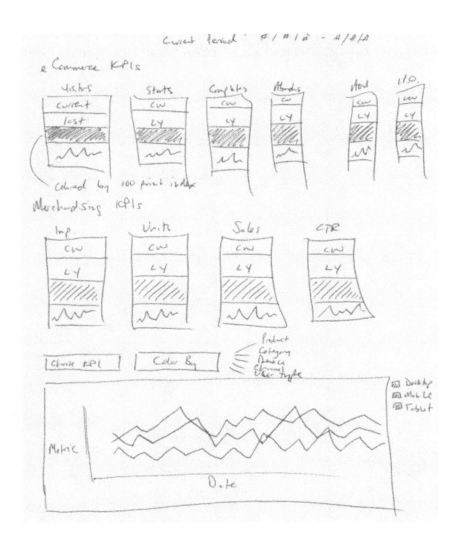

A partially developed workbook

In some cases, there are certain dashboard elements that I know will be included in my final deliverable. If so, I don't mind spending some time building these out and will experiment with sizing, layout, and flow on a dashboard "canvas." When I take this approach, I usually at least have an idea of how the dashboard will be distributed, which will inform the appropriate canvas size (i.e., optimized for mobile, optimized for printing, etc.). Once I have a blank canvas in Tableau, I can begin placing elements to create an initial concept before requesting critiques.

No matter which approach to creating an initial concept you choose, the key is to be open to change at this point in the process. I recommend not investing a great deal of your effort during this step because *your concept will change*—which is discussed in the next step—and you will be happy you saved your effort for later in the framework.

CHAPTER 81

Gather Feedback

As mentioned earlier, there is no one best way to create a data visualization and there are almost infinite factors that can influence a dashboard concept. I have always said that data visualization is a form of art, and with that, "beauty is in the eye of the beholder." One anecdote that I enjoy sharing is that regardless of the Tableau contests I've won, and the popular publications that have picked up my work, and the *hundreds* of times I have created data visualizations...

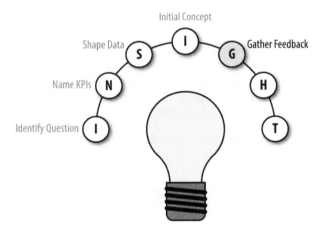

I have yet to build a dashboard that every single viewer thought was perfect.

And that's OK! I understand that it is impossible to please everyone all the time. Among a diverse audience, different people will have different ideas of what the business questions are, opinions on which KPIs should be used to answer those business questions, varying levels of knowledge on data visualization best practices, personal design preferences, and much more.

Gathering feedback should be an expected—and welcome—step in your data visualization process. Gathering feedback on your initial concept from the audience that will be using it provides at least three major benefits:

Improved efficiency

By taking time to gather feedback, you are able to get to the final product faster. When you dedicate a step to gathering feedback in an organized fashion, you are much less likely to receive sporadic, overly detailed feedback after you bring the concept to life.

Reduced frustration

In my personal experience, when I know that incorporating audience feedback is part of the design process, it makes it less frustrating when somebody requests that we move in a different direction.

I suggested in the previous chapter that you shouldn't invest a lot of time on the initial concept. It is easier to hear criticism or varying opinions when you haven't spent time actually building out a vision before gathering feedback.

Ownership

I have found that when you proactively gather feedback from end users, they take ownership in your final dashboard. Things tend to go smoother when the audience has some stake in your work. I don't have any science behind this, but I think subconsciously, people are less likely to criticize something if they had some say in its creation.

How you gather feedback is up to you and is largely dependent on your audience. For example, if you are building a dashboard for a small audience of one to three, you may simply send them an image of your initial concept and ask them to respond with their thoughts. If the audience is slightly larger, you may opt to set up an hour-long brainstorming meeting to think through different approaches as a group.

When designing for a mass audience, consider sending the initial concept to two or three individuals in your personal network to get a sample of how the overall population may look at your visualization. The key with your "preview" audience is that you choose individuals with diverse backgrounds that better reflect a larger, and diverse, public audience.

Even if you are creating a visualization for yourself, I encourage you to at least sleep on your initial concept. By stepping away from the design process, you can determine if you are still happy with the approach or have some ideas for improvement.

In the next chapter, I will share how to incorporate the feedback that you've gathered and hone the dashboard.

CHAPTER 82

Hone Dashboard

After gathering feedback from your stakeholders, you are ready to finalize your data visualization. I call this step "hone the dashboard" because you are refining your initial concept based on the audience input provided in the previous step. At this stage in the INSIGHT framework, the business question (or purpose of the data visualization), the KPIs that will be used to answer that business question, and the dataset that contains those KPIs, should all be in a solid—if not final—state:

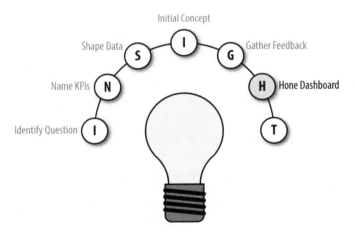

The task that is left to complete is investing the time to actually build out the components of the dashboard and lay them out. Depending on how much time you invested in the Initial Concept step, you may have quite a bit of effort left to get to a working product. In fact, I recommended that in most situations, the initial concept should have very few working components or even none (in the case that your initial concept was a hand-drawn sketch). While this step leaves quite a bit of work to bring your concept to life, it is much more efficient because you only have to build the dashboard elements once (versus building everything only to have the audience make you move in a completely different direction).

While there is no one best way to create a dashboard, here are a few general rules I have in the back of my mind when trying to finalize a view:

- Dashboard dimensions should be determined by the method of distribution. For example, if you know the dashboard will be printed out or attached to an email, consider making the dashboard the same size as an 8½- by 11-inch piece of paper. If you know the dashboard will be consumed on mobile devices, make the dashboard the same size as a tablet or mobile phone.

- Keep dashboard elements to 12 components or fewer. By capping the number of dashboard elements, you keep the design focused and help the story in your data emerge more efficiently and effectively. If you find yourself requiring more than 12 components, consider breaking up the dashboard into multiple views or even multiple business questions. Occasionally I will start with a descriptive overview, but use interior pages to provide more prescriptive analyses.

- *Keep It Simple* in terms of chart selections, user experience, and design. Being clear and concise is another best-practice method for telling your data-driven story, which we will discuss in the next and final step of the INSIGHT framework.

I will close this chapter by addressing one of the biggest questions in any design process: *What do you do if the audience feedback is conflicting or outside of data visualization best practices?* Remember, part of honing the dashboard is the opportunity to incorporate the stakeholder feedback, and there are several benefits to doing so which were outlined in Chapter 81. So what should you do if the audience disagrees with you or each other? Or worse, they want to create a dashboard with 15 pie charts on it?

Ultimately, you are the final gatekeeper of the dashboard and need to prioritize which feedback makes sense and how it fits together. The designing outside of best practices question is one I have struggled with because I really do find it hard to put my name on views that are just a huge spreadsheet or include charts such as pies or packed bubbles. My solution is to provide the views in both ways: (a) the way that was requested, and (b) the way that I recommend. This way everybody gets what they want, and I at least have the opportunity to share the best-practice approach to a specific situation. Sometimes my advice is taken; sometimes it's not. But by providing both approaches, I don't lose any sleep because I know I tried to help.

Honing the dashboard can be an iterative step itself, so don't worry if you don't get it perfect on the very first try. Following the steps in the INSIGHT framework to this point will help make this step as efficient as possible, and you soon will be ready to distribute your work.

CHAPTER 83

Tell the Story

Once you have honed your dashboard and possibly iterated a couple of times to land on a final product, you are ready to distribute your data visualization. I call this step "Tell the Story," because you have hopefully integrated some storytelling tactics into your dashboard and your data has a compelling story to share. Further, I believe that the entire *purpose* of data visualization is to find and share actionable stories that are based in quantitative evidence. If your dashboard does not provide insights that can help inspire action in your organization, it's probably not worth sharing to begin with:

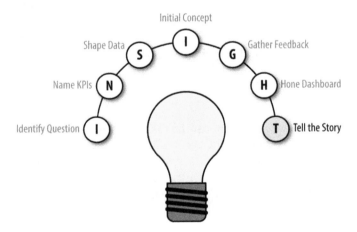

No, there's not always an earth-shattering realization that comes from every single weekly report you may create. That being said, if you have put some strategic thought into identifying the business question that your dashboard is answering and how the

KPIs you're measuring will answer that question, you drastically increase the chances of your dashboard providing actionable insight.

So assuming you've followed the INSIGHT framework to this point and your dashboard is sure to provide valuable insights, your method of distribution once again comes back to my largest factor when creating a data visualization: the audience. In my experience, the audiences for my dashboards are almost as diverse as the factors that go into creating the dashboard itself. They truly live on any and all points of a spectrum in terms of both their analytical sophistication and their technical infrastructure.

For example, I have created dashboards for audiences that have never heard of Tableau. With the analytics partner that I have in mind, I refreshed the dashboard data once per month and saved the dashboard as a PDF that I attached to an email. On the other end of that spectrum, I've worked with several partners that have a very robust Tableau Server implementation in place where I can post the dashboards and set them up to automatically update. This makes it a little easier to tell the story because users can subscribe for periodic email updates, and starting with Tableau 10, you can even subscribe other people to receive your dashboards with the most up-to-date data available.

Regardless of your audience, there are a few specific tactics you can use to help tell the story that emerges in your dashboard:

Context
> You won't always be around to explain your dashboard to end users. Be sure to provide some context for your dashboard so your end users have an idea of what they should be looking for as they navigate your work. This context can be as simple as a title and subtitle on the dashboard itself, but can include additional information such as the source of the data or the date range being applied to the visualizations.

Inline insights
> One of the most effective methods of providing findings and recommendations for next steps is to explicitly write them out within the dashboard. One way to do this is to design in a text box for "inline insights" that the developer or analyst can modify with their own thoughts. Some insights can even be automated through the use of calculated fields that will display a sentence based on the performance of the data.

Annotations
> If a dip on a line graph, for example, is influenced by an event that is not readily apparent in the dashboard, add an annotation to the line graph to provide additional context. In just one hypothetical example, let's pretend that the line graph is looking at daily production. If you know the factory was closed for two days

due to unforeseen circumstances, but this is not data that is normally tracked or reported to the audience, help provide this context by annotating the graph.

I'll close the INSIGHT framework for data visualization part by using the *Do Old Movies Get Better with Age?* example—the winning visualization in the 2013 Tableau Iron Viz Championship—one more time. The three Iron Viz finalists each year are among the best of the best Tableau users in the world. While I pride myself on balancing data and design, I considered one of my competitors more skilled at design than me, and the other competitor more skilled at data. While I think my balance between the two helped, I think the primary reason I was able to win was *storytelling*.

At the end of the Iron Viz contest, each contestant gets to explain their data visualization. While the other two contestants used most of their time to walk through the technical aspects and user experience of their dashboards, I literally told the story behind what motivated my approach. I believe this helped me connect with the judges and gave purpose to my data visualization, providing the edge needed to pull off the win. In a corporate environment, the judges from the Iron Viz are your audience, and pulling off the win equates to finding and sharing a valuable insight that causes positive change for your business.

Part V will discuss more storytelling tactics you can integrate into your dashboard development process.

Storytelling

CHAPTER 84

Introduction to Storytelling

So how exactly do you tell a data-driven "story"? I fear that storytelling in the context of data visualization has become a bit of a buzzword. What's worse is the concept is often mentioned without practical examples of how you can apply storytelling techniques to data visualization. This section offers an introduction to storytelling and aims at providing several tangible tips for incorporating storytelling techniques into your data visualization. If the INSIGHT strategy described in Part IV is the key to taking your work from good to great; storytelling is the key to taking your data visualization from great to *actionable*: the "Holy Grail" of the profession.

Storytelling has been used in every culture as a means of engaging audiences and communicating everything from entertainment to moral values. Stories work because humans are wired to retain stories; not independent facts or statistics. In fact, after a presentation, 63% of attendees remember the stories presented, while just 5% of attendees remember the individual statistics.[1] This is particularly relevant to data, where business insights risk being lost amid a deluge of increasingly large sets of numbers. Think about what you remember after seeing an effective data visualization compared to a raw spreadsheet of numbers. The difference is inherent storytelling at work.

The parallels between data visualization and storytelling are undeniable. Much like stories, data storytelling includes three critical elements:

1. Characters
2. Plot or storylines

---

1 Heath, C. and Heath, D. (2007). *Made to Stick: Why Some Ideas Survive and Others Die*. New York: Random House.

3. Narrative

With data, KPIs and contextual metrics can be considered the characters, storylines can be considered the insights, and the narrative is data visualization—or the style in which the insights are being communicated.

Data visualization practitioners have a lot of say with all three elements of data storytelling: your strategy informs the KPIs that are being used to answer the business questions at hand; your ability as an analyst helps unearth the insights from the data; and the style in which you communicate those insights goes a long way in determining if your visualization will be actionable and cause a change.

Interestingly, not to mention amusingly, data storylines tend to follow another parallel, *The Seven Basic Plots* from Christopher Booker:[2]

1. Overcoming the Monster; the protagonist (us), uses the power of data insight to make a recommendation that overcomes an obstacle to the business.

2. Rags to Riches; we leverage data visualization to add value and maximize our company's ROI.

3. The Quest; we have a business question or know something is impacting the business, but must use data visualization to locate the answer.

4. Voyage and Return; we travel to lengths only data visualization can bring us, returning heroically with business-changing insights.

5. Comedy; it really can be funny when data visualization reveals an insight that was seemingly under our nose for quite some time, but was disguised as a wall of numbers in our monthly Excel report.

6. Tragedy; unfortunately, this may be the most common storyline. At least data visualization helps us find the "tragedy" as efficiently as possible and, when done well, helps us know what to do about it.

7. Rebirth; this one is my favorite. This is when the main character realizes the error of his ways, and uses the power of data to become a better employee.

As our strategy generally informs the "characters" in our analyses and the plot is one of the seven just outlined, these tips will focus on narrative, or style of communication, to maximize the effectiveness of two types of stories:

- You, the visualization creator, know the outcome to the story. In this case, it is your responsibility to communicate the insight as effectively as possible so that action is taken.

---

2 Booker, C. (2004). *The Seven Basic Plots: Why We Tell Stories.* London: Continuum.

- You make the end user part of the story. This happens when you include interactivity that allows users to find storylines about themselves or something they care about.

CHAPTER 85

A Data Visualization Competition—
That's Also an Analogy for the
Data Visualization Process

Before getting into the tips, I want to use the Iron Viz competition one more time to share a bit more about how I think about data visualization. If you have ever seen me present on the topic of visual analytics, you have heard me use Tableau's Iron Viz Championship as an analogy for good data visualization. The "Iron Viz" is a competition held annually at Tableau's conference at various locales throughout the United States. It is the culmination of a year's worth of Tableau users using the latest in Tableau product developments to create innovative Tableau Public dashboards. There is only one way to receive an invite to compete in the Iron Viz, and that is to win one of three Tableau Public feeder contests held throughout the year leading up to the annual conference. During the contest, the three "Iron Vizzers" compete live in front of several thousand conference attendees. Each contestant is given the same dataset, and they have exactly 20 minutes to create the best data visualization they can before being judged by the audience, the previous year's winner, and a panel of Tableau product experts.

It's quite a spectacle—and a lot of fun. As the contest begins, each competitor walks to the stage through dim lighting and heavy fog. Dramatic music is blaring. The competitors even don chef-like jackets—a nod to the contest's format borrowed from the *Iron Chef* television show. After some announcements and introductions from two emcees, the contest is played out on huge projection screens so the audience can watch every competitor's move in real time.

The reason I love this event as an analogy for data visualization is because it is a perfect balance of sizzle and steak—both at their highest levels. The presentation aspect is needed to get the largest audience possible interested in the event and make it an entertaining experience from start to finish. It truly transforms the type of work I do every day into must-see theatre. It guarantees that the event will be (literally) remarkable, enticing the audience to share on social media, write blog posts about it when they return home, and of course, come back in the future for more. At the same time, the three contestants have been thoroughly vetted and are among the best in the world at what they do. The visualizations they are about to pull together promise to be top quality, and are the core of the event. As with data visualization, the data, analysis, and the designer's ability to communicate that analysis are the heart of the work. These key elements are strong enough to stand on their own, but the Iron Viz maximizes their effectiveness by helping make them memorable and shareable.

I argue that the best data visualizations are those that not only incorporate data visualization and analysis best practices, but those that also possess a sense of storytelling —whether that be through usability, graphic design, inline insights, or innovative visual approaches that help make the message of the dashboard stick.

My goal in Part V is to provide actionable tips that will help you round out your existing corporate dashboards in a way that maximizes their effectiveness in your workplace.

CHAPTER 86

Tip #1: Know Your Audience

There are not many tactics that are going to improve the chances of your data visualization making a difference around the workplace more than tip #1: *know your audience*. Before you create a single chart that you intend to share, putting some thought into who will see that chart will dramatically improve your data visualization.

My favorite analogy for this concept is the old Southwest Airlines *Wanna Get Away?* campaign. In one of the commercials, a rapper performing at a concert mistakenly and passionately thanks the audience by saying "Thank you, Detroit—we love you!" The crowd begins to boo and another performer informs the speaker that "Detroit was last night." I have actually been at several concerts where the artist on stage thanks the home crowd by name. Even though the performer surely thanks every stop's hometown in the same way, hearing your own city's name provokes a great sense of pride and is usually an easy way to make a connection with the audience. Get it wrong, however, and the city shout-out has an equally, if not more, negative impact on the crowd.

This same principle can be applied to your own corporate dashboards. Knowing your audience goes a long way to making a connection and maximizes the chances that your end user will understand and happily adopt the reports that you have created. Get it wrong, and you risk permanently damaging the chances of getting your visualizations off the ground around the office. Think about this the next time you undertake a visualization project. Here are just a few examples:

- If your dashboard is intended for a C-level audience, keep your work simple and direct. Focus on KPIs and the progression toward goals. You may also consider creating dashboards that are optimal for being saved as PDFs, to improve the chances that your work is either attached to an email or printed out and handed to a C-level executive.

- If your work is intended for fellow analysts, build in interactivity that allows them to find their own stories in the data. In Tableau, filters, dashboard actions, and parameters are my go-to tools for achieving this.

- If you are using Tableau Public and attempting to make your data visualization connect with a mass audience, don't be afraid to use freeform dashboards, story points, and even incorporate some graphic design elements. Believe it or not, some people think of data as dry! Leveraging some of these tactics will make your visualizations much more shareable.

Data visualization is not a one-size-fits-all practice. Regardless of the storyline you have to share, knowing your audience will help you prioritize and make the most of the data-driven storytelling tips to follow.

CHAPTER 87

Tip #2: Smooth the Excel Transition

Tableau is not Excel. Excel is not Tableau. One of the most common barriers to Tableau adoption is the belief that similar data visualizations can be created more easily in Excel. This may be true for certain situations, but if your goal is to master the art of data-driven storytelling, you must leverage the strengths of each software individually. I do not use Tableau to create and store my datasets. While it's possible, the thought alone makes me cringe with frustration. That is not what Tableau is best at. On the other hand, I don't attempt to use Excel to make beautiful, interactive dashboards. I'm sure with some elbow grease, this could be achieved, but the one million row limit in Excel alone makes this solution impossible in the enterprise-level visual analytics projects I work on. That is not what Excel was designed to do.

And that is OK!

I love both of these programs and use them almost every day, but for different reasons. If Tableau's goal was to replace Excel, Excel would not be one of the primary connection types available in its software. Tableau Personal Desktop users, who are restricted to using flat data files, rely heavily on the ability to interact with their Excel files in Tableau. Tableau knows that it is not Excel.

Nevertheless, the Tableau versus Excel debate is one I encounter regularly. My recommendation for anybody experiencing the same pushback to leveraging the data visualization capability of Tableau, or moving from crosstab views to visual analytics, in general, is to start with highlight tables. The following exercise can be used to help illustrate the power of applying even a very simple visualization to your data. You'll find that even with the most basic visualization, you'll transition your forgettable spreadsheet to a remarkable data story.

First, take a look at the following image, which is what an Excel spreadsheet looks like with no conditional formatting. See how many seconds (minutes, maybe?) it takes you to determine the top three values in the table:

State	Customer Segment			
	Consumer	Corporate	Home Office	Small Business
Alabama	$45,552	$20,843	$52,121	$8,191
Arizona	$27,301	$24,988	$47,291	$20,817
Arkansas	$3,422	$66,134	$11,505	$15,128
California	$229,462	$533,151	$284,838	$114,270
Colorado	$10,172	$38,715	$40,599	$42,725
Connecticut	$10,495	$15,899	$6,469	$9,439
Delaware	$3,543			
District of Columbia	$13,883	$77,912	$29,628	$97,446
Florida	$97,118	$180,177	$151,107	$75,207
Georgia	$23,659	$65,199	$68,561	$38,920
Idaho	$26,695	$28,374	$6,100	$34,474
Illinois	$94,632	$316,880	$152,589	$103,696
Indiana	$23,368	$105,152	$26,336	$39,225
Iowa	$8,548	$33,265	$42,301	$4,587
Kansas	$12,160	$54,677	$21,785	$21,964
Kentucky	$3,139	$32,534	$22,182	$2,905
Louisiana	$13,355	$34,178	$3,734	$15,344
Maine	$28,039	$23,837	$25,106	$20,139
Maryland	$49,992	$19,570	$44,077	$11,266
Massachusetts	$48,764	$111,533	$28,661	$39,494
Michigan	$93,473	$88,627	$79,004	$63,490
Minnesota	$25,044	$82,637	$60,135	$22,673
Mississippi	$9,916	$2,488	$17,883	$11,631
Missouri	$9,110	$61,384	$15,001	$28,207
Montana	$4,613	$5,293	$9,104	$10,394
Nebraska	$67	$18,131	$11,804	$10,920
Nevada	$11,978	$4,937	$3,114	

Next, take a look at the same data, encoded by color. In this case, the higher the sales, the darker the green. Now count how many seconds it takes you identify the three highest values:

		Customer Segment		
State	Consumer	Corporate	Home Office	Small Business
Alabama	$45,552	$20,843	$52,121	$8,191
Arizona	$27,301	$24,988	$47,291	$20,817
Arkansas	$3,422	$66,134	$11,505	$15,128
California	$229,462	$533,151	$284,838	$114,270
Colorado	$10,172	$38,715	$40,599	$42,725
Connecticut	$10,495	$15,899	$6,469	$9,439
Delaware	$3,543			
District of Columbia	$13,883	$77,912	$29,628	$97,446
Florida	$97,118	$180,177	$151,107	$75,207
Georgia	$23,659	$65,199	$68,561	$38,920
Idaho	$26,695	$28,374	$6,100	$34,474
Illinois	$94,632	$316,880	$152,589	$103,696
Indiana	$23,368	$105,152	$26,336	$39,225
Iowa	$8,548	$33,265	$42,301	$4,587
Kansas	$12,160	$54,677	$21,785	$21,964
Kentucky	$3,139	$32,534	$22,182	$2,905
Louisiana	$13,355	$34,178	$3,734	$15,344
Maine	$28,039	$23,837	$25,106	$20,139
Maryland	$49,992	$19,570	$44,077	$11,266
Massachusetts	$48,764	$111,533	$28,661	$39,494
Michigan	$93,473	$88,627	$79,004	$63,490
Minnesota	$25,044	$82,637	$60,135	$22,673
Mississippi	$9,916	$2,488	$17,883	$11,631
Missouri	$9,110	$61,384	$15,001	$28,207
Montana	$4,613	$5,293	$9,104	$10,394
Nebraska	$67	$18,131	$11,804	$10,920
Nevada	$11,978	$4,937	$3,114	

Much less time, right? This is the power of data visualization. This image is called a highlight table, and as you can see, even the simplest forms of data visualization can lead to much shorter time to insight. You can easily create highlight tables in Excel or Tableau, and I have found they are a great way to introduce the power of data visualization. In the tips to follow, I will introduce more complex data visualizations and data-driven storytelling techniques that can be integrated more efficiently in Tableau, but many times, you have to start by helping your audience understand why data visualization plays an important role in analytics.

CHAPTER 88

Tip #3: Leverage Color

> I found I could say things with color and shapes that I couldn't say any other way—
> things I had no words for.
>
> —Georgia O'Keeffe

During his keynote presentation at the 2014 Tableau Conference, Christian Chabot (Tableau co-founder and former CEO) talked about data analysis being a *creative* process. As an analyst, you may not think of yourself as an artist, but by its nature, data visualization is an art form. Visual analysts use data to express insights and provoke action. As Chabot put it, "Analysts and artists are both on a mission to reveal something new—to discover truth, to find meaning." So if you are doing visual analytics, congratulations—you're an artist! If that label makes you feel slightly uneasy, don't worry, this chapter covers several tips on utilizing one of the most powerful forms of artistic expression: color.

While leveraging color is relatively easy to put into practice, it is also one of the most effective tools for discovering and sharing insights.

A Few Benefits of Leveraging Color in Your Data Visualization

- Color makes the stories in your data pop. The primary use of color is a practical one: it helps the insights in your data emerge, both for you and your audience. Color helps accomplish a shorter time to insight by providing (a) a means to identify dimension members so you can quickly recognize strong and poor performers (i.e., each categorical value can have a different color such as as West is colored orange, and East is colored blue), and (b) a scale to illustrate relative performance (i.e., a sequential palette that shows Sales turning a darker green as they increase or a divergent palette that shows positive sales as blue and negative sales as orange).

- Color helps engage your audience. Careful color selections, or even the use of color at all, is an easy way to subliminally capture and keep the attention of your visualization users. I have found that the use of color is often a key ingredient in achieving remarkability in data visualization.

- Color provides an opportunity for you to show your narrative style. Perhaps your company's brand colors work well as primary or secondary palettes (this is not always the case, so consider with caution!). Maybe you want to use color to make an emotional alignment with the story the visualization is sharing (i.e., a darker look and feel when addressing a darker topic).

Customizing Your Use of Color Is Easy with Tableau

The following is one colorful example from my Tableau Public portfolio. Remember, if you ever see something you like in a Tableau Public viz, you can download it to find out how it was created. The same is true with colors—if you see a color you like, you can download the workbook to find the values that generated the color. More on color values in just a moment:

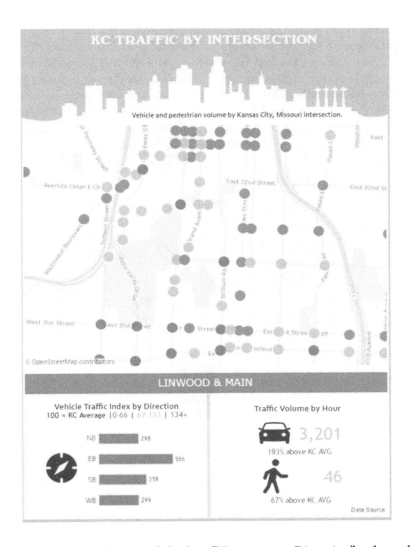

This visualization uses the out-of-the-box "Temperature Diverging" color palette in Tableau. Even though it is typically not best practice to use red and green due to a common color blindness that impacts around 1 out of 10 men, I couldn't resist using these colors for a viz specifically about traffic. Fortunately, the particular hues of red and green used here are actually color-blind friendly. The only downside was that using the color palette in Tableau was not as flexible as I would like because this certain color palette is only available for use when coloring continuous measures (i.e., lower values colored red; higher values colored green). The good news is Tableau allows you to customize colors and how you can use them if you know the values used to generate them.

There are three types of color values that you can use to customize colors in Tableau. The quickest way to customize colors in Tableau is to know either the (a) Hue-Saturation-Luminance, or (b) Red-Green-Blue values. Both HSL and RGB use a combination of three, three-digit numerical codes. You only need to know one of the combinations because when you use one, the other will automatically be generated. For example, if you type in the RGB values of a color, the corresponding HSL values will be generated. Any color can be added and used in Tableau by double-clicking a color in Tableau color legends until you see a color dialog box and enter the HSL or RGB values. The custom color dialog box looks like this on a PC:

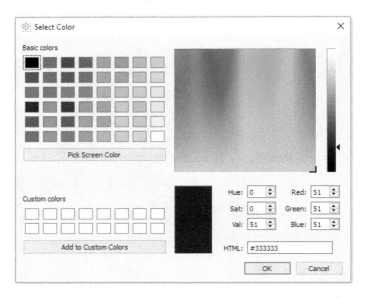

Here are the RGB values for Tableau's temperature diverging color palette if you would like to use them in your own data visualization. The first value is the level of red, the second is green, and third is blue:

Green: 82.153.133

Yellow: 219.207.71

Red: 194.107.81

Orange: 239.180.78

The third type of color value that can be used with Tableau is called hex, which is a six-digit numerical code. Note that all colors have all three types of values (among others): HSL, RGB, and hex. Hex values can be used to create a variety of custom color palettes in Tableau (*http://kb.tableausoftware.com/articles/knowledgebase/*

creating-custom-color-palettes). You can use a tool like ColorSchemer (*http://www.colorschemer.com/online.html*) to find the color values you need.

For more tips on getting the most from color, review Chapter 55.

CHAPTER 89

Tip #4: Keep It Simple

I didn't have time to write a short letter, so I wrote a long one instead.

—Mark Twain

I love this quote from Mark Twain because the author is putting a value on prioritizing content. It is said that Twain's "complete" bibliography remains incomplete due to the volume of his writings, and the fact that they were often completed for obscure publishers—not to mention under a variety of pen names. However, even as one of the most prolific writers of all time, this quote implies that Twain believed the most effective storytelling was done by being clear and concise.

This same idea applies to data visualization: keep it simple. One of the most common mistakes I see in dashboard layout and design is attempting to create silver-bullet dashboards that provide every possible answer to the business question at hand—all in a single view. One of the things I find myself saying often is "just because it is possible in Tableau does not mean you should do it." Tableau makes it easy to add filters, charts, and objects to a dashboard, but there is a point when too many options for the end user actually detracts from your visualization, making it harder for the *story* in the data to emerge.

A concept that' I often consider is Occam's razor, usually described as "the simplest answer is usually the correct one." William of Ockham did not have data visualization in mind when he devised this principle in the early 13th century, but I believe the concept fits quite nicely with the practice. Think about how bar charts have withstood the test of time, and despite their simplicity, continue to be one of the most effective ways to communicate the differences in data.

Less is almost always more when it comes to communicating your data-driven story. 'To help illustrate this tip, let's review one of my most-viewed Tableau Public vizzes to date, which was built using four widgets: one title, two filters, and one chart:

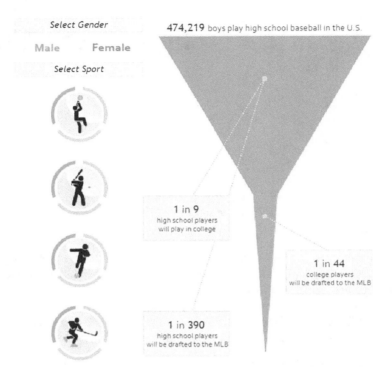

WHAT ARE THE ODDS OF GOING PRO IN SPORTS?

An analysis of high school, college, and pro sports in the United States by gender.

Select Gender

Male   Female

Select Sport

474,219 boys play high school baseball in the U.S.

1 in 9
high school players
will play in college

1 in 44
college players
will be drafted to the MLB

1 in 390
high school players
will be drafted to the MLB

I primarily credit the success of this visualization with its simplicity. The visualization is simple in several different ways:

- It asks and answers a single question.
- It offers only two filters—one with two options; the other with four.
- The story is communicated using a single chart.

The story in this visualization is almost impossible not to understand—and understand very quickly—by analysts and nonanalysts alike. By keeping it simple, you maximize the effectiveness of your data-driven storytelling across the largest audience possible.

CHAPTER 90

Tip #5: Use the Golden Ratio

Without mathematics there is no art.

—Luca Pacioli

The Golden Ratio, or 1:1.618, is a number found in patterns that we see all around us every single day. In fact, the shape of this book and likely the screen you're reading this on (if you're an ebook reader) are probably pretty close to a Golden Rectangle, which is a rectangle where the long sides are 1.618 times longer than the short sides. The Golden Ratio is used in the design of the televisions we watch, architecture, paintings from the likes of Salvador Dali, and even occurs naturally in plants and our own DNA.

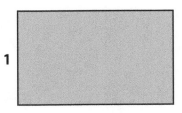

Shapes and patterns created with the Golden Ratio have been found aesthetically pleasing for centuries, and when it comes to data visualization, these patterns offer the added benefit of helping us prioritize the content we share in our dashboards. I've mentioned that I try to stick to twelve dashboard components or fewer, including titles, charts, and filters. The Golden Ratio is one of the tools I use to help guide how to select and lay out those twelve widgets.

The gist of the layout is that the most important data you are communicating should be toward the top and to the left, with lower-priority information appearing further toward the bottom and right of your view. Just as you start reading a page in a book, you can expect your audience to approach your data visualization the same way.

Knowing your audience will help you choose which content earns the prime real estate on your dashboard. For example, if your audience is C-level executives, you should likely have your main measurements of success and your progress toward achieving that success near the top left of your dashboard. If you are creating self-serve reports that your audience is going to use to help answer their own needs, you may want to consider prioritizing the filters, which will be a natural starting point for this type of end user.

The Golden Ratio is effective in both a horizontal layout as well as a vertical layout. The choice of a vertical or horizontal dashboard should be based on how you intend to distribute your data visualization. For self-serve dashboards with many filters that other analysts are going to use to help find stories in the data, I typically opt for a horizontal layout. I prefer vertical layouts for dashboards that I know are going to be saved as PDFs and passed around, and for all of my Tableau Public dashboards, which are embedded in blogs that typically have vertical designs.

Using the Golden Ratio in your data visualization is an easy way to subconsciously provide a familiar and well-balanced layout to your audience. It also serves the practical purpose of helping you prioritize content and think about how your audience is going to consume your dashboard.

CHAPTER 91

Tip #6: Retell an Old Story

Our stories are not new; yet, in the retelling we are reborn as heroes.

—Harley King

I think we've all been there—a few months after introducing a new reporting format, you may start to get the sneaky suspicion that your weekly or monthly updates are not being opened by stakeholders. Or perhaps they are being opened, but that fresh new reporting format that was so well received upon release is no longer being used to gain as much insight as it is capable of providing. This may be due to rarely fluctuating KPIs, a lack of understanding on how to leverage the reporting, or maybe simply a shortage of time to dedicate to finding stories in the data.

The nature of many KPIs used to answer business questions is that they are steady and/or predictable. Think about a website's bounce rate and average time on site—for better or worse, two KPIs often used to measure a company's ability to engage website visitors. Without a site redesign, these two KPIs may never fluctuate more than 5%–10% over the entire life of the website. Once you have seen these numbers two or three times, they become stale, and end users become less and less motivated to use the reporting you're creating for them. In the same vein, you may have KPIs that follow a seasonal pattern, and your end users know exactly what to expect from week to week or month to month; this may make them indifferent to large spikes or dips spotted in your reporting.

The good news is that data visualization provides a means for re-engaging your audience by retelling your data's stories in new ways. Data visualization tools like Tableau enable you to (a) make your dashboards more aesthetically pleasing, (b) add filters and functionality that allows end users to find their own stories in the data, and (c) makes your reporting more usable so that finding insights is more intuitive for the user.

As just one of infinite possible examples of retelling an old story, I took a shot at reimagining sports standings. As a data visualization evangelist, I view data tables as the least effective way of communicating data. As a sports fan, I am forced to view tables almost exclusively to see how my team is doing—and this is true for every league: NFL, NBA, MLB, NHL, MLS, among others. Tables have been used to track league standings in Europe's "football" leagues for over a hundred years. They even affectionately call their standings, "The Table." To show how much more value visualizing sports standings adds compared to the traditional table, I re-created the table in North America's Major League Soccer as a Tableau Public data visualization.

First, take a look at the traditional standings from mlssoccer.com:

Eastern Conference	Points	Games Played	PPG	W	L	T
Kansas City	35	20	1.75	10	5	5
D.C.	34	19	1.79	10	5	4
Toronto	26	17	1.53	7	5	5
New York	24	20	1.2	5	6	9
New England	23	19	1.21	7	10	2
Philadelphia	23	21	1.1	5	8	8
Columbus	23	20	1.15	5	7	8
Chicago	20	19	1.05	3	5	11
Houston	19	20	0.95	5	11	4
Montreal	14	19	0.74	3	11	5
Western Conference	Points	Games Played	PPG	W	L	T
Seattle	38	18	2.11	12	4	2
Salt Lake	32	20	1.6	8	4	8
Colorado	30	20	1.5	8	6	6
Dallas	29	20	1.45	8	7	5
Los Angeles	27	17	1.59	7	4	6
Vancouver	27	19	1.42	6	4	9
Portland	24	20	1.2	5	6	9
Chivas	23	20	1.15	6	9	5
San Jose	20	18	1.11	5	8	5

Now, take a look at the data visualization created using the same data:

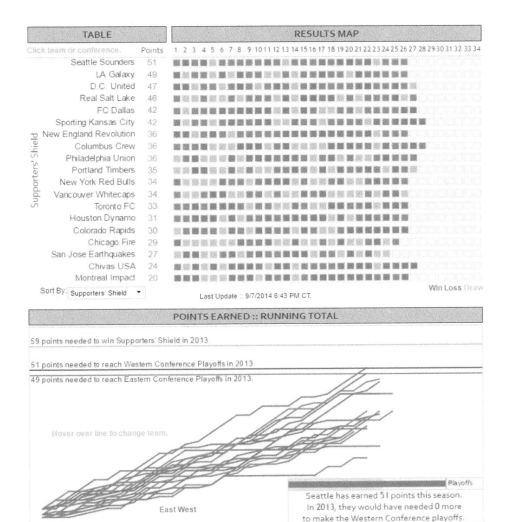

TABLE		
Click team or conference.	Points	
Seattle Sounders	51	
LA Galaxy	49	
D.C. United	47	
Real Salt Lake	46	
FC Dallas	42	
Sporting Kansas City	42	
New England Revolution	36	
Columbus Crew	36	
Philadelphia Union	36	
Portland Timbers	35	
New York Red Bulls	34	
Vancouver Whitecaps	34	
Toronto FC	33	
Houston Dynamo	31	
Colorado Rapids	30	
Chicago Fire	29	
San Jose Earthquakes	27	
Chivas USA	24	
Montreal Impact	20	

Supporters' Shield

RESULTS MAP

1 2 3 4 5 6 7 8 9 10 11 12 13 14 15 16 17 18 19 20 21 22 23 24 25 26 27 28 29 30 31 32 33 34

Win Loss Draw

Sort By: Supporters' Shield ▼

Last Update :: 9/7/2014 6:43 PM CT.

POINTS EARNED :: RUNNING TOTAL

59 points needed to win Supporters' Shield in 2013.

51 points needed to reach Western Conference Playoffs in 2013.

49 points needed to reach Eastern Conference Playoffs in 2013.

Hover over line to change team.

Playoffs

Seattle has earned 51 points this season.
In 2013, they would have needed 0 more
to make the Western Conference playoffs.

East West

| 0 | 7 | 14 Game # | 21 | 28 | 35 |

In addition to the table, you now have the ability to do the following in a single view:

- Filter between conference and league standings.
- See how many games each team has played and how many games they have remaining.
- Hover over every single game to see the teams that played and the final score.
- Determine what it will take for each team to make the playoffs.

- Gain better understanding into how teams are performing relative to each other.

The same principles used to add value to this century-old story can be used to reinvigorate your reporting at work, engage your audience, and maximize the impact of your data visualization. I'm willing to bet that by retelling old stories, you will discover many new "Rags to Riches" storylines in your existing data!

CHAPTER 92

Tip #7: Don't Neglect the Setup

When you tell a story, you don't jump to the climax without first building up the characters and working your way through the plot. If you skipped the setup, the story would not be as effective as possible. Data visualization is the same way.

When you work closely with a dataset for a long time, the insights that emerge may begin to feel intuitive. It is natural to think that the audience for your data visualization will find the seemingly "obvious" stories in the data as easily as you. This may be true occasionally, but why not make it a guarantee by setting the user up for success by adding some context to your work? This will also allow you an opportunity to guide the way your data visualization is consumed and ensure that you and your audience will align on those aforementioned "obvious" stories in your data.

If you don't believe your data visualization will be interpreted differently by each stakeholder, you have likely never seen an Iron Viz Championship. I am always amazed by the diversity of stories that emerge from the same dataset each and every time the competition is held. The designers not only find unique stories in the data, but they communicate the stories using varying chart types, fonts, colors, and *context*.

Here are just a few tips on setting up your data visualization:

- *Always include a title*. This helps set an expectation for what your work is about and can provide valuable information to the end user such as data sources and the date range covered.
- *Ideally, you can ask a single question to open your data visualization*. Each item in your dashboard will then ladder up to answering that single question. Oftentimes, one dataset can be used to answer many different questions, but by stating up front what question you are focusing on answering, you guide how your audience will consume your data visualization.

- *Explain the features available in your dashboard up front.* For example, if your visualization is interactive, explain the filtering options available.

Here is an example of a setup I like from Anya A'Hearn in her 2012 Iron Viz winner, *Does Tornado Alley Deserve Its Moniker?* Notice that the viz asks one question, and the rest of the viz attempts to answer the question. I also like how she saved real estate by building her color legend into the setup. This also helps the end user understand how to read the dashboard right from the start:

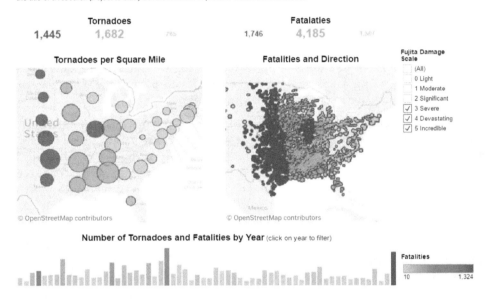

By not neglecting the setup, you help align your message with the audience's expectations by guiding the story that the data is telling.

CHAPTER 93

Tip #8: Don't Use Pie Charts

"The only worse design than a pie chart is several of them."—Edward Tufte

Pie charts have become one of the most recognizable and widely adopted chart types in business and data journalism. Being that the message that pie charts convey is almost universally understood, it is tempting to incorporate pie charts into your own data visualization. However—data visualizer beware—while the message that pie charts convey is immediately recognized (parts of a whole), *the insights that pie charts provide are not*. Using pie charts works against you and your end users because when compared to other visualization choices, they make it more challenging to glean *accurate* stories from your visualization.

The pie chart's primary limitation is that people are much better at comparing lengths and heights, as you would see in a bar chart or line graph, than they are at comparing areas within a pie. Further, the long-tail results, or the thinner pieces of a pie, tend to become unreadable. Pie charts are also a very poor vehicle for communicating changes over time.

Despite the empirical evidence against pie charts, I continue to see them in some of the world's most trusted news sources, stock reports, and corporate dashboards, among many other places. It is easy to make fun of people's use of pie charts, but I want to be clear that when you hear people recommend avoiding pie charts, it is not some kind of elitist-data-visualization-specialist credence—it is a best practice based in evidence. I've always viewed the prolific use of pie charts as a huge opportunity to educate and improve the data visualization space. While graphical methods of statistics date back over 200 years, we still have a lot to improve—which is a great thing for you if you are reading this and are interested in evangelizing the benefits of data visualization.

To help, here is a simple exercise to illustrate the reduction in time to insight from a pie chart to more appropriate chart types.

First, have a look at this series of pie charts, showing the sales by department over a four-year period. Take 15–30 seconds and think of a couple of insights that the charts provide:

You likely gathered that the entire pie was getting slightly larger over time (though it was hard to tell by how much and what that means), but it is pretty difficult to ascertain which pieces of the pie are causing the growth. With an easy tweak in Tableau, look at the exact same data as a line graph (take the same 15–30 seconds to understand what the data is telling you—though it likely won't take you nearly that long):

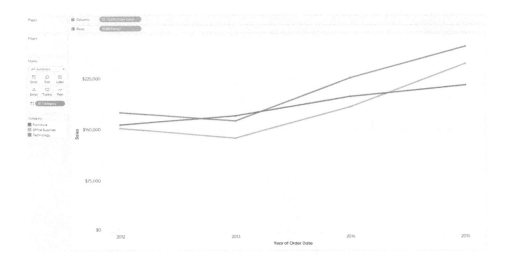

Much easier, right? By converting our pie chart to a line graph, we can easily see that all three categories are on the rise, and by how much. We were able to process the visual and get to the insight much faster. If you are not as interested in the performance over time, and want to see how each category performed compared to each other each year, use a bar chart:

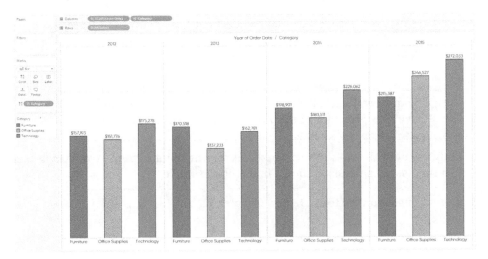

Again, your brain processes heights of bars more easily than it processes areas in a pie. Using a bar chart also provides you more real estate to display the values, either as dollar amounts and/or percentages of the whole (as you were trying to convey by using a pie chart). To take this one final step further, if you only care about comparing how each category performed against the others for one period in time, you can isolate the bar chart to show just the year in question:

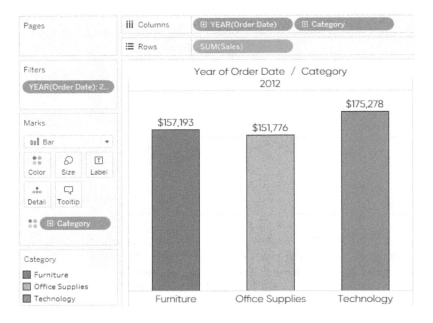

I understand that you may have a stakeholder that has a hard time letting go of pie charts. If you or a boss can't quite go cold turkey, here are a couple of tips for using pie charts while you transition away from them:

- Stick to five slices or fewer, including the "other" category. As mentioned previously, the thinner, long-tail slices become unreadable. If you find yourself saying, "but I have to represent all fifteen of my categories," that is another vote for you moving away from pie charts.

- Only use pie charts to show comparisons for one point in time. Avoid using them in a time-series analysis as shown in the first example.

For more thoughts on the topic, review Chapter 52.

CHAPTER 94

Tip #9: Provide Visual Context

Content is king, but context is God.

—Gary Vaynerchuk

Context is useful in data visualization because it helps you avoid the dreaded question, "So what?" As powerful and simple as they are, fundamental chart types such as bar charts and line graphs are often used in a vacuum. Lack of context makes it difficult for an end user to understand, engage, and eventually *take action*. By building context into the visuals themselves, you help the stories in the data emerge, even if you aren't there to explain them.

For this reason, context helps us tell both types of stories discussed in the introduction to this section. If you as the visualization creator know the endgame, you can use context to make your story stand out and "stick." If you are building a self-service interactive data visualization, adding in context will help your end users analyze the data and find the storylines that are most relevant to them.

In Chapter 92, I shared some recommendations for what to provide at the top of a dashboard. There are several ways to add context to the rest of the dashboard including:

- Index scores (covered in Chapter 61); not only do these scores provide comparisons, they help normalize the data.

- Sparklines (covered in Chapter 24); this chart type is essentially a small set of line graphs that allow you to view high-level trends across several metrics at the same time.

- Bullet graphs (covered in Chapter 26); this chart type is a variation on the bar chart that adds context in the form of comparison points such as prior period performance and/or goals.

- Small multiples (covered in Chapter 25); this chart type is similar to a table of visualizations instead of raw numbers, which allows the end user to compare results across several different dimensions and/or measures at the same time.

The Cost of Attending the Baseball Championship Series is an example of small multiples providing context that led to remarkable insight:

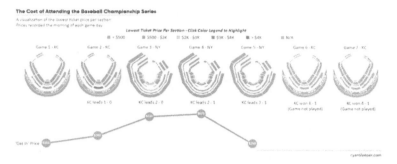

CHAPTER 95

Tip #10: Use Callout Numbers

Callout numbers are one of the easiest ways to communicate what is most important to you in your data-driven story. A Google Images search for "callout" provides several examples of speech bubbles, thought bubbles, and Batman-style "BAM"/"POW" graphics. While I typically do not enclose my callout numbers in such an illustration, they share the purpose of explicitly telling the main story in your data visualization.

Callout numbers, as I'm calling them, are simply oversized numbers that should be in a legible font that is easy to consume. As these callout numbers will be communicating the most important numbers in your view, they should be prioritized near the top and left of your dashboard. For more on prioritizing and laying out content, review Chapter 90.

In Tip #4 (Chapter 89), I discussed keeping your data visualizations simple. This is a critical concept if you want to cut through the noise and be as effective as possible at communicating the story in your data. Callout numbers provide a means for cutting through the noise, even within your own views.

Here is an example from my portfolio using callout numbers. This viz includes two numbers that stand out: 42 (Jackie Robinson's number that is retired league-wide), and 71 (the number of seasons without integration in MLB). The end users can see instantly what the dashboard is about and why I think the content is important. From there, they can decide whether or not they want to explore the data:

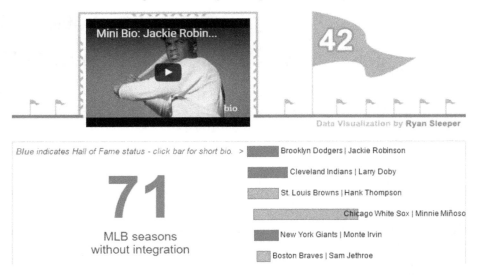

The Integration of Major League Baseball by Team

Mini Bio: Jackie Robin...

bio

42

Data Visualization by **Ryan Sleeper**

Blue indicates Hall of Fame status - click bar for short bio. >

71

MLB seasons
without integration

Brooklyn Dodgers | Jackie Robinson

Cleveland Indians | Larry Doby

St. Louis Browns | Hank Thompson

Chicago White Sox | Minnie Miñoso

New York Giants | Monte Irvin

Boston Braves | Sam Jethroe

If you use callout numbers in your view, they will likely be the first thing that your end users are drawn to. This serves two important purposes: (a) it instantly tells the main point of your dashboard and (b) gives end users a natural place to decide whether or not they need to continue searching for the answers or context they are looking for. This could come into play with C-level executives, who may only want a top-level data point before leaving your visualization—and this is not necessarily bad.

I compare this behavior to a website's bounce rate. There is a common misconception that it is *always* bad to have a high bounce rate (or rate of people that view only one page on your website before leaving). However, a perfectly optimized web page that provides exactly what visitors are looking for without making them search for it on a second page will have a very high bounce rate. In the corporate world, you may have numbers that do not fluctuate very often, and callout numbers will be a valuable tool for either providing what users are looking for or communicating that it's important for them to investigate further.

CHAPTER 96

Tip #11: Allow Discovery

Tell me and I forget. Teach me and I remember. Involve me and I learn.

—Benjamin Franklin

I've always loved this quote from Benjamin Franklin, and especially in the context of data visualization, because I think it applies to the practice in a couple of ways. First, simply telling a stakeholder your results is the least effective way to get your data-driven story to stick. By its nature, visualizing data provides additional context beyond verbally sharing findings, so practitioners are already a step ahead in communicating actionable insights. Second, tools like Tableau allow data designers/artists/developers to build in interactivity that lets end users find stories in the data on their own. When end users are involved, whether it be in the iterative process of a dashboard design or in interacting with a dashboard, the shared sense of ownership goes a long way toward making your data visualization a success. When end users find an insight on their own, they are more likely to remember it, and what's better, *do something about it.*

Allowing discovery is a tip I take personally because, as a huge sports fan in a relatively small market (Kansas City), my teams do not get as much coverage as some of the teams in larger cities on the coasts. With tools like Tableau, there is no longer an excuse to not include relevant information for every fan. This is something I keep in mind every time I create a new data visualization. This same principle applies in a corporate setting, as you now have the capability to provide relevant information to a variety of stakeholders in the same amount of space. For example, you can provide filters that change the view based on product categories or regions. You may have data size considerations, but it is theoretically possible to allow end users to look at every order or every customer individually.

In Tableau, there are three easy-to-implement ways to allow discovery, which gives you the power to make your end user part of the story:

Filters

We'll start with the most obvious tool for allowing discovery: filters. Any filter used in the making of a view can be added to a dashboard. Filters can be shown in two ways:

- From within a sheet view, right-click a filter on the Filters Shelf and select Show Filter. When the sheet is added to a dashboard, the filter will appear with the sheet.

- From within a dashboard view, (a) click the down arrow that appears when you hover over a sheet, (b) hover over Filters, and (c) make the appropriate selection.

What filters look like:

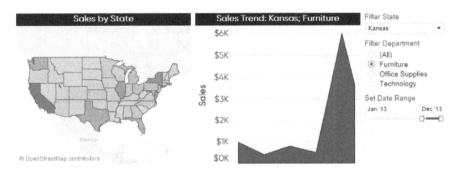

See Chapter 11 for a review on filters.

Dashboard actions

Dashboard actions are a more subtle way to add interactivity to a dashboard. They also have the added benefit of saving processing time if your Tableau workbooks are published to Tableau Server, Tableau Online, or Tableau Public. Dashboard actions are easy to create, but there are many options on how they can be utilized. The easiest way to implement dashboard actions is to click the down arrow that appears when you hover over a sheet and select "Use as Filter." This will create a simple dashboard action behind the scenes that will filter your entire dashboard based on the item clicked in the sheet that you opted to use as a filter.

What dashboard actions look like (clicking Florida filters the area chart on the right):

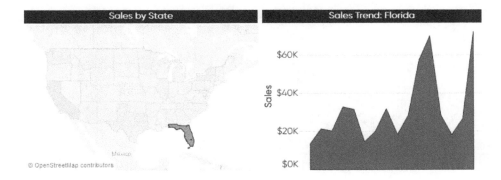

See Chapter 56 for a review on dashboard actions.

Many people do not realize that web-based Tableau workbooks are interactive. This will improve as more and more people are exposed to the functionality of the software and end users become comfortable exploring a dashboard on their own. In the meantime, you may want to include a brief instruction somewhere on your dashboard such as, "Click to filter by the element selected."

You may even want to consider using hover actions so end users that are new to the software may stumble into the interaction capabilities that you've built in. For example, they may accidentally hover over the map in your dashboard, causing a change that makes them realize how to use your data visualization. This option is set when you build a dashboard action; instead of having the action execute on select (or click), choose to have the action execute on hover.

Parameters

Parameters are user-generated values that can be used in calculations. Another advantage of using parameters is that you can provide user-friendly names to the values, making it easier for your end users to understand what each selection will do. By showing the inputs for the parameters on your dashboards, end users can experiment with different scenarios on their own.

What parameters look like:

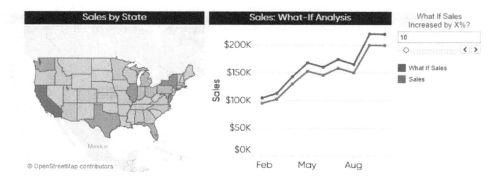

See Chapter 14 for a review on parameters.

Parameters are a slightly more complex way of allowing discovery. To learn how to build the what-if analysis pictured, see Chapter 48.

CHAPTER 97

Tip #12: Balance Data and Design

Data should always be the heart of any data visualization. Obviously, you cannot have a *data* visualization without data—and it is imperative that the data is accurate and honest. If I had to choose one element of a new data visualization to focus on between its data or design, I would make sure the data is right first every single time.

That being said, without making some design considerations, your data visualization is doomed to falling short of its full potential. Balancing data and design is another tip that I take personally because I often hear criticism from data purists that do not see the value in complementing the data with an appealing design. To those I ask:

What is the purpose of data visualization?

My answer is that the purpose of data visualization is to find and share actionable stories that are based in quantitative evidence. To make your insights actionable, this means sharing them with the most relevant, and many times, largest audience possible. If you don't provide your data stories in a well-packaged design, you drastically minimize the chances of your work spreading, and thus, it is consumed and acted on by fewer people.

See Chapter 54 for some tactics for improving your balance between data and design —even if you don't have any design experience. This chapter also shows a before and after to help illustrate the value this balance can provide.

These tips will ensure your dashboard has its best chance at being shared and causing action.

CHAPTER 98

Tip #13: Eliminate Chartjunk (But Not Graphics)

Chartjunk is a term coined by Edward Tufte in his book, *The Visual Display of Quantitative Information*. In it, Tufte defines chartjunk as "non-data-ink or redundant data-ink." My interpretation of chartjunk is that it is any design element that is counterproductive, actually detracting from a data visualization rather than adding value to it. Chartjunk can be as brash as charts that are made to fit within a graphic, with the data almost a complementary element to an illustration (see the work of Nigel Holmes (*http://www.nigelholmes.com/gallery/*)). It can also be as subtle as a three-dimensional bar or extra gridlines. Calling nonessential elements "chartjunk" is a fair criticism, but the same person who invented the term also said the following:

"Only a picture can carry such a volume of data in such a small space."—Edward Tufte

As with most debates, the truth probably lies somewhere in the middle. When the design becomes the primary purpose of a data visualization, it can become distracting and even misleading. Neglect design completely and a data visualization can be unengaging. In the last tip, I explained the importance of balancing data and design in data visualization. The tasteful use of graphics is one way to do that.

Chartjunk is not always composed of graphics. There are several examples of "non-data-ink" outside of graphics, including extra gridlines, shading, and three-dimensional marks. In the same way, graphics do not always create chartjunk. In fact, graphics are one of the most powerful ways to communicate information in a small space, and they also help engage an audience.

Consider the following "symbol map" showing sales by US state. This is technically a scatter plot with a circle on each combination of latitude and longitude. The circle is sized and colored by the sales amount. Here is the scatter plot with no image:

Now see what happens when we add a background image to the exact same scatter plot:

The map graphic helps you decode dozens of latitude/longitude pairs almost instantly, leveraging schemas for state locations that you have been building up in your mind over many years. The map also provides geospatial context, which can lead to additional insight that you may not have uncovered looking at a crosstab or bar chart view. This would be especially powerful with an additional data layer, such as showing sales by zip code in relation to store locations.

To help communicate more efficiently and engage your audience, consider using graphics to help complement your data visualization in these three ways:

Background

An attractive background can be a great way to contain a data visualization while communicating what the piece is about. In my opinion, a background with a clear interior container for the charts and graphs is not a distraction, but I do caution you to leave the background as the background. Once background elements overlap or become the primary message of a data visualization, it is counterproductive and takes the end user longer to find the story that your data is sharing.

Icons

Using icons instead of words to communicate what a number represents helps end users understand what's happening in your data visualization without them even having to read. For example, a dollar icon could be used to represent sales. Icons also help reduce language barriers in the case that your data visualization is viewed internationally.

Marks

Think about a scatter plot showing the sales by three departments: furniture, office supplies, and technology. You could use a unique shape (i.e., Square, Circle, and Triangle) to represent each of the three departments, but this would cause the end user to look back and forth to the legend to determine which shape represents which department. One alternative would be to use graphics as your marks to cut out the middle man and help your end user process the view faster. For example, a chair, stapler, and phone could represent furniture, office supplies, and technology, respectively.

Using graphics is about first engaging your audience, and then helping them process your data visualization more efficiently.

CHAPTER 99

Tip #14: Use Freeform Dashboard Design

Conformity is the jailer of freedom and the enemy of growth.

—John F. Kennedy

Using freeform dashboard design is an easy way to tie several of these data visualization tips together including Tip #5: Use the Golden Ratio (Chapter 90) and Tip #12: Balance Data and Design (Chapter 97). Starting all the way back with Tableau version 8.0, data visualization developers have the option to not only select the overall height and width dimensions of their dashboards, but the ability to place charts, titles, filters, and graphics on the exact x and y coordinates of their choosing—down to the pixel.

This feature is extremely powerful in that it removes all spatial restrictions and offers designers the freedom to use an entire dashboard canvas. Prior to Tableau 8, all dashboard elements had to literally fit inside of a box. The creative freedom that comes with freeform dashboard design provides additional means for engaging end users and making your data visualization worthy of sharing. The biggest benefit that I see from this update is that Tableau users can now create what are essentially *interactive* infographics. Here are just a few of the possibilities:

- Design a background image for your data visualization that is the same height and width as your final dashboard. Place the image in the dashboard first, then float all of the elements over the image.

- Experiment with the sizing and layout of icons and other graphics to create the best look and feel for your data visualization.

- Place dashboard elements in better relation to related content.

To help illustrate, take a look at a data visualization I originally created in Tableau 7, but gave a makeover in Tableau 8. In fact, this was a contest with the specific objective of showing off the new features in Tableau's latest product release— including free-form dashboard design.

Consider the following viz:

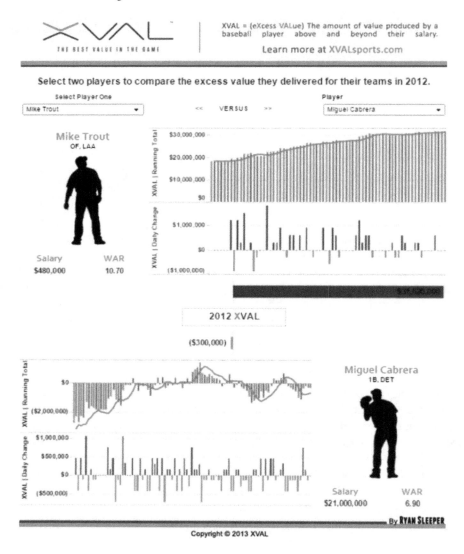

Notice that every item is in its own container, with no overlap. I did not have much choice but to waste a great deal of real estate in the center of the dashboard where the main player comparison takes place.

Now take a look at the freeform dashboard design:

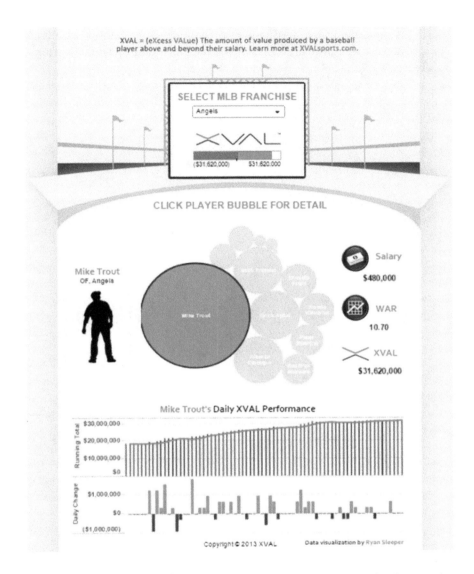

With freeform dashboard design, I was able to create an attractive background image and float everything on top of that image exactly where I wanted it, resulting in an interactive infographic. I was also able to place icons for Salary, WAR (an advanced baseball statistic), and XVAL (an advanced baseball statistic) in better relation to their titles and values.

I would be remiss if I didn't point out that the trade-off for the type of flexibility and precision that floating objects provide is that they require additional effort and attention to detail. Most beginning Tableau users start with tiled objects, and that is the best choice for rapid iteration. Starting with tiled objects is perfectly OK, but as your skills progress, you will find the most flexibility and design-friendly options with floating objects.

Tip 15: Tell a Story

Storytelling is the most powerful way to put ideas into the world today.

—Robert McAfee Brown

In an ideal scenario, the stories in your data are so compelling that they are self-explanatory. Unfortunately, this is rarely the case. What's worse, at times we are so close to the data and insights that we don't realize that our data visualizations need additional context in order to be properly understood.

If we want our data visualizations to be understood, elicit sharing, and—eventually—*cause action*, we need to help tell the data-driven stories in our dashboards. Here are just a few ways to help complement a data visualization with written anecdotes:

- In Chapter 92, I remind data visualization practitioners to "not neglect the set-up." By adding some context to open a dashboard, you clearly communicate what your work is about. This works even better if you are able to ask a single question that the rest of your dashboard attempts to answer. This guides end users and helps them find the answer on their own, giving the discovered insights a better chance to stick with your audience.

- I also use "inline insights" as a tactic for communicating my analysis of the data. To do this, I will simply build a text box into my data visualizations that provides real estate for me to add my own two cents about my findings and recommendations.

- Thirdly, don't underestimate the power of annotations. Many times, the practice of data visualization is extremely dependent on context. For example, if I am analyzing web analytics data and see a large spike in traffic, I would like to know what offline tactics may have driven the spike. I may be able to see that the spike was a result of an increase in direct traffic, but without input from advertising stakeholders, I will not be able to fully explain the trend. Perhaps our company launched a television commercial during the timeframe in question. These are the pieces of context that I like to add in the form of annotations.

- Finally, if you have a chance to be in the room when an end user interacts with your data visualization, try to—literally—*tell a story*. Why did you make the visualization? What were the key findings? What *actions* should we take next?

With a firm grasp on the technical tactics in Tableau, a strategic approach to data visualization, and some elements of storytelling, your work will have the best-possible chance at causing positive actions.

Index

A

actionable data visualizations, 533

actions

    creative uses of dashboard actions, 353-363

        Google Search or Google Image Search from a dashboard, 361

        primer on Tableau dashboard actions, 353

        using every sheet as a filter, 355

        dashboard actions for custom navigation/ filter icons, 298

        leveraging dashboard actions to improve user experience, 320

        using dashboard actions instead of filters, 374

Add Action dialog box, 353

Add Image dialog box, 202

Add Phone Layout, 387

Add Reference Line dialog box, 156, 179

    Distribution, selecting, 158

addressing field (table calculations), 72

Adobe Illustrator, 210

aggregations

    choosing before creating bar chart, 37

    choosing for a measure, 57

    date aggregations, 39, 427

        changing using parameters, 427-428

    in calculated field for measue selection, 416

    in calculated fields, 63-64

    options for, in Tableau, 37

alerts

    adding to dashboards, 307-311

        date settings, 307

        dynamic labels, 309

        heat map dashboard with optional Tableau server email, 310

        of exceptional or poor performance, including, 326

Alteryx, 210

Analytics pane, Cluster feature, 456

Angle Marks Card, 232

annotations, 583

    for points on a background map, 203

    removing, 205

Apply button, 375

Apply to Worksheet option (filters), 59

area graph/dual-axis line graph combination, 493

Area mark type, 163

audience

    aligning your message with through setup, 559-560

    engaging and communicating with, using storytelling, 533

    engaging with use of color, 546

    gathering feedback from, 524

        conflicting feedback or outside of best practices, 526

    identifying, 520

    knowing your audience, 539-540

        dashboard layout and, 554

        examples, 539

    re-engaging by retelling data stories in new ways, 555

Automatic mark type, 111

automation, 7

AVG aggregation, 37

axes

Q

qualitative categorical data, 28
quality control, using Pareto chart for, 257
Quantity bin, 171
Quick Table Calculations option, 393

R

RANK function, 273
rank over time, visualizing with bump charts, 271
rates, caution with stacked area charts, 164
ratios, calculated fields for, 61
records, viewing number of, 24
Red-Green-Blue (see RGB values)
Reddit, using to share public visualizations, 463
reference distribution, 267
    adding to bullet graph, 158
reference lines
    adding for a Box Plot, 179
    adding to a dimension, 409-413
    adding to a Gantt chart, 215
    adding to axes in scatter plots, 127
    creating for bullet graph, 156
    using for highlights, 409
refreshing data source extracts, 16
Reload Shapes option, 316
remarkable data visualizations, 343
    creating remarkable content, 460
Returns table, left join to Orders table, 258
RGB values, 352, 548
rows
    conditionally formatting individual rows, 365-372
    laying out for heat maps, 114
Rows Shelf, 23
    Latitude on, 188
    set field added to, 85
Ryan Sleeper, Tableau training offering, 4

S

Sample – Superstore data source, 12
saturation, 349, 472
scatter plots, 125-128
    creating in Tableau, 125-128
    with a background image, in maps, 199
Scope radio button, toggling from Per Pane to Per Cell, 157, 159

search engine optimization (SEO), leveraging for Tableau Public visualizations, 460
security, 8
Segment dimension
    ranking sales by, 273
    showing highlighter for, 488
segmentation, 455
    bringing data visualizations to life with, 324
    creating a permanent segment from a cluster, 458
    creating and comparing segments, 335-341
    creating quadrant-based segments, using Cluster feature, 456
    customizing, 325
    segmenting data in calculated fields, 65
    segmenting data in scatter plots, 127
    segmenting data in small multiple, 148
Select dashboard action, 355, 360, 362
sequential custom color palettes, 352
sequential path, mapping in Tableau, 195-198
sets, 81-87
    creating from clusters, 458
    creating from segmented scatter plot data into, 128
    creating in Tableau, 81-83
    uses of, 83-87
Sets Shelf, 22, 82
setting up data visualizations, 559-560
The Seven Basic Plots (Booker), 534
Shape Marks Card, 48, 50, 296
    Instructons dimension on, 316
shapes
    custom shapes in Tableau, 296
    mapping custom shapes to icons, 297
    using custom shape palettes to add methodology or instructions to dashboards, 313-317
    using to enhance visualizations, 498
shapes directory, each folder having corresponding palette in Tableau, 315
Shapes folder, 296
shaping data (see data, shaping)
sheets
    reducing, 376
    Source Sheets list for dashboards, 354
Sheets option, 98
Shewhart charts, 265
    (see also control charts)
show all values, 355

About the Author

Ryan Sleeper is a data visualization designer, author, speaker, trainer, and consultant specializing in Tableau. He is the only person in the world to earn all three titles of Tableau Zen Master, Tableau Iron Viz Champion, and Tableau Public Visualization of the Year author.

Colophon

The animal on the cover of *Practical Tableau* is a Malachite Kingfisher (*Corythornis cristatus*). There are five subspecies of kingfisher, and this one is small, measuring around 5.1 inches in length.

Its upperparts are blue, and it has black banding with green and blue on its forehead. Adult birds have bright metallic blue upperparts and bright red legs. Their heads have a crest of black and blue feathers, and there are white patches on the throat and back of the neck. Young birds have black bills, whereas adults have reddish-orange bills.

Malachite kingfishers typically nest in tunnels above water, burrowing upward into the nesting chamber. They lay eggs on a pile of fish bones and other debris. Kingfisher's calls are short and shrill, described as a chuckling *li-cha-cha-chui-chui*.

Many of the animals on O'Reilly covers are endangered; all of them are important to the world. To learn more about how you can help, go to *animals.oreilly.com*.

The cover image is by Karen Montgomery, based on a black and white engraving from *Shaw's Zoology*. The cover fonts are URW Typewriter and Guardian Sans. The text font is Adobe Minion Pro; the heading font is Adobe Myriad Condensed; and the code font is Dalton Maag's Ubuntu Mono.